The Mississippi River immediately below
Itasca Lake

The Mississippi River immediately below
Itasca Lake

The Mississippi River

And Its Wonderful Valley

Twenty-seven Hundred and Seventy-five
Miles from Source to Sea

By

Julius Chambers

Fellow of the Royal Geographical Society
Member of the National Geographic Society

With 80 Illustrations and Maps

G. P. Putnam's Sons
New York and London
The Knickerbocker Press
1910

The Knickerbocker Press, New York

TO MY WIFE
MARGARET

CONTENTS

Contents

LIST OF ILLUSTRATIONS

Illustrations

Illustrations xiii

FOREWORD

THE Mississippi was named "The Father of Running Waters" by natives dwelling amid the forests of its vast valley who knew not of other great rivers upon earth. Those sponsors were not far wrong. In length, it is exceeded only by the Nile; in volume, by the Amazon.

Geographically, it divides, almost equally, the broad territory of the United States of America. It is the proudest, most valued natural possession of the American people: it is revered next to American liberty! Its banks are scenes of traditional and authenticated romance. Its source has been a dreamland for poets; its delta a haven of buccaneers and a rallying ground for worthier heroes.

In American history, it maintains leadership over all other rivers, although many of them are nearer to European discovery and settlement. In finance, its good name was tarnished by Spanish and French schemers: but, self-reliant by nature, the majestic river redeemed itself as a highway for the internal development of a Republic of free men. Its commerce has builded a score of populous cities, has made hundreds of millionaires, and has suggested vast railway systems that, for a score of years, took the burden of traffic from its bosom. But the development of the country has exceeded the capacity of man to build railways and to equip them. Throughout the Mississippi valley confessed congestion exists. Deep waterways are planned that will re-establish the majesty of The River and its tributaries. The Mississippi returns to its own!

In religion, the earliest missionaries of the Holy Faith in North America followed its watery way.

In war, the Mississippi always has had a full share, —savage against savage, white against red, and white against white! As an epilogue to the final conflict with Great Britain, a battle was fought near its mouth, weeks after the signing of the Treaty of Ghent, that guaranteed title to the mammoth Louisiana Purchase. Early in the Civil War, this river became the western " deadline " for revolt against Federal authority. From Saint Louis and from the Gulf of Mexico, wedges of assault were driven southward and northward into the vitals of the Confederacy. Hereafter, it is a bond that must always bind together the faggot of States.

Such a theme is worthy of a wondersmith in words. It deserves the sacrifice of a lifetime's patience and research. The writer had hoped that a worthier hand would give to the task a career and a fortune. His only reason for undertaking this work, amidst the demands of an exacting profession, is that since he traversed the Mississippi's uttermost length, that river has been to him an enthusiasm. Dwellers along its banks have become his friends and associates; mere towns when first known to him have grown into prosperous cities.

During these lengthening years, the mighty river's irresistible flood has pursued its ceaseless journey to the sea, indifferent to the appreciation of man.

JULIUS CHAMBERS.

LOTOS CLUB, NEW YORK CITY, 1910.

The Mississippi

CHAPTER I

The Era of Fable

HISTORY begins with an interrogation mark. An Age of Fable has always preceded the Age of Fact. The mystery regarding the first Spaniard who saw the mouth of the Mississippi River never can be cleared, unless credible records be unearthed in the Royal Library at Madrid that will explain the sources of information drawn upon for " The Admiral's Map," with which the name of Christopher Columbus is associated. This " Admiral's Map " is the earliest known drawing upon which are set down the partly enclosed waters to-day described as the Gulf of Mexico, and the three-pronged delta of a mighty river entering that Gulf from the northward. This map, so intimately identified with Columbus, receives its chief importance, despite many inaccuracies of detail, from the fact that the three-mouthed delta is located notably near the point at which the Mississippi delivers its flood of waters to the sea. Corroborative evidence of the accuracy of the original discoverer, whoever he may have been, exists in the indisputable fact that no other river's embrochure along the entire Gulf coast presents similar peculiarities. The map is veritable,—one of the geographical treasures of this world; —but it was not engraved until 1507, or actually published until 1513, when it appeared as an illustration

3

in a Spanish translation of the " Almagest " of Claudius Ptolemæus, an Alexandrian astronomer-geographer of the early part of the second century A.D. The second book of the remarkable work of Ptolemæus deals with problems connected with determination of the obliquity of the sphere. Not only did this Egyptian believe that the planets and stars revolved around the earth, but he attempted a calculation of the circumference of this globe! A study of this work, many years previously, had warranted Columbus in assuming that the distance from the west coast of Europe to the east coast of Asia was only two thirds of the actual circumference of the earth. Jebb is authority for the statement that the entire theory of Columbus, which led to the discovery of America, was due to the writings and calculations of this Egyptian scientist. Such is the debt of America to Egypt that never has been honoured.

An examination of this sketch chart—for it cannot claim to be more—discloses near the western extremity of the large gulf that stretches westward from the Florida peninsula an unmistakable delta, extending far into the sea and having *three* distinct mouths, through which a river of unusual volume discharges its waters. The location and shape of Mobile Bay, with its two rivers, are also accurately placed. Whether the chart was drawn from hearsay, or was the fruit of Columbus's actual vision, during his fourth and last voyage, cannot be positively decided. But the sources of Columbus's information are not so obscure as might be supposed. On his second voyage, he coasted the south side of Cuba, assumed by him to be a peninsula of Asia, and discovered Jamaica. That was in the summer of 1494. On his third voyage, he kept farther south and, on July 31, 1498, went ashore at Trinidad, following up this discovery by landing upon the continent of South America. The Cabots had already visited North America. On his way home, Columbus reached Santo Domingo, where he was seized and sent to Spain in chains.

The importance of the fourth voyage of Columbus, as associated with the famous " Admiral's Map," cannot be overestimated. Leaving Spain in March, 1502, he called at Santo Domingo only long enough to reprovision and sailed thence to Central America, discovering Honduras on July 30th of that year. The most credible record of that voyage contains little definite information regarding the route by which the explorer reached the Central American coast. If he passed through the Strait of Florida and followed the coast line to the north and west, the " Admiral's Map " is readily accounted for, because he must have sighted the peculiar formation of alluvial soil that carries the Mississippi's flood far into the Gulf of Mexico. After landing at some point on the coast of Honduras, Columbus followed the shore line southward as far as Panama, and then sailed homeward by way of Jamaica. This is matter of record. It has been surmised that Columbus obtained the information upon which this chart was drawn from daring Spanish adventurers at Jamaica,—men who, at that time, had explored the islands of the Caribbean Sea and most of the coast of the vast land-and-island-enclosed gulf to the northward.

Serious attempts have been made by modern savants to link the name of Americus Vespucius to the Missis-

sippi delta; but their arguments have not been conclusive. Vespucius was Columbus's evil genius: he was
an Italian, hailing from Florence, as Columbus did
from Genoa. He was a member of the commercial
house at Seville that outfitted Columbus's third voyage.
His claim that he was absent from Spain between
May, 1497, and October, 1498, engaged in a voyage
of discovery, is hotly contested and apparently con-
trovened by authenticated records of his business activities in Seville during much of that time. Whether
the assertions of Vespucius were true or false, he stole
much of Columbus's glory, and, through the aid of
German geographical publishers, who first suggested
that the continent be named after " its discoverer," he
achieved the immortality his name enjoys. Toward
the close of the nineteenth century, he found an able
defender in Count F. A. de Varnhagen, one time
Ambassador of Brazil to Portugal, who made many
original researches at Seville into the career of Vespucius. His final conclusions were published in 1874.
Count de Varnhagen contends that the so-called first
voyage of Vespucius, previously discredited, actually
occurred in 1497–98; but that it was made to North
America and not to any place south of Honduras. On
his return voyage, he followed the coast northward and
eastward as far as some " undetermined port which he
described as ' the finest in the world,' whence he sailed
to the Bermuda Islands and thence home." The intri-
cate navigation suggested by this latest eulogist of Vespucius through the Bahamas or, in the Gulf Stream, up
the Florida coast, is not creditable to his comprehension
of navigation at the close of the fifteenth century.[1]

[1] Count de Varnhagen has this to say regarding " The Admiral's

The status of the next claimant is even more hazy than that of the Florentine ship-chandler of Seville. Francisco de Garay, Governor of Jamaica, made a report to the Crown (published at Burgos, 1521), announcing the discovery of Yucatan and expressing a determination "to fit out, at his own expense, four ships, with good pilots, and to give the command to Alonzo Alvarez de Pineda, with the object of seeking some gulf or strait in the mainland towards [!] Florida." The meaning of this obscure phrasing is that the Governor of Jamaica believed, as did many other people, that a navigable strait, to be found somewhere, led through the continent to the sea that washed the shores of Asia. He hoped to find it. This report of Francisco de Garay bears date of 1519. The hoped-for channel to Cathay was not found, although Pineda was absent eight or nine months; but the commander reported that he "had entered a large bay, into which emptied a large river." This has been assumed to have been Mobile Bay. He declared the mainland to be thickly inhabited, adding that, after ascending the river sixteen miles, he had "discovered forty villages of natives." These he located in the Province of Amichel, "a good land, peaceful, healthy, and provided with abundance of fruits." Nothing is said about any obstacles to navigation. In another part of the report, Pineda describes the careening of his vessels "upon a sandy beach, to clean their hulls," but whether this occurred at Mobile Bay or elsewhere is not made clear. Recent researches conducted by Mr. Clarence B. Moore

---

Map ": " It was compiled from much earlier ones, the information derived from various sources. ' The River of Palms,' shown on that map, was intended to represent the Mississippi."

appear to prove conclusively that Pineda visited Mobile
Bay, which has two rivers, instead of one, flowing into
it. The shores of this land-locked harbour contain many
evidences of early Indian villages. In fact, no other
port of entry on the coast of the Gulf of Mexico
answers to the condition set down by Pineda. This
Spanish commander may have passed the mouth of the
Mississippi but the claim that he sailed up that river
two hundred miles, or to the present site of Baton
Rouge, is so discredited as to be dismissed. If he ever
saw the Mississippi, he reached it through Lakes Pontchartrain and Maurepas. In that event, Mr. Moore's
theories go by the board.

The chief historical importance of this report of
Francisco de Garay centres in the statement that
Pineda " encountered Hernan Cortes, who had already
occupied Vera Cruz." Pineda's description of the natives also casts a doubt upon his credibility. He says:
" Their stature varied in different provinces. In
some, we saw gigantic people; in others, men of
ordinary stature, and in still other places mere
pigmies."

It is highly probable that Hernan Cortes first accurately charted the Mississippi mouth, as his map gives
it the name of " Arrestiosos "; but the voyage of Pineda
must be immortal because it fixed the boundary of the
Western sea between Florida on the east and what is
now Mexico on the west. Cortes completed the super-
ficial exploration of Columbus by proving the non-
existence of any channel through which vessels could
pass to Asia.

Francisco de Garay sent out another expedition in
1528 with the avowed purpose of conquering and an-

nexing the provinces of the mainland extending from the river Palmas—which may have been the Rio Grande—to the Cape of Florida. This expedition was entrusted to Panfilo de Narvaez, to whom was given the title of " Governor of Florida, Rio de Palmas, and Espiritu Santo." This undertaking had a most unfortunate termination. When nearing the mouth of the Mississippi, they discovered the influx of fresh water but were blown out to sea and were forced to land on what they assumed to be the western coast of Florida. After a council had been held, the main body under Narvaez's command was ordered to march along the coast " until it reached a harbour; and the ships carrying the other members of the troop were to sail in a like direction, until they arrived at the harbour sought for." The land and sea forces never were reunited. The sufferings of the men afoot, among the swamps and rank vegetation of the coast, were terrible. The land forces reached Apalache, an Indian town believed to have been near the present site of Tallahassee. Thence they proceeded to the coast but nothing could be seen or heard of their ships. They set about building boats but as they had only one carpenter among them and were without tools, they erected a forge, making a bellows from horses' hides, and converted their spurs, stirrups, and other iron implements into axes, chisels, and other tools. Hair from the manes and tails of their slain horses was converted into rigging. Stones served for anchors; sails were made from their own shirts. Five vessels are said to have been completed in forty-eight days. Into each of these fifty men were crowded, with such provisions as they could obtain. They sailed on September 22,

1528, following the coast westwardly "until the latter part of October," when they made a landing but were attacked by the natives and lost two of their men,—a fact afterwards reported by Hernando de Soto. This landing is supposed to have been near the present site of Pensacola. The expedition at once put to sea again and the only chronicle extant of the immediate happenings is found in Oviedo's version of a letter written nine years later by one of the only two survivors (the original text does not exist), as follows:

And our people went two more days, at the end of which the boat in which the treasurer was arrived at a point made by the coast, behind which was a river that flowed broad and swollen from freshet; a little behind, the boat of the governor and the others anchored at some islands near by, and the treasurer went to them and made known the discovery of the river. As they found no wood with which to parch the maize they had been eating raw for two days, they agreed to enter the river, of which they took up fresh water in the sea; and on going near to it, the violence of the current at the entrance did not permit them to gain the land. While working to get to it the wind sprang up in the north, and by it and the strong current they were put out more to sea. And they sailed that night and the next day following up to night time, when they found themselves in three fathoms depth, and seeing that evening many smokes on the coast, they did not dare to land in the night time, and anchored.

The "Relation" sent by Nuñez Cadeza de Vaca, described as "the treasurer," to Emperor Charles V. the same year differs in some respects. Here is its text:

We sailed that day until the middle of the afternoon, when my boat, which was first, discovered a point made by the land, and against a cape opposite passed a broad river. I cast anchor near a little island forming the point, to await the arrival of the other boats. The Governor did not choose to come up, and entered a bay near by in which were a great many islets. We came together there and took fresh water from the sea, the stream entering it in freshet. To parch some of the maize we brought with us, since we had eaten it raw for two days, we went on an island, but finding no wood, we agreed to go to the river beyond the point, one league off. By no effort could we get there, so violent was the current on the way, which drove us out while we contended and strove to gain the land. The north wind which came from the shore began to blow so strongly that it forced us to sea without our being able to overcome it. We sounded half a league out, and found with thirty fathoms, we could not get bottom; but we were unable to satisfy ourselves that the current was the cause of the failure. Toiling in this manner to fetch the land, we navigated three days, and at the end of this time, a little before the sun rose, we saw smoke in several places along the shore. Attempting to reach them, we found ourselves in three fathoms of water.

It is not mere guesswork to conclude that the mouth of this river which De Vaca could not enter with his shallow boats was some other stream than the Mississippi. Exactly where he touched must be a matter of surmise, because it may have been any river outlet along the coast of what is now Texas.

With this voyage, we close the conjectural period of Mississippi River discovery, taking up in the next chapter the real hero of the history of the mighty river, Hernando de Soto, Adelantado de Florida, and Conquistador.

CHAPTER II

Dawn of the Era of Credibility

DEALING with fable or with fact, the distinction of original discovery of "The Father of Running Waters" must be accorded to the Spaniards. They were not only first to gaze upon the Mississippi, but, on their return to Europe, first to make it known to the civilised world of their day. The name of the hardy adventurer who first sighted the three-pronged delta never will be known, but he was a Spaniard.

Series of Lakes, supposed route of Pineda, entering Mississippi in 1519 and of Moscoso leaving it in 1543

"It is a remarkable feature in the history of the Mississippi," says Schoolcraft, "that it has been 'discovered' in sections, separated by long intervals of time." When we remember that the river is nearly three thousand miles in length, almost dividing a great continent, nothing else was to have been expected.

Quest for gold brought adventurers to the mouth of the mighty stream, while explorations of the northwest were principally undertaken in the name of religion. Some explorations were not so religious as they claimed to be, because a thrifty spirit of commercialism characterised the conduct of their leaders.

The highly coloured tales of Cabeza de Vaca inspired the formation and despatch of the largest expedition that ever set sail for the American world. A soldier of fortune, Hernando de Soto was born at Badajos in 1500 or 1501, and when fourteen years of age, went to Darien with Pedrarias. He is heard of ten years later in Nicaragua, with Cordoba. In the spring of 1532, he joined Pizarro with reinforcements at the Gulf of Guayaquil and took a prominent part in the conquest of Peru. He returned to Spain, in 1536, loaded with honours and loot. The following year, Charles V. appointed this daring adventurer Governor of Cuba and Florida, adding special instructions to explore the latter country. If we may believe the *Relation of a Gentleman of the Town of Elvas,* written in Portuguese but not printed in English until 1686, the flower of the Spanish nobility joined that expedition. Of the six hundred Spaniards and Portuguese noblemen " in doubtlets and cassocks of silk " every man was intent on winning glory and gaining riches. The entire expedition, when it finally sailed from Havana, is said to have numbered nine thousand men, including officers, sailors, and fighting men. This statement is evidently erroneous because nine ships sufficed to carry the invaders. Soto's total equipment was probably about nine hundred and fifty men, half of whom were arrayed in silk or satin. The little squadron sailed from San Lucar in April, 1538, and after a year in Cuba, left Havana (May 12, 1539) for Tampa Bay, where a landing was made. The ships were sent back to Havana, with orders to return to a designated place upon the northern coast of the Gulf.

The march of Soto during the next three years took him around the top of the Gulf, across territory that is now Florida, Alabama, and Mississippi. He made a great circuit to the northward that possibly carried him into Georgia, the Carolinas, and eastern Tennessee. That is conjectural, however; but it is known that he descended the Alabama River to Mobile Bay. There he had a fierce engagement with the natives (October, 1540). Thence, he pushed north-westward through Mississippi and wintered on the Yazoo River, near to the greater river but unconscious of its proximity. A severe battle with the Indians occurred at this point. (This same ground was fought over by Grant and Sherman during the Civil War, prior to the siege of Vicksburg.) Soto reached the Mississippi at Chicka-saw Bluffs, May 8, 1541, old style, the exact locality of Sherman's defeat in 1863. Soto crossed the Mis-sissippi on May 15th, by what means is not clear, for the river is more than a mile wide at that point and the spring floods must have rendered its current very rapid. He explored the region west of the river as far north as the Missouri and south to the Red River. He did not find the fabulous stores of gold he had expected to discover. His followers were discouraged; two hundred and fifty of them had died of fevers or wounds received in battle. He returned to the Mississippi again, at the mouth of the Red River, on April 17, 1542, fell ill of malarial fever, and after appointing

Luis de Moscoso (generally written Luys Moscoso) his successor, Hernando de Soto died. To maintain the fable of Soto's divine attributes, his body was hidden in a hut for several days and then buried in the darkness of night. But the natives discovered the grave and gathered about it. Moscoso became fearful the Indians might disinter the body; removing it from the grave, he sunk it, heavily weighted, in the middle of the great river with which the name of the Conquistador for ever will be associated. According to "A Gentleman of Elvas," the only chronicler who accompanied the expedition and whose name never will be known, Soto died on May 21st.

The will of Hernando de Soto, made in San Cristobal of the Havana, May 10, 1539, and sent back to Spain, was found at Seville among the papers in the suit of Isabel de Bobadilla, his widow, against Hernan Ponce de Leon, Soto's partner and a co-executor of the estate under the will. It is a long document, gorged with religion, and makes many bequests. Soto directed that his body be buried in the church at Xeres, near Badajos,—a wish that never was realised.

After wandering about in the swamps until December of the same year, the depleted band reached Minoya, above the mouth of the Arkansas,—much farther from the Gulf than the point at which Soto died.[1] Here they constructed and launched seven brigantines, in which, on July 2, 1543, they set out for the mouth of the tortuous river, thus completing their

---

[1] Coronado was in the country west of the Mississippi, probably in what is now Kansas, when Moscoso's troop was in such straits. Had the fact been known and could they have united, the fate of the combined troop might have been very different.—J. C.

knowledge of the lower part of the broad stream to which Soto had given the title of "Rio Grande," or Great River.

Attaining the Gulf, they coasted westward, never losing sight of land in their frail vessels, until they arrived, ragged and disheartened, at the Spanish settlement at Tampico. "They kissed the ground when they found themselves again among their countrymen," according to the Elvas chronicler.

Here the record of Spanish exploration in the Mississippi Valley halts for two hundred years. There were a few private expeditions to Florida, chiefly from Cuba, but all were disastrous. The Spaniards had "discovered" the Mississippi; but they did nothing to utilise it.

CHAPTER III

The French Explorations

WE must now mentally transport ourselves to Canada and to the North-west. As we have seen, the Spaniards made their search for the Mississippi from the sea; the French set out from the region of the Great Lakes. Professor Ogg truly says: "Except as a basis for subsequent territorial claims, its discovery by the Spaniards might as well never have occurred. The whole work of discovery had to be wrought anew nearly a century and a half later by the efforts of a different people."

The fur-traders and the missionaries of New France accomplished a task that the Spaniards, greedy for gold, had abandoned in disgust.

The Roman Church was prompt to recognise the importance of the discoveries of Columbus. Whether the Genoese had found much or little territory, Pope Alexander VI. undertook, as Vicegerent of the Creator of land and sea, to apportion it between Spain and Portugal. By a bull, bearing date of May 4, 1493, the right of discovery—which carried with it possession—of any new lands upon the face of this earth, whether the planet were flat or spheroidal, was accorded to those two crowns. This remarkable document, disposing of all territories, known and unknown, in the Americas, much of Africa, the eastern part of Asia, and the islands of the Atlantic Ocean, fixed as a dividing line the meridian passing north and south through the Azores. A year later, the same authority, presumably at Portugal's insistence, moved the longitudinal demarcation far enough westward to annex to the crown of Portugal the eastern part of the continent of South America. The only part of North America gained by Portugal was the large island of Newfoundland. The remainder of both continents was accorded to Spain! Although Portugal got the worse of that Papal decree, it still holds much of the territory granted at that time, while Spain has lost every foot of the earth's surface thus apportioned except the Canary Islands!

Doubt as to the exact point at which that longitudinal line crossed the mainland of North America afforded a pretext to the French to enter this continent by the Gulf of St. Lawrence. Francis I. was a devout churchman; he respected the majesty of Spain but cared little for the rights of Portugal. That Papal bull was therefore the excuse for the voyages of Jacques Cartier.

I—JACQUES CARTIER

The chart of Sylvanus, from the edition of Ptolemy of 1511, induced Cartier to sail from St. Malo, April 20, 1534, with two vessels of sixty tons each and sixty-one men, for the " Square Gulf," or Gulf of St. Lawrence familiar to us, instead of to the semi-enclosed sea known at that day to lie west of the Florida peninsula. This statement is practically reduced to a demonstration by Justin Winsor, in his recent elaborate volume.[1]

[1] *Cartier to Frontenac*, by Justin Winsor, 1894. (The cartography of this work makes it invaluable.—J. C.)

" Norman, Breton, and Basque had been frequenters of its shores," says Winsor, meaning the " Gulfo Quadrado," and Cartier felt sure of the accuracy of their charts—a contention that has been seriously disputed regarding the " Admiral's map " of the Gulf of Mexico. Jacques Cartier does not belong to the Mississippi any more than do his successors who never reached its banks; but Cartier, Roberval, Nicolet, and Champlain were the inspiration of the subsequent advance of sturdy explorers and earnest French missionaries into the New World.

Before there could be a Groseilliers, a Radisson, a La Salle, or a Marquette, there had to be a New France.

This development of an unknown land took time; and that fact accounts for the long interregnum between the lapse of Spanish enthusiasm for exploration on the Gulf of Mexico and the westward advances of the French from Quebec through the Great Lakes. The failure of Columbus to locate a supposed strait leading to Cathay was admitted. The broad river that flowed into the " Square Gulf " promised much. If Cartier, in his reported voyage to the coast of Brazil during his buccaneer period, had encountered the wide mouth of the Amazon, he might have entertained the same hope of solving the problem that Columbus and his successors had abandoned. Every mile of progress made by his ships up the St. Lawrence to what is now called the Island of Orleans, near the present site of Quebec, must have encouraged Cartier in the belief that he had indeed found the way to the ocean of the Indies. He established winter quarters in a small cove near the mouth of the St. Charles River. On

September 19, 1534, taking one of his vessels, he started up the St. Lawrence, and, on October 2d, reached the present site of Montreal. He named the hill, familiar to every visitor to the hustling Canadian city, Mont Royal. When Cartier climbed that mount, down which athletic Canadians now toboggan during four months of every winter, he saw only the terrors of the Lachine Rapids and recognised a natural barrier that must have ended his dream of a channel to the Indies.

The real value of this inland voyage of Cartier is that the route was developed up the Ottawa, through Nipissing Lake to the sea of the Hurons and the Great Lakes. Its importance was momentous! If Canada ever grows sufficiently rich and enterprising, she will cut a canal from Lake Huron through Nipissing Lake to the upper Ottawa and, by a series of locks on that river, establish a water route that will shorten, by a thousand miles, the distance from Duluth and the vast wheat country of the Dakotas and Manitoba to the sea!

The Frenchmen, like the natives, knew hardly anything about Lakes Ontario and Erie, because their way to the North-west led up the Ottawa, through Lake Nipissing to Georgian Bay, and left those two large bodies of water outside their path.

Cartier's *Bref Récit,* as his report to Francis I. is known, is one of the few veritable guide-posts of modern history. He returned to France twice and died within sound of the sea, on the Brittany coast, September 1, 1557. But Gerard Mercator, the Flemish map-maker, did not recognise the debt geography owed to Cartier. Either he had not heard of the Frenchman's explorations or he disbelieved in him.[1]

[1] The Hakluyt-Martyr map of 1587 was the first to show the

II—GROSEILLIERS AND RADISSON

The claims of these two men as original discoverers of Minnesota have been disputed, reasserted, and discussed ever since the finding of the so-called R a d i s s o n manuscripts in the Bodleian L i b r a r y, at Oxford, and among some records of the Hudson Bay Company now owned by the British Museum. The history of these precious manuscripts—which, in themselves, appear to be fully authenticated—casts a shadow upon them that is probably ill deserved. They were copied and published only in 1885, by the Prince Society of Boston, in a small quarto volume of three hundred and eighty-five pages, bearing this title: *" Voyages of Peter Esprit Radisson,* Being an Account of his Travels and Experiences among the North American Indians, from 1652 to 1654. Transcribed from original Manuscripts . . . and an Introduction, by Gideon

MISSISSIPPI RIVER: PROGRESS OF ITS DISCOVERY.

MORRISON, 1804

Prairie Island GROSEILLIERS AND RADISSON, 1655.

JOLIET AND MARQUETTE, south to the Arkansas River, 1673.

Missouri R.

Mississippi River

Ohio R.

Arkansas R.

DE SOTO, 1541.

Red R.

PINEDA, 1519.

NARVAEZ, 1528.

Atlantic, Gulf, and Pacific coast lines of North America below latitude 50° N.

D. Scull, London, England. Boston: Published by the Prince Society, 1885." In the aforementioned " Introduction," we learn that these priceless manuscripts, if genuine and trustworthy, were " for some time the property of Samuel Pepys, diarist and Secretary of the Admiralty to Charles II. and James II., who probably received them from Sir George Carteret, Vice-Chamberlain of the King and Treasurer of the Navy, for whom, no doubt, they were carefully copied from his rough notes by the author, so that they might be brought, through him, under the notice of Charles II. Some years after the death of Pepys, in 1703, his collection of manuscripts " (meaning Pepys's collection) " was dispersed and fell into the hands of various London tradesmen, who bought parcels to use in their shops as waste-paper. The most valuable portions were reclaimed by the celebrated collector, Richard Rawlinson." Here we have all that is known about the Radisson narratives. Although Mr. Scull, editor of the manuscripts as published by the Prince Society, states in his introduction, " All his [Radisson's] manuscripts have been handed down in perfect preservation, and are written out in a clear and excellent handwriting, showing the writer to have been a person of good education," there are disconnected passages inclining one to fear that many sheets were lost or misplaced. Some of the most vital incidents in the narratives are passed over by mere mention or are vaguely hinted at, while inconsequential matters are given in elaborate detail. It is futile, therefore, at this late date, to discuss these slips and shadows of doubt. We must take the narrative as it comes to us, and allow every reader to have an opinion of his or her own.

The writer of this volume does not intend to enter upon a discussion regarding the credibility of the Radisson accounts of the stay of Groseilliers and himself in the valley of the Mississippi. That they were there is very fully attested by *The Jesuit Relations and Allied Documents; Travels and Explorations of the Jesuit Missionaries in New France, 1610 to 1791.* This series of seventy-three volumes is probably the most valuable bit of Americana ever published in this country (Cleveland, Ohio, 1896–1901). The writer prefers to lean upon the best authority now living on the Radisson manuscripts, Warren Upham, Secretary of the Minnesota Historical Society, and to accept them as they come to the readers of the present day.

Sieur des Groseilliers, as the young Jesuit layman helper in missionary work among the Hurons and Algonquins chose to describe himself, was born Medard Chouart,[1] probably near Meaux, France, in 1621. Before he was twenty, he came to Canada and for six years or more was a devoted servant of the Faith. Then he became a fur-trader. He married a daughter of Abraham Martin, from whom the Plains of Abraham, to the west of the citadel at Quebec, received their name. This wife, Helen, died in 1651 and two years thereafter he took for second wife a sister of Radisson. This appears to have been the tie that bound these two intrepid adventurers together. Pierre Esprit

[1] " The name of des Groseillers, taken from a small property, was Medard Chouart, but he is as little known by that name as Voltaire was known by his real name of Arouet, he being always spoken of by the name of des Groseillers, changed in one affidavit into ' Gooseberry,' the name literally translated into English being ' gooseberry bushes.' "—Canadian Archives, Report for 1895, p. 22.

Radisson was also a Frenchman, hailing from St. Malo, in Brittany. While a boy in his teens, his parents brought him to Three Rivers, a settlement on the northern bank of the St. Lawrence, about midway between Quebec and Montreal. The date of the arrival of the Radissons is fixed by the fact that Groseilliers married Marguerite Radisson shortly after their coming to the country (1651). Radisson had been a sailor, even in youth, and knew most of the ports of the Mediterranean. He had visited Paris, and during a lengthy stay in London had acquired the English language,—not alone a grammatical knowledge, but an idiomatic and colloquial acquaintance, as his written narratives prove. One year after his arrival in Canada, Radisson, while on a hunting expedition, fell into the hands of a band of Iroquois and was taken by the Indians to a point in what is now Central New York, on the Mohawk River. At the end of a year, he escaped to Fort Orange (now Albany), came down the river to New Amsterdam, whence he sailed to Holland. Radisson returned to Three Rivers in the spring of 1654, at which point our interest in his "voyages" begins. Groseilliers, as the elder man, appears to have been accorded command, although Radisson was much the better type of *coureur des bois*. In the two expeditions, for profit rather than fame, that these two commercial adventurers made between 1654 and 1660, they penetrated beyond the great lakes of Michigan and Superior into what is now Minnesota territory. The claims set forth in the Radisson manuscripts to having descended "the great river" to the sea or of having travelled as far north as Hudson Bay need not be discussed. The first is probably a boast

Mats (they told vs that there weare sixteen thousand men this we beliued). they haue as many wiu's as they can keepe. If any one did trespasse vpon the other, his nose was cutt off, and often the crowne of his head. The maidens haue all manner of freedome, but are forced to mary when they come to the age. the more they beare children, the more they are respected. I haue seen a man hauing fourteene wiues. there they haue no wood, and make prouision of mosse for their firing. this their place is environed with pearches which are a good distance one from another, that they gett in the valleys where the Buffes to lepasse vppon which they doe kill. they sow corne but their haruest is small. the soyle is good but the cold hinders it, and the graine very small. In their countrey are mines of copper, of peuter and of lead. there are mountaines couered with a kind of stone that is transparent and tender, and like to that of Venice. the people stay not there all of yeare they retire in winter towards the wood of the North where they kill a quantity of castors, and I say that there are not so good in the whole world, but not in such a store as the christines, but for bech. wee stayed there six weeke, and came back with a company of people of another nation of the Nadueseronons that came along with vs so farr as boats, we weare twelue dayes before we could overtake our company that went to the lake. Others being approaches with the first time to kill the Oriniack a wildman and Indian my brother killd that time aboue six hundred, besides other beasts. we came to the lake side with much paine, for we spent our wildmen before, and we two weare forced to make carriages fiue dayes through the woods, after we mett with a company that did vs a great deale of service for they carryed what we had and arriued att the appointed place before three dayes ended, here we made a fort, att our arriuall we found at least twenty stages full. one faire euening we went to finde what we hid before which we finde in a good condition. we went about to execut our resolution for seeing that we must stay that yeare there for we weare not very sorry being resolued to know what we heard before we waited untill the Ice should vanish but receiued that the Octanaks built a fort on the point that formes that Bay, which resembles a small lake. we went towards it with all speede. we had a great store of booty which we would not trust to the wildmen for the occasion makes the thiefe. we overloaded our slids on that rotten Ice, and the further we went the sun was stronger which made our drainage haue more difficultie. I seeing my brother so strained, I tooke the slid which was heauier then mine, and he mine. being in that extent aboue three leagues from the ground we sunke downe aboue the one halfe of the legge in the Ice: and must advance in spight of our teeth. to leaue our booty was to endoe vs, we strued to that I hurted my selfe in so much that I could not stand vp right, nor any further. this putt vs in great trouble. vppon this I aduised my brother to leaue me with his slid. we put the two slids one by another. I tooke some cloathes to couer me. after I shipped my selfe from my wett cloathes, I stayed my selfe downe on the slid. my brother leaues me to the keeping of that good God. he had not aboue two leagues more to goe. he makes hast and came there in time and sends will men for me and the slids. there we found the perfidiousnesse off the Octanaks.

seeing

A Page of the Radisson Manuscript.
Photographed at Bodleian Library, Oxford, England, under Direction
of Hon. W. E. Lee.
(Courtesy of J. V. Brower.)

and the second is unimportant in connection with the
Mississippi.

With the generous permission of Mr. Upham, who
has placed at my disposal the fruits of years of research and travel, I shall summarise an exhaustive
treatise on the narratives of these " first white men in
Minnesota " based upon a series of addresses recently
delivered by him before the Minnesota Historical
Society.[1]

Radisson "married upward," securing for wife the
daughter of John Kirke, who soon after became a director in the Hudson Bay Company. That corporation, which received its charter from Charles II. as
late as 1670, had been doing business in a practical
manner for many years prior to that date. Radisson
had joined interests with the pioneers of that company,
and, with his brother-in-law, had gone to England to
put up a good front for the acquisition of the charter.
But Radisson was at heart a Frenchman and he was
not a tractable employee of the Hudson Bay Company.
In 1674, he kicked over the traces and transferred his
allegiance again to France, taking with him his inseparable companion, and for ten years did everything
that he believed would advance the interests of his native land. He went so far as to establish a French
trading post near the mouth of the Nelson River and
to turn pirate by seizing a New England ship that had
penetrated into Hudson Bay. This high-handed act
led to negotiations between the two nations, in which
Groseilliers and Radisson were "turned down" by the

[1] Published in *Minnesota Historical Society Collections*, vol. x.,
Part II., pp. 449–594. The maps in this chapter are used by the
courtesy of Mr. Upham and the Minnesota Historical Society.—J.C.

French. They harked back to their English friends and were welcomed with open arms. No doubt, Radisson's father-in-law had much to do with that reception and for the forgiveness of the past. In a few lines of the " Narratives," Radisson states his own feelings, although he does not speak for his companion. He writes: " In May, 1684, I passed over to England for good; so intent was I on engaging myself to the service of his Majesty, and to the interests of the Nation, that any other consideration was never able to detach me from it." Groseilliers, ever a Frenchman, refused the overtures of the Hudson Bay Company; and at this parting of the ways the two brothers-in-law separated for ever. Groseilliers drops out of history as does Civilis, the great Batavian, afoot upon the disconnected bridge over the Wahal at the end of the Sixth Book of Tacitus's *History*.

What these two men had previously accomplished in six years (1654 to 1660) cannot be overlooked by any historian of North American development. Our interest in their " voyages " begins with the first western expedition of the two Frenchmen, which occupies pages 134 to 172 in the Prince Society's publication. Radisson, the chronicler, overlooked the importance of the discovery of the Upper Mississippi, because he entitles his Narrative " The Auxoticiat Voyage into the Great and filthy Lake of the Hurrons, Upper Sea of the East, and Bay of the North." The date of starting is not set down, but it is certain that it occurred in the fall of 1654, because Radisson had returned from France in the spring of that year. They ascended the Ottawa River, with a small company of Hurons and Ottawas, by way of Nipissing to what is now known

as Georgian Bay. Stopping at all trading posts, the
Frenchmen passed that winter in the neighbourhood of
the Strait of Mackinac. Radisson praises the beauty
of Lake Huron; some of the expeditions were extended
as far as Green Bay,
Lake M i c h i g a n.
Early in the spring
of 1655, the two ad-
venturers went to
the southern end of
G r e e n B a y, as-
cended t h e F o x
River through Lake
W i n n e b a g o, ad-
vanced across Wis-
consin, and entered

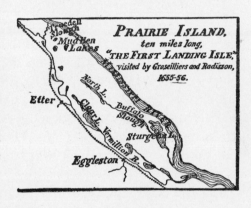

PRAIRIE ISLAND,
ten miles long,
"THE FIRST LANDING ISLE,"
visited by Groseilliers and Radisson,
1655-56.

the Mississippi near the site of Prairie du Chien.
Thence the explorers ascended the Mississippi through
Lake Pepin to Isle Pelée (or Bald Island), now
known as Prairie Island, on the Minnesota side
of the main channel a short distance above Red Wing.
Their stay lasted from April or May, 1655, to June,
1656, about fourteen months.

Investigations made by Upham and Brower regarding the year passed by Groseilliers and Radisson on
Prairie Island have done so much to clear up the mystery that enveloped the Jesuit "Relations" and the
Radisson diaries that we cannot do better than quote
the Upham address on this point:

On this island, which derived its names, both in French
and English, from its being mostly a prairie, a large number
of Hurons and Ottawas, fleeing from their enemies, the Iroquois, had recently taken refuge, and had begun the cultiva-

tion of corn. Their harvest the preceding year, on newly
worked land, was small; but much corn would be needed for
food during the long journey thence to Quebec with beaver
skins, which canoe voyage, requiring a month or more, Groseilliers and Radisson wished to begin soon after their arrival

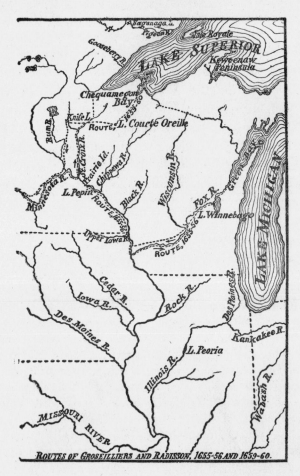

ROUTES OF GROSEILLIERS AND RADISSON, 1655-56 AND 1659-60.

at the island. They were obliged to remain till the next
year, and Groseilliers spent the summer on Prairie Island and
in its vicinity, one of his chief objects being to provide a large
supply of corn for the return journey. Meanwhile Radisson

went with hunting parties, and travelled "four months . . . without doing anything but go from river to river." He was enamoured of the beauty and fertility of the country, and was astonished at its herds of buffaloes and antelopes, flocks of pelicans, and the shovel-nosed sturgeon, all of which he particularly described. Such was the first year, 1655, of observations and exploration by white men in Minnesota, and their earliest navigation of the upper part of the Mississippi River.

During the summer of 1655, while Groseilliers was planting, tending, and harvesting corn for the return journey of himself and his attendants in the following year, Radisson occupied four months of the season in hunting excursions. His account of these trips is so general as not to be satisfactory. Apparently, he desired to have posterity believe that he had descended the great river to the Gulf of Mexico. Here is a verbatim transcript:

We weare 4 moneths in our voyage without doeing anything but goe from river to river. We mett severall sorts of people. We conversed with them, being long time in alliance with them. By the persuasion of som of them we went into the great river that divides itselfe in 2, where the hurrons with some Ottanake & the wildmen that had warrs with them had retired. There is not great difference in their language, as we weare told. This nation have warrs against those of [the] forked river. It is so called because it has 2 branches, the one towards the west, the other towards the South, which we believe runns towards Mexico, by the tokens they gave us. Being among these people, they told us the prisoners they take tells them that they have warrs against a nation, against men that build great cabbans & have great beards & had such knives as we had. Moreover they shewed a Decad of beads & guilded pearls that they have had from that people, which made us believe they weare Europeans. They shewed one of that nation that was taken the yeare before. We understood him not; he was much more tawny than they with whome we weare. His armes & leggs weare turned outside; that was the punishment inflicted uppon him. So they doe with them that they take, & kill them with clubbs & doe often eat them. They doe not burne their prisoners as those of the northern parts.

We weare informed of that nation that live in the other river. These weare men of extraordinary height & biggnesse, that made us believe they had no communication with them. They live onely uppon Corne & Citrulles [pumpkins], which are mighty bigg. They have fish in plenty throughout the yeare. They have fruit as big as the heart of on Oriniak, which grows on vast trees which in compasse are three arme-full in compasse. When they see litle men they are afraid & cry out, which makes many come help them. Their arrows are not of stones as ours are, but of fish boans & other boans that they worke greatly, as all other things. Their dishes are made of wood. I having seene them, could not but admire the curiosity of their worke. They have great calumetts of great stones, red and greene. They make a store of tobacco. They have a kind of drink that makes them mad for a whole day. This I have not seene, therefore you may believe as you please.

Mr. Upham concludes from this narrative that the Radisson party travelled south-eastward, through what is now Illinois, " going by portages from one river to another, until they reached the Illinois River, ' that divides itself in two,' so described, apparently, because it is formed by the junction of the Des Plaines and the Kankakee, each an important canoe route." Descending the Illinois to the Mississippi, Radisson probably went as far south as the junction of the big muddy Missouri, referred to as an important canoe route " toward the west." Upham concludes that neither Groseilliers nor Radisson was aware that the river upon which they were encamped, at Prairie Island, was the eastern or main branch of their "forked river."

The great council held on Prairie Island, prior to the return of the Frenchmen to civilisation, must always command a place in the early history of the Mississippi Valley. It bears so many earmarks of veritability that Radisson must be acquitted of exaggeration in this instance, if not in some others. Probably five hundred Indians of various tribes had assembled, with their flotilla of birch canoes, to accompany the two Frenchmen to Lower Canada. The Hurons, who had accompanied the traders the previous year, were afraid of their enemies, then upon the war paths along the route. The dangers of the return journey took away the courage of the Indians, and they began to talk about waiting until another year. But Radisson, as soon as the "Council of Braves" was assembled, harangued it.

This incident occurred toward the latter part of June. Mr. Upham says:

What a scene for a painter to depict Groseilliers and Radisson pleading before eight hundred Indians! On each side, two miles away, rise the wooded bluffs that inclose this valley and its islands. In a beautiful prairie area, the motley crowd of savages are sitting or lying upon the ground. At the centre of the assemblage, these two courageous Frenchmen are striving to persuade their dusky auditors to set out on the first commercial venture connecting this region with civilisation.

The eloquence of Radisson prevailed. Accompanied by several hundred Hurons and other Algonquins (Radisson says five hundred), and "carrying a most welcome freight of furs," Groseilliers and Radisson arrived in Montreal and Quebec in August, 1656.

The second western expedition of Groseilliers and Radisson did not occur until two or three years later. Historians never will agree whether the two Frenchmen started in 1658 or 1659, although the Radisson account explicitly enumerates the events of two years, which perforce would have marked the summer of 1658 as the time at which the journey began, because the return of the party in August, 1660, is proved by several concurring records. Again there is a clash with the " Journal" of the Jesuit Fathers, which indicates that the party was away only one year. Upham charges Radisson with deliberately adding a year during which he asserted that he made a journey to Hudson Bay. In any event, the charge does not affect the Groseilliers and Radisson explorations in northern Minnesota. The Jesuits might not have known of the year's voyaging to the far North. Upham insists that records at Montreal, Three Rivers, and Quebec show that the party was absent about twelve months. That is vital, so far as affecting the credibility of the alleged Hudson Bay trip, but it does not concern the parts of the Radisson narrative that interest us.

After more elaborate preparations than on the first journey beyond Lake Superior, the two brothers-in-law paddled away from Three Rivers amid the darkness of night, because the Governor of Quebec, Argenson, had expressly refused to sanction the expedition on terms proposed by the explorers and had followed that refusal with a specific prohibition. The journey up the Ottawa River was attended by several skirmishes with roving bands of Iroquois. Some of the best written

passages in Radisson are his descriptions of the craft
and wariness of Indian warfare; he understood the aboriginal nature as well as Fenimore Cooper. Twenty-
two days of frequent danger and constant hardship
brought the canoe flotilla into Georgian Bay, which
Radisson describes as " a sweet sea." Following the
east coast northward they came to the Sault Ste.
Marie, " overflowing from Lake Superior." Jean
Nicolet, with seven Huron canoemen, had ascended the
Sault just twenty-five years before (1634), and had
cast the first European eyes upon " The Big Sea
Water,"—as Superior was known to the Indian tribes
of the region. Groseilliers and Radisson became the
first white men to navigate its length and to enter the
territory now known as northern Wisconsin and Minnesota. Radisson's description of the landmarks along
the south coast of Superior are accurate and prove his
presence there. He makes first mention of the high
sand dunes near Point au Sable, about one hundred
miles beyond the Sault. Fifteen miles farther, south-
westward from Point au Sable, he locates with accuracy the Grand Portal, or Arched Rock, a natural
wonder to this day. Also, the Keweenaw peninsula,
which projects fifty miles into the lake, and the portage,
which saved eight days' paddling around the headland, are described. Five days of canoeing beyond the
western end of the Keweenaw portage brought the
voyageurs to a camp of Crees, on the shore, where they
were welcomed. A few days later, at the mouth of
the Montreal River, some boats' crews of Ojibwas, the
men in which had voyaged with the party from the
Sault, turned their boats into that stream, returning
to their own country. The main party, however, con-

3

tinued westward along the coast half a day's paddling
to Chequamegon Bay, which became their base for departure inland and for their subsequent return homeward. This headquarters was about the site of the
present town of Ashland.

A stockade was erected, to protect the party from
sudden attacks by the natives, until a start for the
interior could be made. Having arrived so late in the
fall, the determination of the Frenchmen not to winter
on the coast is inexplicable. They had heard of a
large Indian settlement about sixty miles in the direction of the St. Croix River, by which in the spring
they intended to descend to the Mississippi. This
community was on the shore of what was later called
" Ottawa Lake." It is now identified as Lac Courte
Oreille. The natives of the tribe had not among them
an organising mind like that of Groseilliers at Prairie
Island to prepare a store of corn for the bleak winter:
the result was that the Frenchmen and their carriers
became a further addition to the half-starving settlement before the rigours of winter began. The situation
grew rapidly worse. Those who have doubted the accuracy of " The Famine," as portrayed in Longfellow's
Hiawatha, will do well to compare the poem with
Radisson's account of the sufferings of himself and
party that winter. According to Upham, " the narra-
tion shows that the winter began while Groseilliers and
Radisson were guests, as we may say, of the Huron and
Menominee Indians, probably at Lac Courte Oreille,
near Hayward, Wisconsin. The first snowfall, and the
ensuing separation of the Indians into parties of two
or three for procuring sustenance by hunting, took place,
as we must suppose, in the later part of October or

early November, 1659. Two months and a half later, that is, shortly after New Year's day of 1660, they came together at ' the small lake, the place of rendezvous ' in the country of the Sioux."

Radisson's description of the reassembling and the famine that followed, turned into modern English, is highly realistic:

We are come to the small lake, the place of rendezvous, where we found some people who had preceded us. We built huts, waiting for those that came in day by day. We remained fourteen days at this place, dismal as a churchyard; for a heavy snow fell, preceded by mist that caused the snow to stick to the rough-barked trees. The snow was so fine that it would not bear our weight and although we made racketts six feet long and a foot and a half broad we could not travel upon them.

The famine grew worse daily. Beasts of the forests had been frightened away, hunting was unprofitable. To augment our misery, we received news from the Octanaks, a tribe of one hundred and fifty, including women and children. They had had a quarrel with the Hurons on the island where we had been some years before in the Lake of the Staring Hairs [Bois Blanc Island, as identified by Campbell, in Lake Huron. —Upham], threatening to make war upon them in the coming summer. Did they bring anything upon which to subsist? Nothing; they are worse provided than are we: not having any huntsmen, they are reduced to famine. O, cursed covetousness, what art thou going to do? It were far better that a company of rogues perish than that we be in danger of a fate so cruel. They kept victuals from their own poor children, those dogs. They are the cursedest, unablest, and cowardliest people I have seen amongst fourscore nations! Every one cries with hunger; the women become barren and the breasts of nursing mothers dry like wood. You men must eat the bow-string, seeing you have not strength to use the bow. Children, you must die! Ye French, who call your-

selves Gods of the earth, hoping to make yourselves feared;
but you, too, shall taste of this bitterness.

Oh! If the music we hear could give to us hope: we need
not for lamentable sounds nor sad spectacles. In the morning, the husband looks upon his wife, the brother upon his
sister, the cousin upon cousin, the uncle upon nephew found
dead in their cabins. The living languish with cries and hide-
ous lamentations. Good God, have mercy upon these unfortunate, innocent people! Of us that acknowledge Thee and have
offended, punish us! True, we also have the executioner among
us. Those of us that are able, seek roots which are found
with much difficulty. The earth is frozen two and three feet
deep and the snow lies five and six feet upon it. Our chief
subsistence is a vine with a rind that grows upon trees like
ivy. We cut this vine into short pieces, boil them until the
skin loosens. This we dry in the smoke and grind to powder
between two stones, making a broth. It causes much thirst,
however.

We ate our dogs during the first fortnight. Next, we devoured the pelts we had reserved for shoes, clothes, and socks,
especially the beaver skins that were the walls of our cottages.
We burned off the hair upon the coals. All these abhorrent
things, we devoured. So eagerly did we eat that our gums
did bleed! The bark mentioned was our only food the rest
of the sorrowful time. We finally became images of Death!
We frequently mistook ourselves, taking the living for the
dead and the dead for the living. We wanted strength to
draw our friends out of the cabins, and when we had to do
so it was to put them four paces in the snow. At the end,
the wrath of God begins to be appeased. A large volume
would not contain the details of our sufferings. There were
above five hundred dead,—men, women, and children. When
we had abandoned hope, a few small, lean stags came our
way. They were easily run down, because their feet stuck
in the deep snow. Their throats were readily cut. I forgot
to mention that the wildmen [Indians] charged us with having
food surreptitiously brought to us by devils. Our sufferings
were as great as any, but we did not give up, as did the
natives.

Except for the fact that the Radisson manuscripts were not discovered at Oxford until many years after Longfellow had published *Hiawatha*, the presumption would be fair that he had drawn his facts and inspiration from them. Here is Canto XX., entitled "The Famine":

O the long and dreary Winter!
O the cold and cruel Winter!
Ever thicker, thicker, thicker
Froze the ice on lake and river,
Ever deeper, deeper, deeper
Fell the snow o'er all the land-
    scape,
Fell the covering snow, and
    drifted
Through the forest, round the
    village.
  Hardly from his buried wig-
    wam
Could the hunter force a passage;
With his mittens and his snow-
    shoes
Vainly walked he through the for-
    est,
Sought for bird or beast and
    found none,
Saw no track of deer or rabbit,
In the snow beheld no footprints,
In the ghastly, gleaming forest
Fell, and could not rise from
    weakness,
Perished there from cold and hun-
    ger.
  O the famine and the fever!
O the wasting of the famine!
O the blasting of the fever!
O the wailing of the children!
O the anguish of the women!
  All the earth was sick and
    famished;
Hungry was the air around them,
Hungry was the sky above them,
And the hungry stars in heaven
Like the eyes of wolves glared at
    them!
  Into Hiawatha's wigwam
Came two other guests, as silent
As the ghosts were, and as
    gloomy,
Waited not to be invited,
Did not parley at the doorway,
Sat there without word of wel-
    come

In the seat of Laughing Water;
Looked with haggard eyes and
    hollow
At the face of Laughing Water.
  And the foremost said: "Be-
    hold me!
I am Famine, Bukadawin!"
And the other said: "Behold me!
I am Fever, Ahkosewin!"
  And the lovely Minnehaha
Shuddered as they looked upon
    her,
Shuddered at the words they ut-
    tered,
Lay down on her bed in silence,
Hid her face, but made no answer;
Lay there trembling, freezing,
    burning
At the looks they cast upon her,
At the fearful words they uttered.
  Forth into the empty forest
Rushed the maddened Hiawatha;
In his heart was deadly sorrow,
In his face a stony firmness;
On his brow the sweat of anguish
Started, but it froze and fell not.

. . . .

"Gitche Manito the Mighty!"
Cried he with his face uplifted
In that bitter hour of anguish,
"Give your children food, O
    father!
Give us food, or we must perish!
Give me food for Minnehaha,
For my dying Minnehaha!"
  Through the far - resounding
    forest,
Through the forest vast and va-
    cant
Rang that cry of desolation,
But there came no other answer
Than the echo of his crying,
Than the echo of the woodlands,
"Minnehaha! Minnehaha!"

. . . .

In the wigwam with Nokomis,

With those gloomy guests, that
    watched her,
With the Famine and the Fever,
She was lying, the Beloved,
She the dying Minnehaha.
    "Hark!" she said; "I hear a
    rushing,
Hear a roaring and a rushing,
Hear the Falls of Minnehaha
Calling to me from a distance!"
"No, my child!" said old Noko-
    mis,
"'T is the night-wind in the pine-
    trees!"
    "Look!" she said; "I see my
    father
Standing lonely at his doorway,
Beckoning to me from his wig-
    wam
In the land of the Dacotahs!"
"No, my child!" said old Noko-
    mis,
"'T is the smoke, that waves and
    beckons!"
    "Ah!" she said, "the eyes of
    Pauguk
Glare upon me in the darkness,
I can feel his icy fingers
Clasping mine amid the darkness!
Hiawatha! Hiawatha!"
    And the desolate Hiawatha,
Far away amid the forest,
Miles away among the mountains,
Heard that sudden cry of anguish,
Heard the voice of Minnehaha
Calling to him in the darkness,
"Hiawatha! Hiawatha!"
    Over snow-fields waste and
    pathless,
Under snow-encumbered branches,
Homeward hurried Hiawatha,
Empty-handed, heavy-hearted,
Heard Nokomis moaning, wailing:
"Wahonowin! Wahonowin!
Would that I had perished for
    you,

Would that I were dead as you
    are!
Wahonowin! Wahonowin!"
    And he rushed into the wig-
    wam,
Saw the old Nokomis slowly
Rocking to and fro and moaning,
Saw his lovely Minnehaha
Lying dead and cold before him,
And his bursting heart within
    him
Uttered such a cry of anguish,
That the forest moaned and shud-
    dered,
That the very stars in heaven
Shook and trembled with his an-
    guish.
    Then he sat down, still and
    speechless,
On the bed of Minnehaha,
At the feet of Laughing Water,
At those willing feet, that never
More would lightly run to meet
    him,
Nevermore would lightly follow.
    With both hands his face he
    covered,
Seven long days and nights he
    sat there,
As if in a swoon he sat there,
Speechless, motionless, uncon-
    scious
Of the daylight or the darkness.
    Then they buried Minnehaha;
In the snow a grave they made
    her,
In the forest deep and darksome,
Underneath the moaning hem-
    locks;
Clothed her in her richest gar-
    ments,
Wrapped her in her robes of
    ermine,
Covered her with snow, like er-
    mine;
Thus they buried Minnehaha.

Warren Upham and J. V. Brower agree that the
"small lake" was Knife Lake, Minnesota, about fifteen miles south-east from Mille Lacs, the latter a large
body of shallow water, with numerous islands, that

drains southward into the Mississippi through the Rum
River. Knife Lake is about ninety miles due west of
Lac Courte Oreille. Had the river St. Croix not been
frozen, the party could have descended to their former
home on Prairie Island, where, no doubt, they would
have had to reconquer the lands from the Sioux that
had driven away the Hurons, whom the Frenchmen had
left in possession three years before. As Radisson reports, five hundred people died of famine and pestilence
at the Knife Lake settlement that winter! He and
Groseilliers narrowly escaped the same fate.

When spring came, the Frenchmen were as intent
as they had originally been upon a great feast for the
Indians of the surrounding country. Prior to going
into winter quarters they had sent word to the eighteen
settlements of Sioux, also to the Ojibwas, and they now
summoned the Crees from the shore of Lake Superior.
That feast caused native and foreigner alike to forget
the terrible winter. Radisson's account of the entertainment would do credit to a society writer. Groseilliers and Radisson were famous among the natives as
" chin-chin men." The latter of the two strangers was
the better orator but the former was probably more
familiar with the Indian languages. The effect of the
three weeks' entertainment by the two Frenchmen was
felt among the Crees and Dakotas for two hundred
years! It probably saved thousands of human lives, as
white settlers began to enter the " wildman's country,"
and it made missionary work among the natives less
dangerous.

At the close of the feast, Groseilliers and Radisson,
inseparable on this journey, accompanied the Tinton-
wan Sioux bands on a visit to their homes, far to the

westward of the Mississippi. Their route is not as clearly defined as could be wished, but authorities agree that the party descended the Rum River to the Mississippi at the present site of Anoka, thence by a land route to the Minnesota River, which was ascended to the prairie country.[1] Mr. J. V. Brower, to whom the people of United States owe Itasca Park, at the sources of the Mississippi, argued that the Frenchmen returned with their Sioux hosts to the sources of Crow River, which joins the Mississippi eight miles above Anoka, and did not go near the Minnesota River. It will be noticed on a map that the Minnesota makes a long detour to the southward before it starts upon its northwesterly course. Brower's argument is based upon the non-reference of Radisson to St. Anthony's Falls, a very tenable reason. Whichever route they travelled to " the Sioux of Buffalo Land " they are believed to have returned by the Minnesota and to have encamped under the bluff upon which Saint Paul stands. The rocky heights of Fort Snelling did not have the picturesque, casemated castle that afterward crowned them.

The return to the stockade at Chequamegon Bay, Lake Superior, was made by very much the same route as that over which they had entered the country. At this point appear several irreconcilable points in the narrative,—probably due to changes subsequently made to introduce the Hudson Bay " diversion," which the best of evidence proves never occurred. But it appears credible that in the early part of 1660, the

[1] Mr. Upham discusses the mystery of non-reference to St. Anthony's Falls by Radisson in *Minnesota Historical Society Collections*, vol. x., Part II, pp. 502–503.—J. C.

western end of Lake Superior was encumbered with broken ice. Mr. Upham cites a paper read before the Minnesota Historical Society in 1898 by John R. Carey, in which the statement is made that he, the speaker, " knew two men who got off a steamboat that had been stuck in the ice in sight of Duluth for several days, on June 9th, about forty years ago, and walked to the shore, a distance of six miles." Residents of Duluth assure me that such conditions are very exceptional. But Groseilliers and Radisson pushed their way across the western end of Lake Superior that June, to trade with pelt hunters of the St. Louis River, not far from the present site of the town of Two Harbours. The Frenchmen returned to their base on Chequamegon Bay and outfitted for the seven or eight weeks' homeward journey to Three Rivers. There is no available space to give to that voyage.

The importance of the two expeditions of Groseilliers and Radisson is such that it is not greatly dwarfed by the incontestable fact that they failed to realise the magnitude of their discoveries. Radisson was not the braggart that others who followed him became. For genuine pioneership these Frenchmen stand unchallenged. Radisson also belongs to literature, because modern spelling and a moderate resort to the blue pencil—the lash under which all inexperienced writers of diaries have to go—would render some of his work equal to Parkman or the best of Cooper. Groseilliers and Radisson have left their footprints so plainly in Wisconsin and Minnesota that time never will efface them.

Mr. Upham sums up the work of these two men admirably when he says:

Among all the very interesting records of negotiations and treaties of "peace and union," made with the Indians of the North-west by forerunners and agents of the French fur-trade, none is more picturesque and dramatic than this. In the late autumn or winter of 1634-35, Jean Nicolet, wearing a fantastic silken Chinese vestment, met the Winnebago Indians for a ceremonious conference, in the vague belief that their country might border on the farthest eastern parts of Asia. In 1660, Groseilliers and Radisson, as we have seen, probably within the area of Kanabec county, in the east central part of Minnesota, taught to the Sioux and the Crees, previously hostile to each other, peace and friendship toward the French. In 1679, Du Luth ceremoniously planted the arms of France in the great village of the Isanti tribe at Mille Lacs, and in other Sioux villages of north-eastern Minnesota, none of which, as he says, had been before visited by any Frenchman; and on the 15th of September in that year, at the west end of Lake Superior, he negotiated a great treaty with the assembled tribes of the north, inducing them to make peace with the Sioux, "their common enemy." During the remaining years of the seventeenth century, Perrot, in 1689, at Fort St. Antoine, on the Wisconsin shore of Lake Pepin, and Le Sueur in 1693 at Chequamegon Bay, later at his trading post built on Prairie Island in 1695 according to the command of the Governor of Canada, and again in the winter of 1700 at his Fort L'Huillier, on the Blue Earth River, were conspicuous by their efforts to maintain peace among the Indian tribes, loyalty to the French, and consequent extension and prosperity of the fur-trade.

We may thank Radisson for his particular care to describe the Sioux who attended the great feast. He thus gave the earliest portrayal of the characteristics of that people, the aboriginal owners of the greater part of Minnesota. It is to be regretted, however, that he recorded only a very meagre account of the ensuing visit of these French traders with the Sioux of the Buffalo Prairies ("the Nation of the Beef") in their own country.

III—ALLOUEZ FINDS A NAME

The pioneer voyages of Groseilliers and Radisson had been inspired by hope of commercial gain; but we are now to witness the powerful influence of religion in the field of exploration.

When the flotilla of native canoes that came every spring to French settlements on the St. Lawrence was ready in the autumn of 1665 to begin the homeward voyage to "The Big Sea Water," Father Allouez joined it.

The party arrived at the Sault Ste. Marie on September 2d. Before the great lake froze, Allouez had proceeded to the western end of Superior and had planted a cross and founded a mission at La Pointe, on Chequamegon Bay, near the site of the present town of Ashland. Of the hardships of that long trip, no record remains. Diplomatist, as well as priest, Allouez made friends with eight hundred Algonquin warriors in the neighbourhood of La Pointe and took sides with them against their traditional enemies, the Iroquois. He recognised the efficacy of the war club, the tomahawk, and the arrow when needed to convince a foe of error. During his intercourse with various tribes along the coast of the Gitche Gumee ("The Shining Big Sea Water"), Allouez first heard the name "Missipi" applied to "The Great Running Water." He was of opinion that the river flowed into the Sea of Virginia (Chesapeake). It is significant that neither Groseilliers nor Radisson had brought back that name! Lack of knowledge of the languages of the region may explain, but hardly to the satisfaction of doubters.

At the Sault Ste. Marie mission, Fathers Marquette and Dablon had been labouring for two years before the former was despatched westward to La Pointe in September, 1669, to relieve Allouez, who voyaged to the head of Green Bay, on Lake Michigan, to exert the reformatory influences of religion upon a band of French *coureurs de bois* that had demoralised the native of that locality. Allouez arrived in early winter and established the mission of St. Francis Xavier among the Pottawattomies. In the spring of 1670, he ascended the Fox River, portaged to the head of the Wisconsin, which, he recorded in his next report to Quebec, "led to the great river 'Messisipi,' six days' journey by canoe." The Jesuit "Relation" of the years 1669-70, to which we shall have occasion to refer frequently, specifically mentions this river again, Allouez adding: " It is more than a league [2.76 miles] wide, and flows from North to South. The natives never have reached its mouth: none of them knows whether it empties into the Gulf of Florida or the Vermilion Sea " (Gulf of California).

This information is somewhat more definite than had been learned four years previously by the same missionary, when he had first heard the name " Missipi." This earnest man filled Marquette's mind with a sincere longing to become an explorer. Accounts of the great stream had appeared in the " Relations," compiled at Quebec from the reports of Jesuit Fathers (Allouez does not appear to have heard of Groseilliers and Radisson), and, as he supposed, Marquette determined to be first of all white men upon the river. He wrote, " If I get a canoe which the natives have promised to make for me, I intend to navigate this stream, to meet the tribes far down its course, and to decide the ultimate direction of its flow." He added that he would take with him a Frenchman (probably a converted *coureur de bois*) who spoke the languages of the natives. He uses the full word "Mississippi," variously spelled. The "Relation" of 1671 reports that Indians who had seen both rivers declared that "for more than three hundred leagues from its mouth it is wider than the St. Lawrence at Quebec."

A new name of which we shall hear much, that of Louis Joliet, comes to the fore. An expedition to the Great Lakes, in search of copper mines, led by him, had returned, unsuccessful. In the spring of 1671, we hear of him as a member of the imposing pageant headed by Simon François Daumont, Sieur St. Lusson, sent to the Sault Ste. Marie to impress the natives with the majesty and glory of France. This ceremonial, fully described in the "Relation" of 1671, occurred on June 14th, of that year. At this durbar, or function, St. Lusson "assumed power for the French sovereign over all the territory from the North to the South Sea and extending to the ocean on the west." Not a signatory of that presumptuous document knew the extent of the territory to which claim was made. It had for fair precedent the bull of Alexander VI! The four immortal names signed to that paper are the Jesuit Fathers Claude Dablon, Louis André, Gabriel Druillettes, and Claude Allouez. The masterly but florid speech of Allouez to the assembled savages, gathered from all parts of the Superior, Illinois, and Michigan regions, is a classic. It was preserved by Father Dablon. When the ceremonial ended, we hear

nothing more of Louis Joliet for two years, when he
and Marquette loom large in history.

It is not necessary to attach great importance to
the only account that has come down to us of the expedition of the Spanish Governor of New Mexico, who,
at an unknown date in 1661, set out from Santa Fé
" to visit the 'Quivera' Indians." The "Relation" is by
the hand of Father Nicholas Freytas, chronicler of the
expedition, and the only possible claim to credibility
that can be set up for it is that it mentions the name
of the great river. If that word were not interpolated
at a later date by some jealous rival of Father Allouez,
Freytas and not Allouez must be given credit for first
introducing the word " Mischipi " to the civilised world.
Here is the paragraph upon which the Freytas claim
stands or falls:

" Through these most pleasant and fertile fields we
marched during the months of March, April, May, and
the kalends of June, and arrived at a large river which
they call ' Mischipi,' where we saw the first Indians
of the Escanxaques nation, who might be to the number
of three thousand, most warlike."

The almost conclusive argument against the Freytas
claim to first mention of this Algonquin name for the
Mississippi is that the Penalosa expedition did not pass
anywhere near the lands in which the Algonquins dwelt.
The name " Quiveras " does not appear in any other
" Relation." If they were adjacent to the Arkansas nation, Tonty, La Salle, or Bienville would have been
very likely to have heard of them and to have left
some record of their location. The distance from Santa
Fé to the Mississippi, as the crow flies, is about eight
hundred miles, which assuredly might have been tra-

versed in the hundred days claimed by the chronicler
for the undertaking. Governor Penalosa was the last
of the Spaniards for whom any original discovery associated with the great American river has been claimed.
Father Freytas locates the Escanxaques as "having
north of them the Land of Fire " (*i. e.* the Maskoutens
country).

IV—WONDERFUL LA SALLE!

A member of a rich Rouen family, René Robert
Cavelier, known to history as Sieur de la Salle, had
appeared at Montreal several years previously. He
had come ostensibly to visit a brother in Canada belonging to the Sulpitian order. Hennepin has declared
that this young man of twenty-three had been a Jesuit
novice in France, but not a particle of proof exists.
An early act of his was to join the Sulpitian Fathers;
next, he applied for and secured a grant of land, on
the St. Lawrence above the rapids—a site suggested
thirty years previously by Champlain for a trading post.
This was about 1667. He formed a small colony, built
a stockade, and began the life of a grand seigneur.
Some Senecas visited him for barter and the tales they
spun about a great river, faring south-west, that could
be followed for eight months to the sea, filled La Salle's
mind with a craze for exploration and wealth. As
Justin Winsor cleverly comments, the Seneca's story
" is comprehensible to-day by combining in one the
courses of the Alleghany, the Ohio, and the Mississippi;
but to La Salle's imagination, it was a vision of the
great waterway that had been sought since the time of
Cartier." He cast religion to the winds!

Mad with passion for fame and wealth, La Salle, who had tied up his money in his stockaded post on the St. Lawrence, hurried to Quebec in hope of raising funds. The Governor, Courcelles, gave him letters patent of the broadest scope but nothing in money. He returned to Montreal and organised a syndicate. Chief among these associates was the Sieur de la Roussilière. La Salle seemed undecided in which direction to travel but a Sulpitian priest, Dollier de Casson, threw the deciding die. During the previous winter, passed in the Nipissing country, he had picked up a renegade French trooper who had claimed to have voyaged far beyond the Great Lakes, and had inspired the local head of the Sulpitians with the dream of pushing his missions farther into the wilderness. The chief of the Jesuits in Canada, Laval, happened to visit Montreal (May 15, 1669) and readily gave to Father Dollier a letter commanding the aid of all Jesuits, wherever met. Laval suggested the valley of the Mississippi as a future field.

La Salle converted his seigneury near Montreal into cash and on July 6, 1669, with twenty men in seven canoes, headed up the St. Lawrence. Galinée, one of the party, left a journal of this trip, the manuscript of which is now in the Bibliothèque Nationale, at Paris. The expedition entered Lake Ontario and made a landing at Irondequoit Bay, August 26th; but when La Salle, Galinée, and others reached the Jesuit mission, the priests of that order had gone away to Onondaga (in what is now central New York) to attend a council. In disappointment, La Salle returned to the lake and passed the outlet of the Niagara River, without seeing the falls, although Galinée says their roar was heard.

Champlain had previously visited and described Niagara (1603).[1]

At the western end of Lake Ontario, Louis Joliet and Peré, returning from the copper prospecting tour previously mentioned, were met. La Salle and Joliet, nearly of an age and equally adventurous, struck up a friendship at once. Here, the two priests, Dollier and Galinée, broke away. La Salle was suffering from illness, caused, according to the sarcastic Galinée, "by a sudden encounter with rattlesnakes," although he was not bitten. It was really a split between the two missionaries and the men actuated only by commercial impulses. The two Sulpitians portaged to Lake Erie and upon its shore went into winter quarters. In the spring, after many mishaps, Dollier and his companion proceeded up the Detroit River and reached the mission at the Sault in May, 1670. Here, they found Fathers Marquette and Dablon. Laval's letter was not favourably received there and the two wandering priests returned to Montreal by the Ottawa route.

From the moment he parted with Fathers Dollier and Galinée, La Salle's movements become vague. He was in eclipse for two years. Perhaps his reputation unjustly suffers from the absence of a chronicler, like Galinée. Many of his men deserted and returned to Montreal. Where La Salle passed the two years that intervened before his reappearance at Montreal is literally unknown! Margry, of Paris, courageously pub-

[1] DES SAVVAGES, OV VOYAGE DE SAMVEL CHAMPLAIN, DE BROVAGE, à fait en la France nouuelle, l'an mil six cents trois. A Paris, Chez CLAVDE DE MONSTR'OEILL, 1603. (Only four copies known. One, owned by Mr. Mitchell Kennerley, recently sold at auction in New York for $2900.—J. C.)

4

lished a curious series of " Conversations " with La
Salle, said to have occurred in Paris in 1678, wherein
a claim is set up to the discovery of the Ohio River in
1670; and that he voyaged thereon as far as the Mississippi. Margry also asserts that, in 1671, La Salle
" went by Lake Michigan to the Chicago portage and,
by descending the Illinois River, again entered the
Mississippi." This would appear to have been spoken or
written by a man who was deficient in knowledge of
geography. Claims to two visits cannot be substan-
tiated. No information regarding the return routes
eastward in either the first or the second alleged trip
is presented. Gravier was a warm defender of La
Salle. Parkman believed the Frenchman descended the
Ohio as far as the falls and that his men deserted him
there, instead of at the Mississippi, as stated by Margry.
As a matter of fact, the Ohio rapids at Louisville are
readily run in canoes—the fall being only twenty-seven
feet in two and a half miles. Upon the slender thread
of an anonymous publication, impossible of verification,
rests La Salle's claim to have visited the upper
Mississippi ahead of Marquette.

The determination and energy of the man from
Rouen was such that he made two subsequent efforts
to reach the great river, the second from the Gulf of
Mexico. In this last voyage he was accompanied by
his brother, the Sulpitian priest, John Cavelier, whose
chronicle, as far as it goes, is wholly authenticated.

V—JOLIET AND MARQUETTE

Prior to the finding of the Radisson manuscripts
at Oxford, the claim of Joliet and Marquette to a first

sight of the upper Mississippi was uncontested, except by the upholders of the La Salle contentions. There had been arguments that Deguerre (1652), Drocoux (1657), Allouez (1668), Pinet (1670), and Augustine Meulan de Circe (1670) had visited the Mississippi by the Illinois River route in the years mentioned. The late Dr. Shea devoted many years of his life to clearing up Marquette's record, and ultimately established the credibility of the missionary's narrative. In the statuary room of the Capitol at Washington stands a marble effigy of the good priest who first explored the river that gives name to the State of Wisconsin: it was erected by the citizens of that State.

In far away Paris, Colbert never lost sight of the vast possessions that lay beyond and south of the Great Lakes of North America. His ambitions, if we are to believe Charlevoix, exceeded his knowledge. Apparently, the English had not detected his intention to seize all North American territory as far as the Gulf of California, into which he believed, as did nearly everybody, that the widely heralded Mississippi emptied.

The Comte de Frontenac was Governor at Quebec. Although a staunch Catholic, he hated the Jesuits.[1] On impulse, he is alleged to have stopped the publication of their "Relations," a misfortune of the most lamentable character. Frontenac hoped to divert attention from his own unpopularity in New France by sending men to carry out Colbert's ambitious dreams. Joliet had already been selected and he was responsible for the choice of Father Marquette, a member of the order

---

[1] *Discovery of the Mississippi*, John Gilmer Shea; Redfield, New York, 1852. Also, *Collections of the Wisconsin Historical Society*, vol. iii.

that Frontenac feared and disliked.   Joliet was a Canadian, son of a waggon-smith; but the only man who objected to the appointment was silenced by a reminder that Paul of Tarsus was a tent-maker.   Joliet had had experience in the wilderness, as we know.   La Salle, who understood him, was absent on his vaguely-defined visit to Ohio and Lake Michigan, and, unfortunately, did not return until a month after Joliet's departure in August, 1672.   Joliet wintered at Mackinaw, where he cultivated the acquaintance of Marquette, who had been at the head of the Jesuit mission there for two years.   His experience among the natives exceeded that of Joliet, and the latter fixed upon him as a valued coädjutor.   Whether or not Father Marquette secured the consent of Monseigneur Laval to accompany Frontenac's agent, Joliet, may never be known, but he decided to go.

Joliet was chief of the expedition; but Marquette kept "the log," which accounts for the minor figure that the former cuts in the narrative of this memorable voyage.   An opportunity presents itself to the writer at this point to display vast erudition regarding the peaceful conquest that the Governor of New France was planning, but he puts it aside.   A publishers' war of the keenest sort between map-makers had broken out in Europe.   Sanson, the boldest guesser among them, had issued a chart of the Great Lake region in 1669, in which he made Lake Michigan larger than Superior.

Father Marquette's "Narrative," as printed by Margry, of Paris, takes two forms.   The text was originally sent from the wilderness to Father Dablon, at Quebec, and by him embodied in his "Relation,"

which was forwarded to Paris. The original was
retained at Quebec; when the two versions were printed,
some discrepancies were pointed out. They are not
serious and do not affect the credibility of the documents. Dr. John G. Shea first published Marquette's
journal in English.

The party started from Mackinaw in two large
canoes, seven men in all, on May 17, 1673, going by
the route to Green Bay that Jean Nicolet had followed
thirty-eight years before. Thence, they ascended the
Fox River, as Groseilliers and Radisson had done, and
made the mile and three quarters portage into the Wisconsin River,—although Marquette does not appear to
have known its name. The narrative of that trip to
the Mississippi is so full of details that doubt of its
occurrence is removed. Every bend in the Wisconsin
and many of its natural features are mentioned.

The two canoes emerged from a sheltering headland upon the broad, swift current of the Mississippi
on June 17, 1673,—just one month after starting.
Marquette says he " found nineteen fathoms of water "
(one hundred and fourteen feet!), an error due to enthusiasm, doubtless. Remembering Father Allouez's
reports upon his return, he recorded the river's name
as " Missipi." The priest gives the latitude as $42\frac{1}{2}°$
N., approximately correct. Prairie du Chien, which is
to-day near the mouth of that river, is in north latitude
43° 3', and the distance from the portage to that point
is one hundred and eighty miles.[1]

Marquette's party then descended the great river
and at a point below 40° (or about sixty leagues)

---

[1] Marquette's Map on page 248, Justin Winsor's book. Houghton,
Mifflin & Co.

they discovered a foot-path " leading into a beautiful prairie." (Marquette does n't say upon which bank, although it becomes apparent later in the narrative.) He and Joliet undertook to follow the trail alone. They discovered an Indian village at the end of two leagues (about five and a half miles). Near-by on a river, were two other villages. The smaller stream upon which these teepees stood would appear to have been the Des Moines, which fixes the field of exploration in what is now Iowa. Priest and trader were hospitably received; they smoked the calumet and many speeches were exchanged. Marquette causes the Illinois, who were away from their home upon a hunting excursion, to talk like the Mohicans in Fenimore Cooper's novels. The sachem gave to the visitors a dog-feast.

The stay with the Illinois was brief, and toward the end of June, priest and pelfer resumed their journey with the current, noticing mulberry and persimmon trees. They passed cliffs upon which were painted the images of two monsters: these palisades are known to this day as " the Painted Rocks," although the designs that gave to them name have long vanished.

The entrance of the muddy, or coffee-hued, Missouri is graphically described by Marquette, who, being physicist as well as priest, reasoned that the Mississippi was driven as nearly south as possible by the impetuosity of its added tributary from the north-west and that its mouth was on the Gulf of Mexico instead of the Vermilion Sea. He so declared, without reservation, and his opinion, formed by deduction, is almost as great a mental triumph as was subsequent physical proof, supplied by Tonty and the Ursuline Sisterhood. As every visitor to Saint Louis will recall, the waters of the two streams have not mixed, even at that point. Marquette rightly conjectured that it would be possible to ascend the Missouri and its tributaries and find a portage into some great river that delivered its waters into the Gulf of California. It was a good guess; the headwaters of the Platte almost interlock with the Colorado.

The site of Saint Louis was a dense forest. The next great affluent entered from the east, twenty leagues below the Missouri. It was the Ohio, known to the natives as the Ouabache (Wabash). Joliet, or his chronicler, does not record any traces of La Salle's previous visit to that place. They then " entered the mosquito country" as called in Chippewa-land to-day. Soon after, they saw natives with fire-arms, the Chicachas, who, after parleying, received the travellers. As other voyagers had been told, Marquette was assured that not more than ten days' journey separated them from the sea. Everywhere, the natives were friendly,—indeed they continued to be until the white man treated them with injustice. The voyageurs redoubled their paddling and arrived at Akamsea, the mouth of the Arkansas River, which Marquette locates 33° 40′ N. latitude,—probably not far from the Indian village of Guachoya, where Hernando de Soto had breathed his last, one hundred and thirty years before. It will be recalled that the Spaniards under Moscoso, Soto's successor, attained the mouth of the Mississippi from this point after sixteen days. This would appear to prove that Soto died near the mouth of the Arkansas, instead of that of the Red River.

Here, again, Marquette was told that the sea was " only ten days distant." Stories they heard about the warlike character of the tribes between Akamsea and the Gulf and distrust of the Spaniards, into whose clutches they must fall, caused priest and trader to agree that the voyage had lasted long enough. A desire to send his report of the trip to Quebec greatly influenced Marquette; the Spaniards might seize the records and prevent their use.

The return voyage was begun, therefore, on July 17, 1673. It may be disposed of in a few sentences. Marquette turned into the Illinois and passed by the familiar route (of the present Chicago drainage canal) to Lake Michigan. He was detained at the mission of St. Francis Xavier, in Green Bay, during the entire summer of 1674. In November of that year, he set out for the Illinois country but an illness, from which he had thought himself cured, returned, and " he died gloriously at the age of thirty-eight years." His last words were, " I believe that my Redeemer liveth." The description of his last hours, near the site of the present city of Chicago, by Father Dablon, is worthy of any literature. Years later, some Kiskakon Indians, dwelling at the Sault Ste. Marie, removed the body of Father Marquette to the shrine he had established at Mackinaw,—the church of St. Ignatius.

Joliet was welcomed on his arrival at the Sault Ste. Marie. As he had been very ill, he wintered there and went forward to Quebec in the summer. Joliet lost all his records in the Lachine Rapids, where two of his men were drowned.

VI—LA SALLE TRIES AGAIN

The reports that Joliet brought home threw La

Salle into a white heat. He accepted Marquette's reasoning and Joliet's statements, based on talk with natives at the Arkansas River, that the Gulf of Mexico received the floods of the Mississippi. He hurried to France and obtained a commission.

In the fall of 1675, Louis Hennepin, a Recollect friar, arrived at Quebec from France. He was welcomed by Frontenac with joy as offering a foil for the Jesuit dominance under which the Governor chafed. La Salle came on the same ship with Hennepin. Also on board was Duchesneau, the new Intendant, to replace Talon, sent as a spy upon Frontenac.

La Salle went to Fort Frontenac, at the western end of Lake Ontario, under the terms of his grant and spent thirty-five thousand livres in strengthening its walls. Hennepin set up a mission among the Iroquois near that fort. La Salle cherished dreams of curbing the British advances to the south. His probable plan was to open trade with the Mississippi, through the Alleghany and Ohio rivers, but hostility of the natives defeated it. La Salle suddenly departed for Quebec and in November, 1677, sailed for France. There, he floated on the high tide of success; he secured confirmation of his seigneural rights at Fort Frontenac and convinced his sovereign that the valuable peltry regions of the West could be more easily reached from the new base that he had created.

Money poured into his hands; but the greatest treasure he secured in Paris was Henry Tonty, an Italian soldier of fortune, who, in good or evil report, for ever after remained staunch in his fidelity to and respect for La Salle. To this day, the one-armed Tonty is the hero of the Mississippi.

Accompanied by Tonty, La Salle set sail from La Rochelle in August, 1678, with fittings for a vessel that was to be built on Lake Erie. At Quebec, after a conference with Frontenac, La Salle decided to send Cadillac and Hennepin ahead to the Illinois country to establish food stations and arrange for trading posts before his coming the following spring. Cadillac stopped at the mouth of the Niagara River, where he was well received by the Senecas, who " burned an Indian prisoner for his entertainment." La Salle and Tonty joined Cadillac and together they selected the mouth of Cayuga Creek, on Niagara River opposite the Grand Island, as the place to lay the keel of a fifty-ton (Tonty says forty-ton) vessel in which to navigate the northern lakes. Leaving Tonty with a score of ship-carpenters, La Salle went to the mouth of the Niagara River, built a blockhouse named Fort Conti, and then to Fort Frontenac.

In May, the *Griffon* was launched, and for safety from the Senecas was anchored offshore. She carried five small guns.[1] Tonty, with a small party, went ahead by Lake Erie to the Strait (Detroit) where he arrived August 10th. The bark, *Griffon,* started for Detroit late in July and after much difficulty in getting out the Niagara River into the lake, overtook the Tonty party at the entrance to the " strait." All were taken aboard. Without mishap, they sailed to Lake Huron and anchored at Mackinaw on September 17, 1679. A start was made for the river of the Miamis

---

[1] From this point we follow the " Relation of Henry de Tonty, written from Quebec, Nov. 14, 1684, and addressed to Abbé Renaudot, who was his patron near the Prince de Conti and who introduced Tonty to M. de La Salle."—Margry.

(St. Joseph River) on October 5th, and coasting Lake Michigan one hundred and twenty leagues they landed at their destination November 12th. There, La Salle was found building a fort. An attempt to murder La Salle was made by one of the twenty-nine Frenchmen during the portage to the Illinois River. The mental grief he must have suffered when he became conscious that poison had been given to him by disloyal companions, who hoped by his death to avoid the dangerous trip ahead of them, must have been infinitely greater than any physical agony he endured. His despair was indicated by the name he gave to the stockade he built, soon after, at the Illinois portage, *Crève Cœur,*—the fort of the " Broken Heart." On December 15th, a conspiracy among the men to take the boats and desert was discovered and frustrated. Tonty describes the descent of the Illinois in admirable manner. An Illinois village was seen on January 4, 1680; and although the weather was very cold, the Indians were naked. While visiting with these natives, poison was found in La Salle's porridge and six of his men, probably implicated in the plot, deserted. The building of a forty-ton vessel was undertaken for the descent of the Mississippi.

Meanwhile, Father Louis Hennepin was sent northward into the land of the Sioux. For some unaccountable reason, La Salle declared his intention to return by land to Fort Frontenac, on Lake Ontario, " a journey of four hundred leagues." He departed on March 10th. Tonty, with a few men, remained through the summer and fall of that year, and his description of an attack from the Iroquois is a graphic picture of Indian warfare. After wandering about all that winter,

the retreat to Green Bay was accomplished and Mackinaw saw the sorely famished party on Corpus Christi
day, 1681.   La Salle arrived next day: his purpose to
return to the Mississippi quest was inflexible.   His
account of his long tramp across what is now Illinois,
Indiana, and Ohio to Lake Erie was listened to with
much interest.

Back went Tonty, under La Salle's orders, to the
mouth of the St. Joseph River, arriving November 10th,
and on December 19th, La Salle joined him.   Finding
the river full of ice, the party coasted the lake (Michigan) " to a certain little river called Chicago," from
which stream they portaged a league and a half into
another creek that emptied into the Illinois.   Sleds
were used to transport the packs.   At this point, Tonty
gives a complete roster of the twenty-three Frenchmen
and eighteen " savages."   After dragging their outfit
for seventy leagues, open water was found, more canoes
were constructed, and the descent to the Mississippi accomplished on February 6, 1682.   This was Tonty's
first sight of the great river, which La Salle named
" Colbert," after his patron.

Tonty describes the camp life at the mouth of the
Illinois, with its hardships and diversions.   He mentions the catch of a catfish so large that it " supplied
ample food for twenty-two men."   This recalls the later
Southern negro story of the same sort of fish that was
" six feet between the eyes,—go as you please on its
length."

Tonty's account of the descent of the Mississippi
to the mouth of the Arkansas is rather more graphic
than is Marquette's, abounding in incidents such as
Pierre Proud'homme, the gun-smith of the expedition,

getting lost in the woods; the finding of large quantities of bean-bearing vines clinging to trees; the ceremonial of the calumet, and the forming of an intrenched camp that would have delighted Violet le Duc, or Vauban. La Salle "took possession of the land at the mouth of the Arkansas, in the name of his Most Christian Majesty, and set up the king's arms."

During the trip down-stream to the Taensas, "beaver and otter were not found, owing to the presence of crocodiles" (alligators). Buffalo were seen all the way to the sea! The western bank was followed until March 22 (1682), when Tonty visited a remarkable native village, having houses of clay, with dome-shaped roofs that were rain-proof. The chief received him seated upon a couch instead of upon the ground. More than sixty elderly warriors, habited in long white shrouds, stood around. A torch of dry canes burned in this audience chamber and, strangest of all, the four walls were decorated with paintings and hung with yellowish copper shields. An alcove was the chief's sleeping quarters. Camp cots were used for the occupancy of the chiefs of the eight villages that were his dependencies. (These are the descriptions appropriated by M. Châteaubriand.) With their hands raised to their heads, these old men shouted, like coyotes, "Ho, ho! Ho, ho!" (This is the Chippewa form of greeting to this day in the Itasca country. "Ho!" uttered singly, means "Thank you"; but repeated several times it is a friendly welcome.) In very many ways, the Taensas showed the effects of a foreign civilisation. Among other evidences, Tonty mentions the fact that food was served to each guest in a separate glazed earthenware bowl; that nobody passed between the torch

and the chief, and that the cooking showed signs of
the culinary art. The chief had pendants containing sixteen large pearls hanging from his ears. He told
Tonty they were taken from shells, plenty in the river.
When Tonty returned to La Salle's camp after his
visit to the Taensa chief, the commandant insisted that
he go back after the pearls. He did so and received
them in exchange for a cheap bracelet. They were as
large as peas and La Salle took them. The Taensas
had a temple facing the chief's cabin, containing an
altar. Upon the top of the lodge were three eagles
looking toward the morning sun, and upon its exterior
walls were exposed heads of enemies slain in battle.
A redoubt with watch-towers of hard wood enclosed
this house of worship. Guards watched day and night.

Ten leagues' farther progress toward the mouth of
the Mississippi was made on March 25, 1682. Next
day, going southward, a log canoe (pirogue) was seen
crossing the broad river. Savages appeared on both
banks. La Salle reluctantly sent Tonty with the peace
pipe. When he landed, the natives received him seated,
which was a sign of peace, and then cheerfully smoked
the calumet. A knife was given to the chief, " which
he hastily hid in his robe as if guilty of a theft." The
chief clasped his own hands to signify his friendship.
Tonty says he imitated the native's action ("*je le
contrefis*"). Some commentators have smiled at this
statement, because Tonty only had one arm. It is
known, however, that he had a bronze hand which he
might have clasped with his real one. Two warriors
were despatched to La Salle, across the river, Tonty
remaining as hostage. After a conference, they returned with all the Frenchmen of the party, including

La Salle. The commandant accepted an invitation to go to the neighbouring village of the tribe, called Nahy (Natchez, according to Parkman) and passed the night there. The Taensas practised slavery: Tonty speaks of buying a boy slave and his mother from them.

Next day, La Salle's party, accompanied by many friendly natives, went ten leagues down-stream to a village of the Cordoas. On Easter Day, another start was made for the sea, said to be ten days distant. At the end of eighty leagues (two hundred and twenty miles), Indians were descried on the western bank and the war drums were heard. The French disembarked at the mouth of a small creek and Tonty constructed a fortified angle as a defence against arrows. Four men sent to reconnoitre were attacked with a shower of arrows. The French party, with native followers, re-embarked and proceeded two leagues (five and one half miles) to a village on the eastern bank, the name of which proved to be Tangibaho. The village was depopulated and evidences of a recent battle were on every side. This is what Tonty says: "We found only corpses. The people had been defeated by Chouchoumas. Blood was ankle deep! Five great lodges were filled with dead bodies. The rest of the village had been destroyed by fire. This place was distant thirty leagues (sixty-seven and one half miles) from the sea."

Following our river route, the voyageurs came in sight of the sea on April 6 (1682). "As the river here divides into three channels," writes Tonty (thus conclusively proving that the three-pronged mouth of the "Admiral's map" belonged to the Mississippi), "M. de La Salle undertook the exploration of the one to the right [the South-west pass of to-day], I took the central one, and the Sieur d' Autray (Jacques Bourdon) that to the left. We found all of them excellent, broad, and deep. When we had reassembled on the 9th, M. de La Salle set up the arms of the King of France and a cross. A Te Deum was sung. After firing three salutes, and burying a lead tablet engraved with His Majesty's arms, M. de La Salle took possession of the river in the name of the most exalted and glorious prince Louis the Great, King of France and of Navarre."

The return voyage began on April 10th, and was enlivened by several pitched battles with the natives. The most serious affair occurred over a slave woman who had been presented to La Salle by the Arkansans on the downward voyage but belonged to the Quinipassas, near the mouth of the Mississippi. She was recognised and a night attack by her people was made on La Salle's camp. Considerable bloodshed resulted but the slave was not surrendered. The French were again well received by the Cordoas, but messengers from the Quinipassas [1] had preceded them: treachery was only prevented by La Salle's undaunted courage. Escape was made up-stream to the Taensas where several very happy days were passed. A neighbouring chief sent two bands of music (!), to the cadence of which the paddlers worked. The reception ceremony concluded with a prayer to the sun. May 3d saw them

[1] Any philological defence of the orthography of many of the obscure Indian names is impossible. The spelling differs in nearly all the Jesuit manuscripts,—in several instances, varying in the work of the same relator. Along the lower Mississippi, many Spanish names were retained by the French; along the upper river, French spelling has been followed. But, as stated, that is not uniform.—J. C.

under way again. Desiring to hasten northward, La
Salle preceded Tonty, but a few days later at a landing, a letter written by Jacques Cochois was seen fastened to a tree announcing La Salle's dangerous illness
and summoning the surgeon of the expedition, Jean
Michel. Tonty started immediately. La Salle was
found at Fort Proud'homme,—named for the place at
which the gun-smith had gone astray in the woods on
the downward voyage,—dangerously ill. After remaining until June 4th, La Salle being no better, Tonty
was ordered to proceed to the river of the Miamis taking
three Frenchmen and one Indian. He parted with La
Salle, as he supposed, for ever. Just north of the
Ohio, the little party had a narrow escape from massacre at a village of mixed tribes. A friendly native
discovered the plot, and on June 27th Tonty arrived
safely among the Illinois. The water in the Wisconsin
being low, the party went afoot to Winnebago Lake,
where Tonty bought a boat and returned by the usual
Green Bay route to Mackinaw (July 22, 1682). There,
he received word of M. de La Salle's recovery, after
forty days' sickness. The commandant arrived in person during the summer. He was anxious to go to
France to report to the King (Louis XIV.) but being
too weak from his illness, sent his despatches by Father
Zenoble, who had accompanied him throughout the long
voyage to the Gulf of Mexico. Tonty was sent by La
Salle to build a fort for the protection of the Shawanoes,
his devoted allies. La Salle joined Tonty on December
30th and during that winter " Fort Saint Louis was
built upon an impregnable rock." Peace was made
between all the Illinois tribes except the Iroquois.

Then it was that La Salle renewed his determina-

5

tion to return to France. After La Salle had sailed, Tonty was harassed by envoys from Quebec and, throwing up his job, returned to the capital of New France in the autumn of 1684, to compose the "Relation" which we have briefly summarised.

VII—LOUIS HENNEPIN

Sparks, and other authorities on the missionaries, consigns Father Louis Hennepin "to that amiable class who seem to tell truth by accident and fiction by inclination." At most, all that can be claimed for Hennepin is that he was first to get into print an account of any voyage on the Mississippi from the mouth of the Wisconsin northward to the Fall of St. Anthony. He is doubtless entitled to that great place in Mississippi history. All students of that period must remember that Hennepin was a Recollect priest and had not been well treated by the Jesuits at Quebec, Montreal, or Sault Ste. Marie, owing to the fact that he had striven to eclipse Allouez, Marquette, Dablon, and other Jesuits.

The Hennepin narrative begins at Fort Crèvecœur, the well-known point on the Illinois about midway between Lake Michigan and the Mississippi, on the 29th of February, 1680. It describes the Illinois as having the width and depth of the Seine, at Paris. The date on which the Mississippi was reached is not mentioned, but on March 12th, Hennepin describes the "Colbert," as he insisted upon calling the great river, "running south-south-west, between two chains of mountains which wind with the river, in some places far from the banks. Between the river and the hills are large prairies, on which wild cattle are often seen browsing. This great river is almost everywhere a short league in width, and in some places two or three leagues."

Hennepin gives the first graphic description of the Lake of Tears (Pepin), " about a hundred miles below the Fall of St. Anthony." This cataract he describes thus: " It is forty or fifty feet high, divided in the middle by a rocky island of pyramidal form. I called the cataract St. Anthony of Padua, in gratitude for favours done to me by the Almighty, through the intercession of that great saint, whom we had chosen as patron and protector of all our enterprises."

The Sioux believed, according to H. L. Gordon, an authority on Dakota traditions, that the Great Unkte-hee, who created earth and man, originally dwelt in a cavern under the Fall of St. Anthony, and often appeared to mortals in the form of a buffalo-bull. In such form, like the ancient Egyptians at Memphis, they worshipped him. Recently, when standing in the Apis tomb at Sakkara, the vast campo-santo of Memphis where the god-bulls were buried, I recalled this feature of the Sioux religion. A very curious fact about the rock-hewn mausoleum at Sakkara is that one of the large, black granite sarcophagi, highly polished and inscribed, lies, with its lid, inside the entrance to the vast tomb. It never was put in place! Why was the work left uncompleted? Did a revolt against the deification of bulls, a protest against a disgusting religious ceremonial, occur at that place, because the folly of worshipping a god that could die was proclaimed and conceded?

Father Hennepin had much trouble with the natives. They were suspicious of his prayers and use of

the rosary. Finally, he and his party were captured
and Indian paddlers put into their canoe. " Five
leagues below St. Anthony's fall," the Indians broke
up Hennepin's canoe, and distributed the members of
his party " as prisoners to three heads of families in
place of three of their children killed in war." The
unfortunate Frenchmen were made to swim streams
filled with floating ice and subjected to many other
hardships. A favourite trick was to set fire to grass
in the path of the prisoners.

In this part of the narrative, there is complete confusion of dates. Hennepin describes a sort of Turkish
bath to which he was subjected as a remedy for a
severe cold. He was cured, after several treatments.
He speaks of " Indians who came as ambassadors from
five hundred leagues to the West." He mentions a
trip that the three Frenchmen made with a single Indian to the mouth of the Wisconsin in the hope that
" the Sieur de La Salle had sent to that place a re-
inforcement of men as he [La Salle] had promised."
That trip to the Wisconsin, whether it occurred or not,
is graphically described. What became of the Indian
guard is not stated, but Hennepin and his other companions arrived at Mackinaw late that fall and wintered
there. In the spring of 1681, the party returned to
Quebec by way of the Detroit, Lakes Erie and Ontario,
and the St. Lawrence.

VIII—LA SALLE'S LAST VISIT

Whatever may be said of La Salle, he assuredly
possessed determination. Although his tales of travels
in the New World were somewhat discredited, he

Father Hennepin's Discovery of St. Anthony Fall.
(Painting by Douglas Volk, in the State Capitol.)
Copyright, 1905, by Douglas Volk.

ascribed the disbelief to jealousy and secured funds enough to fit out a squadron of four ships in the winter of 1684 and sailed from La Rochelle. His own ship, *Le Joli,* encountered a storm in which she fared so badly that the four vessels put back to the port of departure for repairs. Again, they sailed, about the last of December, but ran into a storm and were separated. A Spanish cruiser captured the *St. François,* but the other three came to a rendezvous at Petit Goave, Santo Domingo. We shall follow the narrative of Cavelier, a brother of La Salle and, although a member of the Sulpitian order, not always trustworthy.

At the period in which the Rev. John Cavelier's "Narrative" begins, Europeans possessed only one lodgment on the Mississippi, namely Tonty's stockade. La Salle hoped to ascend the great river from the Gulf to that haven of safety.

Father Cavelier's first important statement is a distinct allegation that Captain Beaujeu, commander of La Salle's little squadron, deliberately caused the foremast of *Le Joli,* the flagship, to be sawed so that it went overboard in the first gale thereafter encountered. This commander refused to proceed beyond L'Espirito Santo Bay (February 4, 1685). He sailed homeward from this port on the Gulf of Florida (Mexico) on March 14th, leaving La Salle with only one ship, *La Belle.*

La Salle, undaunted, founded a village, and built a fort to protect himself from the Indians, who thought the newcomers Spaniards, instead of Frenchmen. He finally made peace, and the Indians guided him to the interior, where they showed to him a copper plate,

dated 1588 and carrying the arms of Spain, fastened
to a post. This proved that the Spaniards had preceded
him.

With thirty men, La Salle set out by land from
his fort to the mouth of the Mississippi. They tramped
two months and ten days—the chronicler omits to state
in what direction. At an Indian village, he learned
that his party was only forty leagues from the sea. He
was told of a river that probably was the Rio Bravo.

Shortly after La Salle's return to his port at
L'Espirito Santo (or St. Louis Bay, as he renamed
it), his small frigate, *La Belle,* was wrecked. The
disaster was due to the lack of sufficient sailors. All
the men aboard, except eight, were lost. In this dire
extremity, La Salle undertook to reach Canada. With
Cavelier, three other Frenchmen, and two Shawnee Indians, he started on April 13, 1685 [according to Le
Clerq, the real date is 1686], to make his way north
to the Illinois River, the route up which to Lake Superior he claimed to know. Nearly all the members of
the party were prostrated with fever, and at the end
of forty days, they returned to Saint Louis Bay.
Abandoning hope of reaching Canada, La Salle waited
a year in expectation that his King would send a
rescuing ship: but when the beginning of 1687 came,
he determined upon a second attempt to ascend the
Mississippi. He selected only twenty-eight of his most
vigorous men, [Anastasius says 20: Joutel, 17], and
started on January 6th. From that date to the
16th of February, when the " Narrative " of Cavelier abruptly ends, we have each day's march set
down.

Not the slightest evidence exists that La Salle

reached the banks of the Mississippi. On January 17th, at an Indian village, they witnessed a bull fight, in which Indians on horseback armed with lances fought bulls exactly as the picadores of Spain do to-day. From that tribe, La Salle bought thirty horses for thirty knives, ten hatchets, and a few needles.

La Salle died about this time, which accounts for the cessation of his brother's "Narrative." The latter returned to Canada and ultimately to France, but concealed the fate of La Salle for two years.

There is a note of suspicion in every line of Cavelier. Whether La Salle was saint or imposter must always be in doubt, owing to the curious, irreconcilable record left by Cavelier.

IX—ST. COSME'S VOYAGE

The scene again shifts to the North-west. Francis Joliet de Montigny, born at Paris in 1661, had been ordained priest at Quebec in 1693. Accompanied by Fathers Davion and St. Cosme, he intended to found a mission of the Jesuit Seminary of Quebec on the Mississippi. He bore the appointment of Vicar General of the Bishop of Quebec. This expedition was outfitted at lavish expense; but M. de Montigny returned from this trip disgruntled, gave up his post at Quebec, went to France, and refused to take further interest in American missions. Exactly what occurred to sour him never will be known. He was sent to China, but returned to Paris and died, 1725. The "Narratives" of St. Cosme and Davion are equally valuable and interesting.

The letter of J. F. Buisson St. Cosme, missionary priest, to the Bishop of Quebec is one of the most valuable of all documents concerning the opening of the upper Mississippi. To it, largely, we owe a proper appreciation of Henry de Tonty. As a lieutenant of La Salle, Tonty had directed affairs in Illinois with tact. He was one of the founders of Detroit.

Montigny, Father St. Cosme, Father Davion, the Sieur de Vincennes,—here first mentioned and apparently a nephew of Louis Joliet,—and Tonty, the Neapolitan, left Mackinaw on September 15, 1698. The intrepid Tonty agreed to pilot the party to and down the Mississippi as far as the Arkansas. The expedition followed the usual course into Lake Michigan, to Green Bay, at the head of which they found a Jesuit mission. The direct route thence to the great river was through Green Bay and down the Wisconsin; but the Foxes were hostile and this party was obliged to go by the Chikagu (Chicago) route. They coasted down the west side of Lake Michigan, arriving at the site of Milwaukee on October 7th. There, the Sieur de Vincennes parted with the missionaries, as he was going to the country of the Miamis. Arriving at the Jesuit mission near the present site of Chicago, Montigny, Davion, and St. Cosme were hospitably received. On the 24th, a start was made up the Chicago River. The route to the Mississippi followed that of the present drainage canal into the Illinois. Lowness of water in both rivers made the journey tedious. Of this trip, lasting about six weeks, owing to halts at various missions, Tonty was the hero. He proved himself diplomatist, as well as leader. The Italian had been among the Illinois three years before. Tonty's shibboleth always was, "We do not fear men!"—meaning that they only feared God.

The Mississippi was sighted on the 5th of December. St. Cosme thus describes it at the mouth of the Illinois: "Micissippi is a large and beautiful river, that comes from the north. It divides into several channels, which form beautiful islands. It makes several bends but seems to me to keep always the same direction to the south as far as the Akanseas. It is lined by very fine forests."

Embarking on the 6th, after making six leagues, the party came to the mouth of the Missouri. "It comes from the west and is so muddy that it spoils the waters of the Micissippi, which, down to that point, are clear."

Upon a lofty headland, on the west bank, a cross was planted, to the singing of *Vexilla Regis*. They camped on the night of December 15, 1698, a short distance below the mouth of the Wabache.[1] Nothing befell the party until they reached the Arkansas's mouth, except the discovery and description of the first pelican,—" as large as a swan, its bill a foot long and the throat of such extraordinary size that it will hold a bushel of wheat." Christmas was celebrated with high mass; and an earthquake occurred at one o'clock in the afternoon. Even the earth was busy.

A large Indian village was reached on St. John's day, where the calumet, or peace pipe, was smoked.[2]

[1] The Ohio was called " Wabash " by the French from its mouth to the source of the present Wabash; the Ohio being the part from Fort Duquesne (Pittsburg) to the mouth of the Wabash. (See Gravier's Journal.) Shea, 69.

[2] Marquette had first described the calumet. Father Gravier also gives an account of this ceremonial. 3 Shea (St. Cosme's voyage, 73).

Here they parted from Tonty, who had to return to the land of the Illinois. St. Cosme thus speaks of him: " He is the man who knows the country best. He has been twice to the sea: he has been twice far inland to the remotest nations. He is loved and feared everywhere."

This letter of Father Cosme to the Bishop of Quebec was accompanied by a brief missive from Sieur de Montigny, detailing the establishment of Father Davion among the Tonicas on the Mississippi sixty leagues below the mouth of the Arkansas. He speaks of his own stay among the Taensas, first mentioned by Father Membré, and a projected visit to the Natchez. He describes their " rather fine temples, the walls of which are of mats." Their religion " is serpent worship." In another place, he says " the serpent is one of their divinities." He adds: " They do not dare to accept or appropriate anything without taking it to the temple." Among the Taensas, the death of a popular chief was accompanied by the killing of all the braves who volunteered to go with him to the happy hunting grounds. " Last year," writes Montigny,[1] " when the chief of the Taensas died, twelve persons offered to die. They were tomahawked."

The same courier took a letter from the Rev. Dominic de la Source, also with the Montigny expedition. It does not add any details. All these communications bear final date of January 2, 1699.

X—IBERVILLE BANISHES ALL MYSTERIES

Although La Salle had really established the connecting links between the great river of Hernando de

[1] Shea, *Early Voyages Up and Down the Mississippi*, 78.

Soto and the mighty stream far to the northward with which the names of Radisson, Joliet and Marquette, Hennepin and Tonty are associated, his statements and those of his chroniclers did not carry conviction. The honour of converting assumption into established fact remained for another Frenchman, Pierre Le Moyne d'Iberville, seventeen years after La Salle's expedition of 1682. Sieur d'Iberville was born at Montreal, July 16, 1661. He entered the French navy at the age of fourteen and saw active service in command of a frigate as early as 1692. He was sent to Hudson Bay in 1694 and again in 1697. Going to France, he was commissioned during the winter of 1698–99 to establish direct commercial relations with the lower Mississippi. Collecting all previous data, he made a thorough examination of the coast line of the Gulf west of Florida. He it was who finally cleared up all doubts about the Mississippi emptying into the " Bay of Saint-Espirit," or Mobile Bay. This bay was the rendezvous of his vessels and he decided that neither of the two rivers entering it could be the one of which he was in search. He coasted westward until he found a haven that afterwards received the name of Biloxi. Acting on information obtained from the natives, Iberville left his ships at anchor and, on February 27th, set out with a party in small boats toward the west. He had been told that the large river which the Indians called the " Malbanchia," the same that the Spaniards described as the " River of the Palisades," lay fifteen or twenty leagues in that direction. He put into the mouth of the Mississippi River on the night of March 2, 1699. Commenting on the momentous importance of this event, Brower says:

Up to this time, the Spaniards seem to have acted like dogs in the manger in respect to the lower Mississippi, and the shores of the Gulf of Mexico to the east and west. Although the entire coast line had long before been explored by their ships, no information concerning it had been directly published. They evidently knew about the embrochure of the river, for they called it "the River of the Palisades," on account of the bristling appearance presented by the trees that had drifted from upstream and lodged at the outlets of the delta, where they helped to form bars. The Spaniards assured Iberville that, by reason of these bars, there was not any entrance. Fortunately, he did not believe them.

Iberville and his brother, Bienville, made a thorough and systematic exploration of the lower part of the Mississippi. Exactly how far northward he penetrated is uncertain. The best opinion is that he ascended to the Red River. He could not reconcile many of the statements made by La Salle and his chroniclers with the topography as he found it; but when he received from an Indian chief a letter—"the speaking bark" he called it—that Tonty had left in 1685 to be delivered to La Salle, when he should ascend the river, Iberville knew that he had solved the greatest mystery of the New World. This first voyage of Iberville closes the story of French exploration on the lower two thirds of the Mississippi. Contemporaneously, Le Seuer, as we shall see, was seeking a blue clay in the Minnesota region, overlooking the fact that unless he found sapphires and turquoises his merchandise would not admit of transportation to an eastern market.

XI—LE SEUER AND BLUE MUD

The first mention of Le Seuer, a Canadian and

relative of Iberville, is as a *coureur de bois* at Chegoimegon, on Lake Superior. His thorough acquaintance with the Dakota language gave high value to his services as mediator for the Quebec government between the Chippewas and Dakotas.

Les coureurs des bois were of a class that made themselves popular by terrorism,—anticipating the cowboys of the western plains. They were lawless, half traders, half explorers, wholly bent on divertisement, and not discouraged by misery or peril. They lived in utter disregard of all religious teaching, but the priesthood, among savages, were fain to wink at their immoralities because of their strong arms and efficient use of weapons of defence. Charlevoix says that " while the Indian did not become French, the Frenchman became savage." Not until Frontenac's day were these French vagabonds brought under control. Of such antecedents was Le Seuer.

The account of Le Seuer's long voyage on the upper Mississippi in 1699–1700 is here summarised from Bernard de la Harpe's transcripts of Le Seuer's journals. He was sent out to Canada from France with the ships *Renommée* and *Gironde* to form " an establishment at the source " of the Mississippi. Reports of the existence of a mine of green or blue earth, somewhere on the upper Mississippi, had reached France. As Shea very truly says, such a mine does n't seem an over-valuable thing to cross the ocean and half a continent to seek. By order of Frontenac, Governor General of Canada, Le Seuer, had, in 1695, built a fort on an island in the Mississippi " two hundred leagues above the mouth of the Illinois to maintain peace between the Sioux [See-ous] who dwelt in the Minnesota country and the Ojibwas (Chippewas or Sauteurs) of the Lake Superior region." It was then that he discovered the green or blue earth in Minnesota. He went to France in 1697 to solicit a grant of the mines. Obtaining it, he embarked at La Rochelle in June of that year, but, off the Newfoundland banks, his vessel was taken by an English fleet of sixteen ships and he was carried prisoner to Portsmouth. Peace being declared, Le Seuer hurried to Paris to secure a new commission, —having thrown his former one overboard to prevent his identity being known. A new commission was issued, bearing date of 1698. When he reached Canada, Frontenac turned against him and prevented him from proceeding to the Mississippi region. He returned again to France and arrived in the colony of Louisiana on December 7, 1699. He made a trip up the Mississippi and was gone about two years, reappearing at Fort Biloxi, near the mouth of the river, on February 10, 1702. The account of this long up-stream voyage and return is the most valuable of all early Mississippi chronicles, because it carries conviction regarding its truthfulness, but it is not interesting reading, kept, as it is, in diary form.

A letter from Le Seuer, dated Paris, 1701 [evidently this date is an error or has been tampered with], exists in which this trader denounces as an imposter one Mathieu Sagean, who had appeared in France with a wonderful tale of his explorations of the Mississippi far above the mouth of the Illinois River. His story was that he had been associated with La Salle and Tonty in the expedition of 1683 and had obtained permission of his chief to penetrate far toward the headwaters of the mighty river. But, as his narrative did

not appear until after Hennepin had announced the
discovery of the Fall of St. Anthony, Sagean's account
of " a high fall, around which it was necessary to make
a portage of six leagues " did not impress anybody.
Sagean was an imposter of the Glazier type, and, as
Brower says, " had he been other than an illiterate man,
he would have written a book "—claiming everything
set down by previous chroniclers.

XII—PHILOLOGY OF MISSISSIPPI

The Mississippi River has borne many names; different parts of the long stream have carried titles of
their own.   Prior to Hernando de Soto's arrival, the
aboriginal tribes along its banks had separate designa-
tions for the river traversing their own possessions.   The
Cortes map gives to the river the name " Espiritu
Sancto," which never was accurately applied to the lower
Mississippi.   A list of all known appellations, gathered
by J. V. Brower, is as follows:

Meche Sebe, the original Algonquin designation.
Chucagua, an Indian name, noted by Soto's expedition.
Tamaliseu, an Indian name, noted by Soto's expedition.
Tapatu, an Indian name, noted by Soto's expedition.
Mico, an Indian name, noted by Soto's expedition.
Rio Grande, a Spanish designation, noted by Soto's ex-
pedition.
" The River," a Spanish designation, noted by Soto's ex-
pedition.
Palisado, a Spanish designation, from floating trees seen
near its mouth, giving the appearance of a palisade.
Escondido, a Spanish designation; hidden from sight by
the innumerable passes, cut offs, bayous, etc., at and above its
mouth, making it difficult to discover the main channel.

St. Louis, a French designation.

Conception, a French designation, by Marquette.

Buade, so called by Joliet after the family name of Gov. Frontenac.

Colbert, after Jean Baptiste Colbert, an eminent French statesman.

Mischipi, Nicolas Freytas's visit to the Quivira tribes, 1661.

Messipi, Father Allouez, in "Relation" of 1667.

Meschasipi, Hennepin map of 1697.

Michi Sepe, Labal's version.

Misisipi, Labatt's version.

Missisipi, Marquette's spelling.

Mississipi, a later French version.

Mississippi, the American spelling, adopted in the nineteenth century.

Minnehaha Fall.

(Copyright, 1908, by T. W. Ingersoll.)

CHAPTER IV

Jonathan Carver to William Morrison

A LTHOUGH Jonathan Carver is the next visitor to the upper Mississippi region whose record is beyond dispute, much had been written in the meantime about the locality. From his dungeon in the Bastile, Antoine de la Mothe Cadillac, long stationed at Mackinaw and Detroit, wrote in his " Mémoires ":

As regards the source of the Mississippi, we can say that it is in 48° N. latitude and 96° W. longitude. It apparently has its origin in some lake, which forms another river, going to the north and discharging itself into the great lake of the Assiniboines, which forms rivers without end that empty themselves towards Fort Nelson, and into other great bays. This lake is called by the savages " The Grandfather of All Lakes," meaning that it is incomparably greater than all others.

An English traveller and astronomer, David Thompson, entered the service of the North-west Company in 1797 and in his capacity as a trader crossed the country lying between the western end of Lake Superior and the Manitoban region. He traversed the Messaba district, and had he been a geologist, as well as astronomer, might have discovered the richest deposits of iron ore on this continent. He first suggested a junction, at their sources, of the waters of the Red and the Mississippi rivers. He left the Mouse River, February 25, 1798, with a dog train. He passed up the Red River of the North to Red Lake River and

arrived at Red Lake on April 17th. Turning southward, he came to Turtle Lake on the 27th. He declared that "Turtle Brook," which flowed to the
southward from that lake, was the Mississippi, and that
Turtle Lake was the source of the great river. Thus
it is seen that he anticipated Pike, Cass, and Beltrami
by many years. He was only guessing, as were they.
Thompson descended Turtle River to Red Cedar Lake
(Lake Cass) and thence passed by the main stream to
Sandy Lake River, going to Lake Superior over the
well-worn trail that marked the "carry" to the St.
Louis River. His reports make the first mention of
Lake "Winnipegoos," the largest body of open water
in the Mississippi's path. He was unqualifiedly the
first white man to traverse that part of the upper stream
between Lake Cass and the mouth of Sandy Lake
River. Curiously, he does not make mention of Pokegama Fall, an obstruction that he could not possibly
have overlooked.

M. de La Verendrye very narrowly escaped association with the search for the sources of the Mississippi
River. He was familiar with the route from Lake
Superior to Lake Winnipeg, through the Lake of the
Woods, and should have possessed a fairly accurate
knowledge, by hearsay, of the region directly to the
southward of that well-travelled water route; but, in
1737, he sent to Paris what purported to be a map of the
country west and north of Superior in which Red Lake
is set down as emptying into the Red River of the North
and reaching Lake Winnipeg through the channel of
the latter. Nothing could be more erroneous. Verendrye coasted Lake Superior and passed to Winnipeg
by the well-known route through Rainy Lake and Lake

of the Woods. He ascended the Assiniboine and Sas-
katchewan rivers to the Rocky Mountains. He was
very near the sources of the Mississippi, if he went by
Red Lake, as some versions of his narrative claim, but
he never visited them or saw any part of the stream.
He seems to have possessed some acquaintance with
Turtle River, flowing into Lake Cass, and thought
to be the continuation of the Mississippi by Beltrami,
Pike, Cass, and all predecessors of Schoolcraft. This
is said without prejudice to William Morrison, who did
not announce his visit to Lac la Biche in 1802 until
January 16, 1856, when the narratives of Schoolcraft and
Nicollet had been in print for more than twenty years.

The claim of William Morrison, which has been
conceded by J. V. Brower, the First Commissioner of
the Itasca State Park and the highest authority upon
Mississippi exploration in Minnesota, rests entirely
upon a letter written by Mr. Morrison to a brother,
dated from Berthier, January 16, 1856. Omitting only
references to family matters, it runs as follows:

MY DEAR BROTHER:—Your letter of the 26th ultimo has
come to hand. . . . I note what you say concerning the source
of the Mississippi. You wish to know who was the first person who went to its source. For the information of the Historical Society, I will state to you all about what came to my
knowledge, by which you will perceive that H. R. Schoolcraft
is in error and that he was not the first person who made the
discovery of the source of the Mississippi.

I left the old Grand Portage, July, 1802, landed at Leech
lake in September. In October, I went and wintered on
one of the Crow Wing streams near its source. Our Indians
were Pillagers; in 1803-4, I went and wintered at Lac La
Folle. I left Leech lake, passed by *Red Cedar lake,* up river
Lac Travers to the lake of that name, then up river La Biche

or Elk river, to near Lac La Biche, when we made a portage
to fall into Lac La Folle. Lac La Biche is near to Lac La
Folle. Lac La Biche is the source of the Great River Mississippi, which I visited in 1804, and if the late Gen. Pike did
not lay it down as such when he came to Leech lake it is because he did not happen to meet me. I was at an outpost
that winter. The late Gen. Pike laid down on his book *Red
Cedar lake* as the head of the Mississippi river. I did not
trace any vestige of white men before me. In 1811-12, I
wintered again at Lac La Folle near to the plains. We went
down river La Folle some distance. I then overtook a gentleman with an outfit from Michilimackinac, Mr. Otepe, with
whom I parted only at Fond du Lac. He took the south
towards Mch'a and I north to our headquarters, which had
been changed to Fort William north of the Grand Portage.
This I expect will explain that I visited in 1804, Elk lake, and
again in 1811-12. With respect to the first Fond du Lac
traders, we all came from Mackinac. Some came by Lake
Superior and others up by Prairie du Chien, up to Crow Wing
and some went to Lac La Que de l'Outre—Otter Tail lake—
Messrs. Reaume, Cotton, Casselais, Sayers, Letang and several
others, some came by Lake Superior and others up the Mississippi by way of Prairie du Chien. These persons were persons who preceded us. The French had trading posts on Lake
Superior, but not in the interior of F. D. L. that I could ever
discover. The late Mr. Sayers returned from Mckina and
found that his bands of Indians had died by the smallpox
—1780—I think.

Perhaps it is not amiss to mention that I went to the
Indian country engaged to Sir Alexander McKenzie & Co.,
who had joined stock with the X. Y. Co., formerly the Richard-
son & Co. . . .

Your affectionate brother,
WILLIAM MORRISON.

Mr. Morrison was born in Canada in 1783, and died
there August 7, 1866: records indicate that he became
a naturalised citizen of the United States.

CHAPTER V

The Louisiana Purchase

THE purchase of the Louisiana Territory had stupendous results and largely made most of the history of the United States for the sixty years that followed the act. By thus securing this vast region from France, Jefferson not only doubled the existing area of our country but secured possession of the Mississippi River from its source to the sea. Napoleon comprehended the sacrifice France was making when he exclaimed, " I have given to England a maritime rival that, sooner or later, will humble her pride." The far-reaching effects of this event are well stated by John W. Foster in *A Century of American Diplomacy* (page 204) :

It made the acquisition of Florida a necessity. It brought about the annexation of Texas, the Mexican War, the thirst for more slave territory to preserve the balance of power, the Civil War, and the abolition of slavery. It led to our Pacific coast possessions, the construction of the trans-continental lines of railway and our marvellous Rocky Mountain development, the demand for an Isthmus Canal, the purchase of Alaska, the annexation of Hawaii. It opened up to us the great field of commercial development beyond the Pacific in Japan, China, and the islands of the sea. It fixed our destiny as a great world power, the effects of which we are to-day just beginning to realise.

The history of the undefined region described as the Louisiana Territory is exceedingly complex and the ablest historians have never been able to disentangle truth from fiction concerning the early period. Religion and love of gold had equal parts in opening and fixing the nationalities of nearly every section in the Mississippi Valley. Francis Parkman has told the wonderful story of what the black robe of the Jesuit did for the North-west and the delta of " The Father of Waters." La Salle was responsible for dedicating the whole region to France under the name of " Louisiana." His chief thought was to outrival Champlain on the St. Lawrence. He secured footing in the upper Mississippi region ahead of the English and by a chain of forts from New Orleans to Blue Earth, in Minnesota, he planned to keep them out. La Salle did not live to carry out his dream, but the idea survived him. In 1699, the first settlement was established in Louisiana and in 1712, Antoine Crozat obtained a grant from Louis XIV. which defined its boundaries so amazingly that the country of Louisiana included the entire Mississippi watershed from the Alleghanies to the Rocky Mountains. The text, taken from Martin's *Louisiana,* (i., 178), is as follows:

The territory is bounded by New Mexico on the West; by the English lands of Carolina on the East, including all the establishments, posts, havens, and principally the port and haven of the Isle of Dauphin, heretofore called Massacre; the River St. Louis, heretofore called Mississippi, from the edge of the sea as far (north) as the Illinois (country); together with the River St. Philip, heretofore called Missouri, the

River St. Jerome heretofore called Ouabache (Ohio), with all lakes and rivers mediately or immediately flowing into any part of the river Saint Louis or Mississippi.

The northern boundary of this immeasurable tract of land was defined by the treaty of Utrecht (1713) to be the forty-ninth degree of north latitude. Crozat could not find any gold on his concession and surrendered his charter to the Crown in 1717.

" The Western Company," with which John Law was connected, took over the Crozat concession and, so characteristic of the " frenzied financier " as subsequently revealed, claimed the whole of the Illinois country as having been included in the charter, but the question never was decided.

According to a painstaking historian, John W. Monette, who published two large volumes on this subject in 1846, " The project of purchasing New Orleans and Eastern Louisiana was entertained from the beginning of Washington's administration." [1] Had New France and Louisiana grown together as La Salle dreamed, France would have become a dominant power in North America, from which Great Britain never could have dislodged her; but personal infatuation for the court life of Paris overcame ambition for dominant power in the New World. The effect of these influences upon the swaggering French royalists of Quebec is admirably described in a recent novel entitled *Le Chien d'Or*. New France passed into English hands (1763); Louisiana was neglected. In 1717, as mentioned above, it had been handed over to

[1] Monette's *History of the Discovery and Settlement of the Mississippi Valley*, vol. i., 503.

John Law and was used by him as the pretext for the
most high-handed financial scheming known to history
until emulators in the United States outshone him during the unwatched period of do-nothing Presidents,
extending from 1868 to 1901.

While Louis XIV. lived, he was "The State," as
he claimed, but he was a weak monarch and the kings
that followed him were cursed with weaker advisers
than he had possessed. In 1762, France ceded her
possession to Spain and for nearly forty years the
people of Louisiana led a semi-tropical existence, hardly
conscious of the yoke they carried. "Under what king,
Bezonian?" never was asked in the absinthe taverns of
the Orleans in the New World.

Her people hardly noticed "the shot heard around
the world"; or, if they did, failed to realise its import
to them. Doubtless, the American Revolution was of
much less interest to the French of New Orleans than
was the Revolution in Paris that hurried fast upon
the conclusion of the former. The two great social
upheavals of the eighteenth century were of minor interest to New Orleans at the time, but both vitally
affected her destiny.

Diplomacy recognised the importance of the trans-
Mississippi region. Napoleon and Jefferson had a
simultaneous thought. The effect of the French phi-
losophers upon Jefferson's mind was apparent in every
act of his public career. Voltaire, Diderot, and Rous-
seau had taught that "the sovereignty of the State and
the people were one,—liberty, equality, and fraternity
of mankind."

The young American Republic was a real thing.[1]

[1] Those interested in the policy of France toward the Mississippi

During the period between 1783 and 1793, Washington shoe-buckles and Franklin snuff-boxes were a fad of Paris. Out of the French Revolution rose Napoleon, in many respects the greatest figure of all time. Neither Europe nor Africa confined his ambition or his thoughts; his eyes often turned toward America, the soil of which had been consecrated to France by La Salle and Montcalm. Napoleon brought sufficient pressure to bear upon the Spanish monarch to compel the retrocession of the Louisiana Territory to France in 1800. The exact date has been disputed. It was a secret treaty of necessity, because England could and would have seized New Orleans. The truth came out during a suspension of hostilities between France and England but any defence of the colony by Napoleon being impossible, Louisiana was obviously in the market for sale. Almost contemporaneously with the general diffusion of the knowledge that France had regained her former possession, a high-handed act of inhibition against the traders of the Mississippi Valley was committed. These sturdy pioneers had enjoyed the right to send their goods to New Orleans, as " a place of deposit," whence they could be shipped to all parts of the world. It was a great market. The closing of it meant dickering with the fur-traders of the North-west and the Great Lakes, men who drove hard bargains and paid slowly. On the other hand, at the great port of New Orleans one part of the commercial world bid against the other. A crisis was inevitable.

Valley during the administrations of Presidents Washington and Adams will find the subject elaborately treated by Frederick Jackson Turner, in *The American Historical Review*, January, 1905.

President Jefferson was prompt to comprehend the importance of this arbitrary act to the pioneers who had won the lands they occupied inch by inch from the savages and beasts of the forests. Although not to be described as a pioneer himself, Jefferson, as Governor of Virginia, had aided in the formation of Kentucky. While Secretary of State, he had insisted upon the right of navigating the Mississippi and had tried to negotiate a treaty to that effect, vainly, until 1795; but when the French closed New Orleans as a place of deposit of merchandise in 1802, Jefferson showed the energy of which he was capable.

Robert R. Livingston, his Minister to France, was directed to make overtures to Napoleon. The latter had vast schemes of colonisation. The pioneers of the Ohio and upper Mississippi were in a threatening mood and wanted to descend the river to take forcible possession of New Orleans. Jefferson, wishing to avert war, which such a filibustering expedition would have forced, sent James Monroe, afterwards President of the United States, to France as Special Envoy. Events in Europe contributed to Jefferson's success. Monroe had hoped to secure all of Louisiana east of the Mississippi for $2,000,000 which Congress had appropriated. Instead, Napoleon made a counter proposition. He offered the entire Louisiana Territory for 125,000,000 francs. This was finally reduced to 80,000,000 francs, about $16,000,000, a fourth of which was to be paid to American citizens for claims against France. (Thus were founded the French Spoliation Claims, about which one hears to this day in the corridors and committee rooms of the Capitol at Washington.)

That treaty was signed April 30, 1803, and on December 29th of that year, at noon, the French tri-colour was lowered from its pole facing the official residence in New Orleans and the Stars and Stripes of the Federal Union replaced it.

The "Louisiana Purchase," including part of Texas, was in area twenty-six times larger than the State of New York. Since the acquisition of that territory the following States, " cut from the web of a splendid imperial property," have been admitted to the Federal Union: in 1812, Louisiana, 48,720 square miles; in 1821, Missouri, 69,415; in 1836, Arkansas, 53,850; in 1845, Iowa, 56,025; in 1858, Minnesota, 83,365; in 1861, Kansas, 82,080; in 1876, Colorado, 103,925,—a portion of this State lying west of the Rocky Mountains was not included in the " Louisiana Purchase " but was secured by the " Guadalupe Hidalgo Treaty," which brought with it Utah, Arizona, etc.; however, fully 60,000 square miles of Colorado territory come from the " Purchase ";—in 1889, North and South Dakotas, aggregating 150,932 square miles; in the same year, Montana, 146,080; in 1890, Wyoming, 97,890; in 1907, Oklahoma, and what is left of Indian Territory, equalling 55,000 square miles,—if what was ceded by Texas to the United States on December 13, 1850, be omitted. The acquisition of the Yellowstone National Park, 3575 square miles, must not be overlooked as part of the " Purchase." Its area is chiefly in Wyoming, although a strip on its western side extends across the Idaho border and to the northward into Montana. The natural features of that region are so marvellous that when John Colter returned to Saint Louis to tell about them, he was ridiculed and denounced. Henry M. Stanley had the same experience after his return to England from the Livingstone expedition.

There is no necessity to discuss the Oregon question in this connection: much pleasanter is it to feel that Oregon came to the Union by right of discovery by Captain Gray, of Boston, who entered the Columbia River in May, 1791, supported by the additional fact that John Jacob Astor established the first permanent trading post at Astoria. The land was not only discovered but actually settled by Americans!

The United States paid less than two cents for each hundred acres of land conveyed by France!

It is usual to refer to the purchase of Manhattan Island for $24 by Peter Minuit, acting for the Dutch West India Company, as an outrageous bargain, driven by civilised men with untutored savages; but, by comparison, the Indians of Manhattan were treated liberally. Jefferson's deal with Napoleon was the greatest real estate transaction ever made. Its consequences were disastrous to the Emperor, precipitating the war with England and her allies that culminated at Waterloo. Under Napoleon, France, mounted and afoot, had faced the troops of all Europe; but that secret treaty with the American Republic, which only half a generation earlier had cast off the British yoke, threw England into a rage and cost Napoleon his crown.

CHAPTER VI

Lewis and Clark

WHEN the purchase of the Louisiana Territory had been completed, President Jefferson began to feel anxiety regarding the value of the acquisition. He had traded with Napoleon " sight unseen," except the part embraced in the lower Mississippi Valley. The great North-west was literally an unknown land. The vastness of the new possession was not comprehensible. And right here, it may be said that one of the most marvellous exhibitions of our national development is the rapidity with which the primeval area has been opened to civilisation.

In the third year of the nineteenth century, Captain Meriwether Lewis and Captain William Clark, with a party of thirty men, pitched camp on the west bank of the Mississippi where is the present site of Saint Louis and began building three flat-bottomed boats. They were preparing for an epoch-making voyage of exploration, nothing less arduous than the ascent of the Missouri River! This trip, inadequately as it was outfitted, was the initiative of approximate knowledge of a territory exceeding five hundred thousand square miles in extent!

Saint Louis, in 1803, was a small trading post and

its few white citizens were indifferent to the fortunes
of the Lewis and Clark expedition; but the young
leaders were exactly the men for the undertaking.
They were Virginians, experienced woodsmen, and had
seen service against the Indians.   Lewis was four years
the younger but was pre-eminently the man to command. He was twenty-nine and Clark thirty-three
years of age. Lewis had been appointed Private
Secretary to President Jefferson when the latter took
office in 1801.   Therefore, when on April 30, 1803,
Jefferson's Special Commissioner, Monroe, and the
regularly accredited Minister from the United States
made the purchase from the French nation, the arduous
task of examining and reporting upon the property
was intrusted to the President's Secretary and a companion of the latter's selection, Captain Clark. The
President gave to the chief of this expedition elaborate
instructions and the report of that three years' task,
readily accessible in Washington, might serve as a model
for all explorers since that time. Lewis was the scien-
tific and Clark the military director.

When the boats were completed and their stores
aboard, the intrepid men pulled twenty miles up-stream
to the mouth of the Missouri, but at this point, the
actual beginning of their journey, they were stopped
by a Spanish officer who commanded a fort at the junction of the two rivers. It must be remembered that
the western boundary of the United States was the
Mississippi, and the Spanish flag floated over all
territory to the west of that river, from the British
possessions on the north.

France had ceded to Spain, November 13, 1762,
" The country and colony of Louisiana and the posts

thereon depending," thereby parting with her entire American dominions; but when Spain, on February 10, 1763, ceded to England all of her American possessions east of the Mississippi except the town of New Orleans, the American Revolution was a foregone consequence. The result of that war so embarrassed England in the control of Florida that she retroceded it to Spain in 1783 and the Spanish flag again waved from the east coast of Florida to the Pacific Ocean.   By a secret treaty October 1, 1800, Spain transferred "the colony or province of Louisiana back to France, without restrictions as to limits but with her ancient boundaries as they were when France, in 1762, had ceded the territory to Spain."

Very probably that Spanish commander at the mouth of the Missouri River in the summer of 1803 had not heard of the last two transfers,—transferrals, namely, of Spain back to France and the sale by the latter to the United States. His name has obscure mention in the Lewis and Clark journal but he is lost to history. His arbitrary act, however, caused one year's delay in the setting out of the expedition. A messenger had to be sent to Washington for instructions and Lewis and Clark went into winter quarters on the Illinois side to await his return.

Having back of them all the power of the young republic and bearing official documents showing the details of the transfer from France to the United States, Lewis and Clark started on their voyage up the Missouri River, May 4, 1804. There we leave them, as one might have said farewell to Jason and the good ship *Argo,* as she disappeared behind the Cyanian rocks at the entrance to the Bosphorus. The extent and wealth of the "Purchase" has been dealt with in a preceding chapter.

Lewis and Clark occupied two years, four months, and nineteen days in their weary journey from the Mississippi River to Portland, Oregon, and back. To-day, luxurious trains traverse much the same route in either direction, in three days. A cargo of two thousand tons of tea from Yokohama arrived at Tacoma, on Puget Sound, recently. It was consigned to Chicago and New York. Ten freight trains were required to move this cargo over the Northern Pacific Railroad, part of which route was traversed by Lewis and Clark.

In little more than half a century after Lewis and Clark had pushed their explorations beyond the Mississippi, the great West was won! This is in contrast to the rate of progress as told in all stories of history. Centuries elapsed during the advancement from Assyria to Egypt, Egypt to Greece, Greece to Rome, and the progress across the Alps to north-western Europe. The Trojan war gave to literature the *Iliad,* the *Odyssey,* and the *Æneid;* Cyrus's invasion of Asia Minor, the *Anabasis;* the conquest of Europe, after the fall of Rome, *The Song of Roland, The Nibelungen Lied, Romance of the Rose, The Cid, Beowulf,*—the hero of an Anglo-Saxon epic poem the scenes of which are laid in Denmark and Sweden (eighth century),—the Icelandic tales of Magnussen (1663), the *Heimskringla,*—the most important prose work in old Norse literature (1178), written by the Icelander Snorri Sturluson,—*Orlando Furioso,* a metrical romance of forty cantos by the Italian poet Ariosto (1515), and *Jerusalem Delivered* by Tasso.

Lewis and Clark gave to English literature Irving's *Astoria* and *Captain Bonneville,* Parkman's Histories, Theodore Winthrop's *John Brent,* Bret Harte's Tales, Joaquin Miller's verses. That is what a peaceful journey did for American literature.

7

CHAPTER VII

Zebulon M. Pike to Giacomo C. Beltrami

LIEUTENANT ZEBULON M. PIKE was directed by the government to proceed up the Mississippi,—as Lewis and Clark had previously been ordered to explore the Missouri,—to its source. He set out from the present site of Saint Louis on August 9, 1805, at the head of twenty men in keel boats. After many hardships, the expedition went into winter camp on November 1st, on the west bank of the river at a point in what is now Morrison County, Minnesota. After erecting a blockhouse, Lieutenant Pike started on December 10th on a sledge journey. He camped on Christmas day a few miles above the present site of Brainerd. He reached the mouth of Pine River December 31st and three days later discovered an Indian village over which a British flag was floating. A fire occurred in the camp of the expedition on the night of January 4th that destroyed the tents and an explosion of the ammunition was narrowly averted. Exhausted, the detachment reached Leech Lake February 1st, on snow-shoes, dragging their supplies on bark toboggans. In his report, Lieutenant Pike commits himself thus: "I will not attempt to describe my feelings on the accomplishment of my voyage, for this is the main source of the Mississippi." When, on February 12th, he had reached Red Cedar Lake, now known as Lake

Cass, he added: " This lake may be called the *upper* source of the Mississippi River." The natives, seeing that Pike's party was not composed of French or Englishmen, described his followers as " white Indians." After several pow-wows, at which the aborigines were made acquainted with the fact that a new and very different " Great Father " ruled over them, Pike began his return march to the blockhouse, where he arrived in March, 1806. When the river opened in the spring, the party returned to Saint Louis, aften an absence of eight months and twenty-two days.

Lieutenant Pike wrote his name large upon the early history of this country. He was only twenty-six years of age when he made the terrible mid-winter trip to Lake Cass. He was mortally wounded during the second war with Great Britain, while leading an American attack upon York (now Toronto). He had then attained the rank of Brigadier-General, at the age of thirty-four years. As J. V. Brower is careful to point out, Pike's information was " entirely hearsay and he accepted the stories told him about the Turtle Lake source." He did not do any actual exploring; the lakes and rivers were frozen, rendering such work impossible. That his trip was considered remarkable at the time is shown by the place accorded to it in contemporaneous literature. He was deceived, just as Beltrami was seventeen years later.

General Lewis Cass was appointed Governor of the Territory of Michigan in October, 1813, and held the post for eighteen years. As *ex-officio* Superintendent of Indian Affairs in his territory, he addressed a letter to John C. Calhoun, Secretary of War, on November

18, 1819, proposing an exploring expedition through Lake Superior and to the sources of the Mississippi. Secretary Calhoun endorsed the suggestion and ordered the equipment of the expedition. The party set out from Detroit, May 24, 1820, accompanied by a detachment of troops. Here we first hear of Henry R. Schoolcraft, who went along as mineralogist. Capt. D. B. Douglas was attached as topographer and astronomer and a few Indian hunters were added. At the end of the forty-third day, over the route travelled by missionaries and *coureurs de bois* for a century and a half, Governor Cass arrived at the mouth of the St. Louis River, near the present site of Duluth. Sandy Lake trading post, on the Mississippi, was reached on July 15th. As J. V. Brower remarks, "Lieut. Pike had preceded Cass at this place by fourteen years and it is probable that Le Sueur had ascended the Mississippi as far as the mouth of Sandy Lake River." Leaving his principal force in camp at this point, Governor Cass proceeded with two canoes, bearing Mr. Schoolcraft, Major Forsyth, Captain Douglas, Dr. Wolcott, and Lieutenant Mackay, "to explore the sources of the Mississippi."

Starting from Sandy Lake on July 17th, Red Cedar Lake was attained on the 21st. Mr. Schoolcraft at once renamed the body of water Cass Lake, in honour of the chief of the expedition, and so it is known to this day. From Chippewas, Cass learned that "the source of the river was *Lac La Biche,* about fifty miles *west-north-west* of Red Cedar Lake." Turtle River, a considerable stream, entered the lake from the north. Remarkable as it appears, nobody undertook to find the source of Turtle River or to circumnavigate the large,

shallow lake called after Governor Cass, for other inlets.   Had this been done, the entrance of the main
stream, leading to the *Hauteurs des Terres,* would have
been found by Cass in 1820.   The weather was pro-
pitious, the expedition was well equipped, but, like
Pike, whose opportunities were limited by snow and
ice, the untrustworthy statements of the natives were
accepted as facts.

Governor Cass began his return journey on July
21, 1820, " after a stay of a few hours " at Cass Lake!

Taking up their detachment at Sandy Lake, the
party descended to St. Anthony Fall, traversed Lake
Pepin to Prairie du Chien, then ascended the Wisconsin, portaged to the Fox River, and landed in Green
Bay, as many had done before them.   Governor Cass
arrived at Detroit, September 15, 1820, having crossed
the southern peninsula of Michigan in the saddle.   His
entire trip occupied one hundred and fifteen days.   It
gave to him international fame and largely contributed
to obtain for him the nomination as Democratic candidate for the Presidency of the United States twenty-
eight years afterwards.   Its fame endured more than
a quarter century.

The only real importance that attaches to the Cass
expedition is that it pointed the way for Henry R.
Schoolcraft, who, twelve years later, followed the same
route, camped where the Cass party had camped, and
imitated its movements in every respect except coming
home without investigating the shore line of Cass Lake.
The map resulting from the Cass expedition, which
was drawn by Schoolcraft, is highly valuable, because
it establishes the existence, although in a wrong direction, of *Lac La Biche,* at a point independent of Turtle

River.   Of course it should have been south-west instead
of north-west of Cass Lake.   Here is the map:

The next visitor of record to Lake Cass, Giacomo
Constantino Beltrami, did not receive during his life-

Section of a map showing the track pursued by the
Expedition under Governor Cass in 1820
Drawn by Henry R. Schoolcraft

time proper recognition of his efforts to locate the
source of the Mississippi.   This was largely due to the
jealousy of Major Long, U. S. A.   No less an au-

thority than Jean N. Nicollet pleads the cause of Beltrami, who was born at Bergamo, Italy, in 1779, his
father being a customs official of the Venetian Republic.
After a superior education, he entered the army but
soon began the practice of law in the courts at Mace-

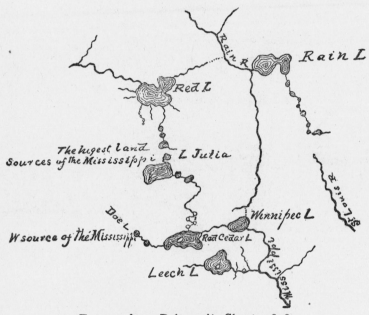

Extract from Beltrami's Chart, 1828

rata. We hear of him in Florence about 1812, where
he gained powerful social alliances that secured to him
the Presidency of the Court of Forlì. He was ambitious and probably became enmeshed in some political
intrigue, because he was banished in 1821. He came
to America, imbued with a desire for exploration and
discovery. He made his way to Saint Louis and thence
to Fort Snelling. From this place, he addressed a

letter to his most influential social sponsor in Florence, Madame La Comtesse Compagnoni, born Passeri and popularly known as " Countess of Albany." This letter would not appear to have brought financial assistance in time to have aided him in accompanying Major Long, who had been commissioned to conduct an expedition up the Minnesota River and down the Red River of the North to Pembina. Beltrami said in his journal: " My first intention, that of going in search of the real sources of the Mississippi, was always before my eyes." When Long and Beltrami quarrelled, the latter engaged two Chippewas and set out for Red Lake. He was soon deserted by his guides and he reached Red Lake alone, after many hardships. Securing a guide and interpreter, Beltrami left Red Lake, August 26, 1823, and two days later reached a place that he described as " the highest land of North America." There he found a deep lake, which he named " Julia " after his patroness. He did not stop at that, but without investigating whether or not the lake had an outlet, announced it " the Julian source of the Mississippi "! As Pike and Cass had done, he accepted statements of the savages. One very singular thing about Beltrami's journal is that he distinctly says " this Julia Lake is formed in the shape of a heart, and it may be truly said to speak of the very soul." Such is the form of Itasca! It must also be admitted, in Beltrami's behalf, that his guide described to him *Lac La Biche* and he charted it as "Doe Lake, West source of the Mississippi." Three quarters of a century's discussion followed the claims of Beltrami. His chart is worthy of a place in all volumes dealing with this subject. Its similarities to that of Lieutenant Pike will be observed. Here is a portion of his map of the region north-west of Lake Superior, setting forth his claims.

Beltrami descended Turtle River to Lake Cass, as Thompson had done, twenty-six years earlier, and ultimately made his way down the Mississippi to New Orleans. There he published, in 1824, *La Découverte des Sources du Mississippi*. From New Orleans, he went to Mexico, and claimed to have crossed the peninsula to the Pacific coast before he returned to London in 1827. In that city, his *Pilgrimage in Europe and America* appeared in two volumes, from which Châteaubriand and other French writers drew copiously. In the museum of his native city, Bergamo, Beltrami deposited the trophies of his explorations in northern Minnesota and there they may be seen to this day. A county in Minnesota has been named in his honour.

CHAPTER VIII

The Schoolcraft Expedition

HENRY R. SCHOOLCRAFT organised his own expedition to Cass, or Red Cedar, Lake at St. Mary's, on Lake Superior, in the spring of 1832. It was not intended, primarily, for exploration, but to effect a settlement of existing hostilities between the Sioux (See-oo) and Chippewas. Lieutenant Allen, U. S. A., with a battalion of infantry, accompanied Superintendent of Indian Affairs Schoolcraft; Dr. Douglas Houghton went along as botanist and Rev. W. T. Boutwell was a guest. George Johnstone acted as interpreter. There were thirty men, in all. It was the year of the Black Hawk War.

As the pretext for the Schoolcraft expedition never was made plain in the reports of Mr. Schoolcraft himself or of Lieutenant Allen, I wrote to Rev. W. T. Boutwell, in June of 1880, asking him to tell me what he knew about the matter. His generous response, made at the sacrifice of much effort, deserves to be given in full as final words from the last survivor of a historic episode. It bears date of June 23, 1880, and is as follows:

Nothing but the infirmities of age (seventy-seven) has prevented an earlier reply. You ask for incidents in relation to Mr. Schoolcraft's expedition to Itasca in 1832. To explain the purpose of the trip, it is necessary to go back as far as

1805, when Lieutenant Pike made his expedition under direction of our Government and, at that early day, reached Leech Lake and pronounced it the source of the Mississippi. He found the country occupied by British [traders] and under English influence. The Indian chiefs were flaunting English flags and displaying English medals. A brief extract from a letter, addressed to Hugh McGillis, one of the traders, will explain the cause of his (Pike's) expedition: " You will give immediate instructions to all posts in the territory under your direction that at no times or on no pretence whatever are they to hoist, or suffer to be hoisted, the English flag. That, on no occasion, will you present a flag or a medal to an Indian, or hold counsel with any of them on political subjects."

Nearly thirty years later (1831), when I came to this country, the old English traders had given place to a new class of men. Most of them were Americans, such as Lyman M. Warren, Charles H. Oaks, John Fairbanks, Allen Morrison, and W. Holiday. The Am. F. Co.'s depot was at Mackinaw, in charge of Robert Stuart. Ex-Governor Sibley was at that time a clerk in the Company's office.

Personal influence has a long life,—as some say, it never dies. Although many of the early English traders had long since died, their influence had become enduring by presents of ammunition, goods, flags, tobacco, and medals from the then traders at all the frontier posts. The chiefs and braves visited these posts every summer and there received large presents. To counteract this influence was one of the objects contemplated by the United States Government in despatching Mr. Schoolcraft upon his mission to Cass Lake. The chief of every band of any note that we visited displayed the English flag and English medals; but they promptly exchanged them for United States flags and medals when Mr. Schoolcraft made such proposition to them. Each band received a present of Indian goods, ammunition, and tobacco; they were civil and respectful in their responses to Mr. Schoolcraft, who counselled them to abandon the war path and to be at peace with their old enemies, the Sioux, until we reached Leech Lake. Flat-Mouth's band, at that place, numbered seven hundred, besides a band of three hundred on [word undecipherable] island. Mr. Schoolcraft made to them a large and valuable present of powder, shot, ball, Indian goods, medals, and flags in exchange for English flags and medals. After Mr. Schoolcraft had addressed the Indians, as he had done on other occasions, old Flat-Mouth rose and replied: " I suppose our Father will be displeased if I do not speak. We are very poor, and when we heard you were coming to visit your children we were in hopes you would pity us and bring us something to make our hearts glad." Pointing to a pile of the richest Indian goods embraced in Mr. Schoolcraft's gifts and amounting in value to several hundred dollars, he continued: " The ' Big Hats,' "—by which he meant to designate the English,—" are more generous to us than that! I would have been on my way to visit them had I not heard you were coming. You tell us to abandon the war path! You would have us sit still while our enemies kill our young men? The words of ' the Long-Knives,' "—meaning the Americans— " have been like the wind that shakes the trees for a moment and is gone. You promised us that if we sat still and our enemies came and killed our children you would punish them; but you have not kept your promises and have restrained us from punishing our enemies."

During this address, Flat-Mouth had held his blanket about his body with one hand, but at its conclusion, he allowed the blanket to fall from his shoulders to his feet and stood before us naked, except a breech cloth. Addressing Mr. Schoolcraft, the chief continued: " I will not hide the truth from you, Father. We have just returned from war, in which we were successful against our old enemy. I tell you, further, that if my people go on the war path and I do not lead I will not be slow to follow." Every member of the speaker's band grunted approbation. Here we saw the true feelings of all the border bands. They were more warmly attached to their long-while English friends than to the Americans.

The Schoolcraft expedition reached the Mississippi from Lake Superior by ascending the St. Louis River and portaging into Sandy Lake River, thence

descending it to Libby's trading post, at its mouth,—
where the main stream was three hundred and thirty
feet wide, according to Lieutenant Allen's measurement. Turning northward, the party ascended the big
river through the Thundering Rapids,—now called
Grand Rapids,—to Pokegama Fall; thence through
the Great Savannah, crossed Lake Winnebagoshish, and
entered Lake Cass, the ultimate point of previous official exploration. Camp was made on Grand Island.

In the first week of July, 1832, Schoolcraft started
across Cass Lake to the westward to find the entrance
of a large stream that Yellow Head, the principal chief
of the lake tribe, assured him was the continuation of
the Mississippi. His party consisted of five small
canoes, carrying three men each, with stores for the
voyage. The remainder of the party was left in camp
on Grand Island.

From the western end of Cass Lake, the ascent of
the river was resumed. Forty miles of paddling
brought Schoolcraft to the pretty lake that has nearly
retained its Chippewa name, Pa-mid-ji-gum-aug, or
Cross-water Lake. The Mississippi merely flows
through the southern end of Pemidji Lake, which is
very nearly cut in two by sharp promontories that
approach from the east and west. Schoolcraft named
the southern part of this lake after Washington Irving,
but the name has not been retained.

After leaving Lake Pemidji, the course up-stream
soon became almost due south. Five miles farther, the
ultimate forks of the river were encountered, the western branch being the larger. The guide recommended
the eastern branch as easier of ascent. Schoolcraft
named it " Plantagenet." It expanded in two places

into small lakes, which were called Marquette and La
Salle, in the order of their discovery. Late in the day,
a larger lake, with a fine evergreen forest upon its
southern side, was entered. The following day, rapids
and falls were met. A portage was made over a ridge,
through a region of Alpine plants. Small pines, of
the grey species, cedar, and spruce were abundant, and
the borders of the river were overhung with grey wil-
lows. A lake formed the ultimate reservoir of this
branch of the river, and from this lake a crossing was
to be made to the headwaters of the western or main
branch of the Mississippi.

This portage of six miles was made with several
rests. Reaching the brow of a ridge, the bright gleams
of sunshine upon a lake burst into view. It was the
goal of the explorer's hopes! The five canoes were
soon in the water and the party embarked. We now
quote Schoolcraft's description:

This was the 13th of July, 1832, being three hundred and
five years after the discovery of the mouth of the Mississippi
by Narvaez, and two hundred and nineteen years after the
actual discovery of its interior channel by Hernando de Soto.
It was a calm and bright day. Itasca Lake, as we named it,
is about five miles long.[1] We found the outlet quite a river,
with a swift current. We were two days and nights in its
descent [i. e., to Cass Lake]. There is a cascade, a few miles
below the lake (Itasca) called Ka-bi-ka, which we ran. We
found this stream the larger branch, and about one-third longer
than the Plantagenet fork.

The most cursory examination of Mr. Schoolcraft's

[1] Commissioner J. V. Brower fixes the geographical position of
Schoolcraft Island, north latitude 47° 13′ 10″, longitude west from
G., 95° 12′.

Recent View at Southeastern Extremity of Itasca, Showing
the Point across the Lake at which Schoolcraft
Reached it, in 1832.

map, as found in his report, shows that he did not
enter the west arm of Itasca Lake.   As a "sketch
map" it is about as inaccurate as a map could be made.
In the drawing, B indicates the point of entrance to
the lake, C the island upon which the party stopped,
and A the outlet of the lake.

The truth about the naming of Schoolcraft's lake
was brought out in 1872, as a direct result of a visit

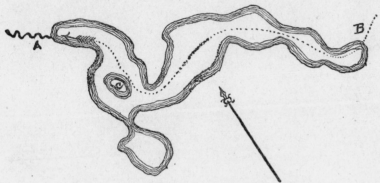

Schoolcraft's map of Itasca Lake, 1832

to the region made by the writer of this volume.   In
a letter to the New York *Herald* the statement was
publicly made by him that Schoolcraft had coined the
name I-tas-ca from two Latin nouns, supplied by the
Rev. W. T. Boutwell,— "veritas caput,"—by eliminat-
ing the first three letters of the first word and the last
syllable of the second word.   It became a matter of
discussion in various parts of the country.   Eight years
later, the author of this book wrote to the Rev. Boutwell
and received the following reply:

DEAR MR. CHAMBERS: As you say, it was in 1872 that in-
quiry was raised regarding the origin of the word "Itasca."

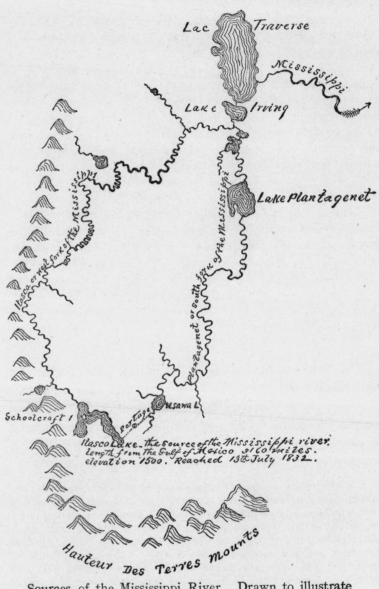

Sources of the Mississippi River. Drawn to illustrate
Schoolcraft's journey to Itasca Lake, 1832

112

The Secretary of the Minnesota Historical Society, knowing I had accompanied the Schoolcraft expedition, addressed a note to me with the request that if I had any knowledge regarding the origin of the name I would favour him with a reply. I gave to him the time, place, and circumstances under which I first heard the word uttered by Mr. Schoolcraft. Here are the facts:

As we were coasting along the south shore of Lake Superior one beautiful morning, the lake as calm and smooth as a mirror, Mr. Schoolcraft turned to me with this question: " Mr. Boutwell, can you give to me a word in Greek or Latin that will express ' true head ' or ' source '? "

After a moment's reflection, I replied, " I cannot; but I can give you two words." I gave to him " veritas caput." He wrote out the two words and, shortly after, turning to me, said, with animation:

" I have it! " Then and there, I first heard the word " I-tas-ca."

With much esteem, yours,
W. T. BOUTWELL.

STILLWATER, July 27, 1880.

Of course, Mr. Boutwell should have given to Schoolcraft the words " ve-rum ca-put," the adjective agreeing with the gender of the noun. From those words, the name " Rum-ca " might have been framed: it would have had a " true " Chippewa ring, albeit suggestive of " fire-water." [1]

[1] In the entire range of history, sacred and profane, only one episode exists as curious and interesting as this one. It is said a Jewish maiden, pitying the sufferings of the Saviour staggering under the weight of His cross on the road to Calvary, handed to Him her handkerchief. Jesus wiped His brow, returned the dainty linen to its owner, and pursued His painful journey. A perfect likeness of the Christ was upon the handkerchief! The precious article was called *vera iconica* (true likeness), and that gentle Jewess has been known ever since that dreadful day as Sainte Veronica (Ver-a iconica). One of these handkerchiefs is preserved in St. Peter's, Rome; another is shown at Milan.—J. C.

Dr. Douglas Houghton, who accompanied the Schoolcraft expedition, kept a journal of the trip which was not published until 1882, when it appeared in the Detroit *Post* and *Tribune*. It explains several obscure points in the narratives of Schoolcraft and Allen. Most startling is its disclosure of the fact that the party was at Itasca only three and one half hours of one afternoon. Having described the voyage to Lake Cass, where the party arrived on July 10, 1832, the Houghton narrative continues:

Our party was reorganised for a further prosecution of the exploration. Indians and voyageurs declared that the Mississippi had its origin in a lake called *La Biche,* sixty miles in a north-westerly direction: actually nothing was known of the situation above Cass Lake. Lieut. J. Allen announced that he could not prevail upon his men to accompany us farther. Our party, as reorganised, numbered sixteen men: H. R. Schoolcraft, Lieut. Allen, Rev. W. T. Boutwell, George Johnson, myself, and eleven voyageurs and natives.

At five o'clock A.M. (Wednesday, July 11th), Schoolcraft, Allen, Boutwell, Johnson [*sic*], and myself embarked. Each of us occupied a separate canoe, paddled by one voyageur and one Chippewa. We ascended the river beyond Lake Cass to a body of water called by the voyageurs *Lac Travers.* Proceeding, we passed a series of small lakes and encamped at a point of woods.

July 12th, Thursday, we embarked at 5 A.M., and continued to ascend the stream until 4 P.M., when the guides advised a portage, owning to the tortuous character of the river. [This is the Eastern, or Plantagenet, branch of the Mississippi, be it remembered.—J. C.] We portaged two miles across country, soil of diluvial character, containing boulders of trap rock, syenite, and quartz. The course of the stream had been southerly. We camped on again reaching the insignificant creek.

July 13th, Friday.—The sun had scarcely arisen when we embarked and ascended the winding brook at which we had encamped the evening before, for twelve or fifteen miles, when we arrived at an expansion of water one or two miles in length, called by the guides Ossowa Lake. Its waters were blackish and bordered with aquatic plants. This lake receives two small brooks, and may be regarded as the source of this branch of the Mississippi. The head of this lake is one hundred and twenty miles from the forks. The chief, Yellow Head, pushed his canoe through the weeds of the shore and soon announced his discovery of the portage which would lead to *Lac La Biche* of the French. Having reached the source of this branch of the great river, it may be noted that its existence as a separate fork of the Mississippi has been hitherto unknown in our maps. Immediately after landing we followed the portage in a westerly direction, wading for some distance before the soil became firm. The course led through a tamarack swamp for about two miles. Thirteen rests were deemed the length of the portage. Having passed over, or rather through, the marshes, we arrived at a series of sandy ridges, supporting a growth of grey pine covered with lichen. These ridges separate the headwaters of the Mississippi and its tributaries from those of Red River. Having passed over these ridges near four miles, making in all six miles of portage, we arrived at Lake Itasca, near its head. This lake is considered the true source of the Mississippi, and our party was the first which had ever reached it. The lake is small and irregular, having many bays proportionately deep. It is eight miles in length, and has an average width of three fourths of a mile. The shore rises gradually to a considerable height from the water, but the soil is of the same barren, sandy kind already mentioned. The principal timber is grey and yellow pine and aspen. Near the foot of the lake is a small island, upon which we landed, and Mr. Schoolcraft ordered the American flag to be hoisted, and it was so secured as to remain a long time. This was the first flag ever hoisted at the head of the Mississippi River.

We arrived at the lake at about one o'clock P.M., *and having coasted through it and made some examinations, our sole object of visiting the Mississippi was accomplished, and, at*

*4.30, we commenced descending the outlet of the lake, which
was a mere brook, about ten feet in width.*

A final word about Beltrami. Mr. Schoolcraft and
Lieutenant Allen have only words of sarcasm and disrespect for the adventurous Italian. One is puzzled,
after comparing their reports, to account for their
bitterness except upon the meanest of motives,—
jealousy at finding their work anticipated. In Beltrami's narrative,[1] published ten years before Allen's
report,[2] he fixes "the source of the great river in Lake
Moscos-Saguaiguen." O-mush-kos Saw-gaw-see-gum
is clearly the same lake; and, if they are not the same
words, the French name, which Beltrami gives, would
settle the identity of the lake. Beltrami adds, "It is
also known as *Lac La Biche,* the first one above *Lac
Travers*" (Pemidji Lake).[3] Beltrami further antici-
pates both of his critics, because he states that "the
large river flowing into *Lac de la Cedre Rouge* [Cass]
on the west is the continuation of the Mississippi." He
says it is called *Demizimaguamaguen-sibi* and leads
directly into *Lac Travers.* Much additional philological proof might be given to strengthen Beltrami's
position and to identify the main stream as located by
him.

Again, Beltrami does *not* claim (as Allen alleges)
Tortoise, or Turtle, Lake as the "true source of the
Mississippi," but only describes it and its feeders as
"the Julian sources." Yet, on the map attached to

[1] Beltrami's *Pilgrimage in Europe and America,* 2 vols. London,
1823.
[2] Executive Reports, 1st Session, 23d Congress. (1833.) Vol. ii.,
page 323.
[3] Beltrami's *Pilgrimage,* vol. ii., page 434.

Itasca Lake, Looking South from Bluff at Northern End.
(Schoolcraft Island Shown at Left.)

Lieutenant Allen's report to the President of the United States, a mark of disrespect for Beltrami's work is placed by affixing to that locality the words, "False source of the Mississippi." Schoolcraft and Allen subsequently quarrelled; but at the time of their journey they appear to have agreed that they possessed letters patent to everything associated with the upper Mississippi. They write as though the river belonged to them; men who had shown them the route are warned off. This feeling accounts for the perpetration of "ver I-tas ca-put," and nothing else does. Mr. Boutwell's letter narrates the circumstances under which the word was coined: but I frankly admit not to have understood Mr. Schoolcraft's motive for insisting upon stamping *"true* source" upon Itasca Lake until I examined Lieutenant Allen's map.

Recurring to the various theories and explanations that had been put forth in former years, to account for the selection of the name "Itasca," I may say that after the Boutwell announcement was made by the Minnesota Historical Society, considerable merriment was created over a letter that had appeared in a Saint Paul newspaper in May, 1872, addressed to A. J. Hill, of Saint Paul, by Mary H. Eastman, of Washington, D. C., in which she had repeated a remarkable legend that had appeared in her collection of Indian Folk-lore, known as *Eastman's Aboriginal Portfolio.* Here is the lady's story, as taken from her letter:

Itasca was the daughter of Manabazho, Spirit God of the Chippewas. I have printed, in my *Aboriginal Portfolio* an account of the exciting scene of the discovery of the Mississippi, and the tradition of Itasca, after whom Mr. Schoolcraft named the lake. The Chippewa guide gave the tradition to

Mr. Schoolcraft who gave it to me.   It is a lovely little tradition, and reminds one of Ceres and Proserpine.

Itasca was beloved by Chebiabo, keeper of the souls of the
dead, and was about to be torn from her family and borne
to his gloomy abode, she having refused to go with him.   The
storm spirits interfered in her behalf, but too late to save
her.   In the confusion of the struggle in which the gods took
part, Itasca was buried under hills of sand, forming a mound
that the Chippewa guide showed to Mr. Schoolcraft as her
grave.   The rills that flow from the rocks and sand, forming
the lake, are made by the tears of Itasca weeping for ever
for home and friends,—the sorrow produced by the revenge
of this terrible (Pluto) Chebiabo.   The name and tradition
of Itasca are as reliable as any other.   It is a subject for a
grand poem.

What can be thought of the statement that Mr.
Schoolcraft is responsible for this yarn?

CHAPTER IX

The Jean N. Nicollet Expedition

THE first real investigation of the sources of the Mississippi was made by a Frenchman, Jean Nicolas Nicollet, who came to the United States in the same year that Schoolcraft visited and named the Itasca region. He was born at Cluses, not far from Geneva, in Savoie, in 1790. His parents were poor; he learned the watchmaker's trade and pursued the study of mathematics. He went to Paris, was admitted to the first class of L'Ecole Normale, and soon received an appointment as Professor of Mathematics in the College of Louis le Grand. He became distinguished as an astronomer,—having discovered two comets, for which he received the decoration of the Legion of Honour.

Nicollet arrived in New Orleans, according to the most credible authorities, in 1832, where he was assisted by Bishop Chance of Natchez. He communicated to the War Department his wish to engage in a voyage of exploration on the upper Mississippi. He set out from New Orleans on a tour to the north in 1835. At Saint Louis, he made the acquaintance of P. Chouteau, Jr., a successful merchant, who furnished him with means to prosecute his journey. Henry H. Sibley, who met Nicollet at Fort Snelling, asserts that the Frenchman's visit to Itasca occurred during the summer of 1835, instead of 1836, as claimed by the traveller himself.[1]

Nicollet arrived in Washington after his exploration of Itasca in 1838, published his reports, and was sent on a mission to chart the vast region between the Missouri and Mississippi. The career of John C. Frémont may be said to have begun with that expedition, he having been assigned thereto by the Secretary of War. Nicollet ascended the Missouri, much as Lewis and Clark had done, and returned by way of the Minnesota River, opening a new country to civilisation. He died, full of honours but poor in purse, at Washington on September 18, 1844.

J. V. Brower summarises Nicollet's preliminary report in such masterly fashion that he brings out its best features. This summary is given without comment on the discrepancies between Nicollet's measurements and those of Schoolcraft[2]:

The Itasca region is covered with American larch and white cedars. The hills to the east of Itasca rise one hundred and twenty feet above the water. No sign of the flag set up on Schoolcraft Island. So, this is Itasca Lake,—it may be lik-

[1] See *Minnesota Historical Collections*, vol. i., p. 188. It is a curious and highly interesting coincidence that M. Nicollet should have had the same Christian name as his distinguished predecessor in Northern exploration, Jean Nicolet, who is mentioned in the "Relations" of the Jesuit Fathers as arriving in Canada in 1618, and, after spending a season at Nipissing Lake, was sent by the Company of New France to *Les Gens de Mer*, or People of the Sea (the Winnebagoes), to negotiate a peace between them and the Hurons. The Nicollet of 1836, who had appreciative words for everybody that had preceded him, was savagely attacked and a contemporary critic asserted that his baptismal name was Joseph. It was probably a mean, unjustified assertion.

[2] Brower's *The Mississippi and its Source*, vol. vii. of *Minnesota Historical Society Collections*.

Nicollet's Creek, beyond Itasca.
("The Cradled Hercules.")
Courtesy of J. V. Brower.

ened to the mysterious source of the Nile! (Pliny, lib. v.)
Five small creeks enter this lake, all but one mere trickling
rills, oozing from clay beds at the bases of the hills that
consist of an accumulation of sand, gravel, and clay, intermixed with erratic fragments.

The elevations are flat on top, varying in height from eighty-
five to one hundred feet above surrounding waters. They are
covered with thick forests, in which coniferous plants predominate. South of Itasca Lake, they form a semicircular
region, with a boggy bottom extending to the south-west several miles: thence these *Hauteurs des Terres* ascend to the
north-west and north, and then, stretching to the north-east
and east through the zone between 47 and 48 N. latitude,
make the dividing ridge between the waters that empty into
the Gulf of Mexico and into Hudson Bay. The waters supplied by the north side of these heights—still on the south
side of Itasca—give origin to the five creeks referred to.
These are the utmost sources! Those that flow from the
southern side of the same heights form Elbow Lake, the source
of the Red River of the North. They are close together.

Of the five streams mentioned, one empties into the east
bay of the lake and the other four into the west bay. I visited
them all. I explored the principal one (August 29, 1836).
At its entrance into Itasca it is between fifteen and twenty
feet wide, and has a depth of two to three feet. I paddled
against a brisk current for twenty minutes; stream full of
obstructions. Leaving my canoe, I sought the springs among
the hills on foot. After a walk of three miles, into the hills,
found a small lake, from which the Mississippi flowed in a
current a foot deep and two feet wide. At no great distance,
however, this rivulet, uniting itself with other streams, supplies a second minor lake. From this lake issues a rivulet,
larger and stronger,—"a cradled Hercules,"—giving promise
of its strength and its maturity, for its velocity has increased.
It transports the smaller branches of trees; it begins to form
sand-bars; its bends are more decided, until it subsides again
into the basin of a third lake, larger than the two preceding.
Having here acquired renewed vigour and tried its consequence

upon an additional length of two or three miles [*sic*] it finally empties into Lake Itasca, the principal reservoir of all the sources to which it [the Mississippi] owes its subsequent majesty.

M. Nicollet was evidently in the dark as to the origin of the name Itasca. (See " Report," p. 59.) This is what he says of the island:

There is only one island in Itasca Lake, not more than two hundred and twenty-two yards long,[1] with a sandy, gravelly soil but covered by a full growth of northern trees that give to it a picturesque appearance. [Again, he says:] The Mississippi, as it issues from Itasca, is sixteen feet wide, fourteen inches deep, beautifully transparent, and swift in current. The temperature of the water (August 29th) at 7 A.M., was sixty-two whilst the air was fifty-six. After an hour's descent, the stream enlarged to twenty-five feet, three feet deep.

In view of discussion regarding the actual achievements of Jean N. Nicollet, we cannot do better than to quote, literally, his official report to Congress, published January 11, 1845,—nearly nine

[1] It is interesting to compare this statement with Lieutenant Allen's report (of the Schoolcraft expedition) in which he says: " The island, which I called ' Schoolcraft,' in *Lac La Biche*, is 150 yards long (450 feet), 50 yards broad (150 feet) and elevated 20 or 30 feet in its highest part; a little rocky in boulders and grown over with pine, spruce, wild cherry, and elm." (See Executive Documents, 1st Session, 23d Congress, vol. 4, p. 44. Also p. 323.) Here is what he says of the region: " The lake is surrounded by hills 300 feet high, of irregular shape, conforming to the bases of these pine hills, which for a great part of its circumference rise abruptly from its shores. The lake is deep, very clear, and cold. . . . It would seem that no kind of animal life was adapted to so gloomy a region."

years after his journey and four months after
his death. He had given many of his last hours to
a revision of the proofs.[1] We begin with the conclusion of the final portage from Leech Lake into
Itasca:

The last in the series [of ridges], also the highest, is one
hundred and twenty feet above the waters of Itasca Lake.
This ridge, with a rapid descent, led us to the borders of the
lake, where I took a barometrical observation at noon.

My next move was to pitch my tent on Schoolcraft Island.
The staff, at the top of which that gentleman informed us he
had raised the American flag, had been cut down by Indians.
I made use of what remained to fix upon it my artificial horizon, and immediately proceeded to make astronomical observations, and to take up the exploration of the sources of the
Mississippi.

The Mississippi holds its own from its very origin; for it
is not necessary to suppose, as has been done, that Lake
Itasca may be supplied with [from] invisible sources, to jus-
tify the character of a remarkable stream, which it assumes
at its issue from this lake. There are five creeks that fall
into it, formed by innumerable streamlets oozing from the
clay beds at the bases of the hills, that consist of an accumulation of sand, gravel, and clay, intermixed with erratic fragments, being a more prominent portion of the great erratic
deposit previously described and which here is known by the
name of " *Hauteurs des Terres* "—heights of land.

These elevations are commonly flat at top, varying in height
from eighty-five to one hundred feet above the level of the

[1] The text is taken from a copy of the Nicollet " Report " in the
possession of the American Geographical Society, which is a presenta-
tion volume inscribed, " To His Excellency, Baron Alexander von
Humboldt,. from his fervent admirer, J. G. Flügel." Doc. No. 52,
House of Representatives, 28th Congress, 2d Session, 1845; page 56
et seq. Jean Godefroi Flügel was a German lexicographer who served
as a German consul in the United States and died in 1855.—J. C.

surrounding waters. They are covered with thick forests, in which coniferous plants predominate.[1]

The waters supplied by the north flank of these heights of land—still on the south side of Lake Itasca—give origin to the five creeks of which I have spoken above. *These are the waters which I consider to be the utmost sources of the Mississippi.* Those that flow from the southern side of the same heights, and empty themselves into Elbow Lake, are the utmost sources of the Red River of the North; so that the most remote feeders of Hudson Bay and the Gulf of Mexico are closely approximated to each other.

Now, of the five creeks that empty into Itasca Lake, *one* empties into the east bay of the lake: the *four* others into the west bay. I visited the whole of them; and among the latter is one remarkable above the others, inasmuch as its course is longer, and its waters more abundant: so that, in obedience to the geographical rule, " that the sources of a river are those which are most distant from its mouth," this creek is truly the infant Mississippi; all others *below,* its feeders and tributaries.

The day on which I explored this principal creek (August 29, 1836), I judged that, at its entrance into Itasca Lake, its bed was from fifteen to twenty feet wide, and the depth of water from two to three feet.[2] We stemmed its pretty brisk current during ten or twenty minutes; but the obstructions occasioned by the fall of trees compelled us to abandon the canoe, and to seek its springs on foot, along the hills. After a walk of *three miles* [2] (*sic*), during which we took care not to lose sight of the Mississippi, my guides informed me that it was better to descend into the trough of the valley; when, accordingly, we found numberless streamlets oozing from the bases of the hills. [Remarks about temperature at this point are omitted.]

[1] A brief omission of matter quoted by Brower, and of a few sentences describing the dividing ridge between the Mississippi and Red River of the North, occurs here. The latter is not pertinent (p. 58).

[2] The reader is asked to refer to the Government survey map in the front of this volume.

The Mouth of Nicollet's Creek, where it Enters Itasca.
(Taken since the Building of the Dam at the Outlet of the Lake.)

As a further description of these head-waters, I may add that they unite at a small distance from the hills whence they originate, and form a small lake, from which the Mississippi flows with a breadth of a foot and a half, and a depth of a foot. At no great distance,[1] however, this rivulet, uniting itself with other streamlets coming from other directions, supplies a second minor lake, the waters of which have already acquired a temperature of 48°. From this lake issues a rivulet, necessarily of increased importance—a cradled Hercules, giving promise of the strength of its maturity; for its velocity is increased; it transports the smaller branches of trees; it begins to form sand bars; its bends are more decided, until it subsides again into the basin of a third lake, somewhat larger than the two preceding.[2] Having here acquired renewed vigour, and tried its consequence upon an additional length of two or three miles [!], it finally empties into Itasca Lake, which is the principal reservoir of all the sources to which it [the Mississippi] owes all its subsequent majesty. [Some comments on Schoolcraft, Lieutenant Allen, and Beltrami are omitted.]

After having devoted three days to an exploration of the sources of the Mississippi, I took leave of Itasca Lake, to the examination of which the expedition that preceded me by four years had devoted but a short time.   (Allen's report, 44.)

M. Nicollet's account of his descent of the river to Lake Cass does not differ greatly from that of Lieutenant Allen, who accompanied Schoolcraft. From that point, he went " through intermediary lakes and portages " to Leech Lake, where we leave him.

Mr. J. V. Brower, who gave the best years of his life to maintaining the worthy, if confusing, claims of

---

[1] Among the articles enumerated in M. Nicollet's kit was " a measuring tape " and it is to be regretted he did not use it.

[2] All of which is very confusing, unless we are to understand that the stream grew *larger* as it neared its ultimate source. Nicollet in his ascent, " took care not to lose sight of the Mississippi." Mr. Brower's explanation is ingenious (see next page).

Jean N. Nicollet, admitted the difficulty of explaining Nicollet's report.   He says [1]:

The discovery of three small lakes by M. Nicollet, up the channel of the main tributary, so graphically described by him, and the manner in which he located them upon his map, without careful courses and measurements, has misled observers of the locality as to his three lakes. Hopewell Clarke was led to presume that his third lake was a small body of water (now a dry bed) to the eastward of his middle lake, while my casual examination of 1888, in the confusion of location in which M. Nicollet placed these three bodies of water, indicated that the third lake up the tributary did not exist, and a belief accordingly was publicly expressed. No one question has been more puzzling than the identity of Nicollet's third lake. There is a probability that M. Nicollet in passing up the valley and affluent discovered by him became bewildered in the thickets of the locality, which precluded the possibility of his correctly delineating the topography of the spot. It is absolutely impossible to certainly and accurately trace his steps after he left his canoe and passed along the brow of the hills, being careful to remain within sight of the stream, that he might not become lost. It is possible, since it is certain that he passed up the valley on the east bank of the stream, that he only saw two lakes, for the peculiarities of the topography there, in passing up the valley on the brow of the hills on the *east* side of the stream, bring the middle lake in sight *first,* and continuing, the lower lake comes in sight, thence passing up the stream the middle lake *again comes to the view*.   Query: May it not have been that Nicollet, passing the middle lake *first,* reaching the lower lake *second,* and then again arriving at the middle lake, may have made the mistake of describing the two lakes as *three,* having arrived in sight of the middle lake a *second time?*   Such a view is forced upon the reader of his report, in the light of a survey in detail of Nicollet's lower

[1]*The Mississippi River and its Source*, by J. V. Brower. *Minnesota Historical Society Collections*, vol. vii., 162.

The Outlet of Nicollet's Middle Lake.

and middle lakes; especially so, since it is known that the waters, in abundance, ooze from the base of the hill immediately above Nicollet's middle lake, and uniting form a stream of continued surface flowage to Itasca Lake. It is very doubtful if Nicollet ever saw the pool of water which has been designated as his third lake, for purposes of correct geographical delineation. It, however, is the only pathway out of a dilemma at this time.

After an exhaustive consideration of the question, it is believed that the underground channel, now distinctly defined between Nicollet's upper and middle lakes, possibly might have been, in 1836, a surface channel, and, accordingly, a declared determination upon the question of the three lakes has been made with much doubt.[1]

Just how much this explanation explains is left to impartial readers. The author of this volume does not express an opinion; and he venerates Mr. Brower.

In this immediate connection (although it does not belong here chronologically), I annex to M. Nicollet's report the account of Hopewell Clarke's special survey of the Nicollet valley, made in 1886, at the instance of Henry D. Harrower.[2] Mr. Clarke's standing and

---

[1] ST. PAUL, MINN., DEC. 18, 1889.
After due deliberation, and with a copy of Nicollet's original map of the sources of the Mississippi and North Red River before us, we conclude the three lakes noted by Nicollet on the principal affluent to Lake Itasca, as shown by his said map, are the two lakes in the south-east quarter of section 21, and the small lake in the south-west corner of section 22, township 143, range 36.
Signed: HOPEWELL CLARKE,
J. V. BROWER.

[2] Mr. Henry D. Harrower, representing the educational publishing house of Ivison, Blakeman, Taylor & Co., had previously issued a small volume dealing conclusively with the claims of Captain Willard Glazier, made by Glazier as a result of a trip to the Itasca country in 1884. On page 21 of that book, Mr. Harrower says: " Some time after most of this paper was in type I learned the name and address of the New York *Herald* correspondent of 1872. Mr. Julius Chambers at once kindly placed his note-book at my service, and a

experience are recognised. With two assistants, he entered the Itasca basin from the southward, by way of Park Rapids, and arrived at Itasca Lake, October 13, 1886. His report bears date of December 7th, of that year; and his survey map, taken therefrom, is much more detailed than that of the Government surveyor, Edwin S. Hall.

DESCRIPTION OF THE CLARKE MAP

Nicollet Creek is the largest feeder of the lake. It is 16 feet wide and 2½ feet deep at its entrance to Itasca. My exploration of this stream was the most complicated and difficult of our undertakings, and it was with considerable difficulty that we were able to identify the three lakes which Nicollet describes: but, while on the ground, we concluded that Nicollet's three lakes are those marked on my map A, B, and C. At first sight, it would seem, from Nicollet's description, that these are not the ones to which he referred; and I have given much study to the points involved, endeavouring to reconcile his description with some other theory.

. We followed the stream to the first lake at the edge of the hills and through the swamps; the course of the brook is two miles in length and seemed like four. Distances on the ground double up very fast when one follows crooked streams, —as you will remember when you compare the length of the stream between Itasca and Elk lakes (1084 feet) with the actual distance between the two lakes (350 feet). If we add to the actual length of the course of the stream from the lake A to its outlet at D, which is in reality two miles, the difficulties Nicollet encountered wading through the tamarack marsh, we

copy of his note-book map is here reproduced for the first time. See page 22." On page 26, he adds: " Mr. Chambers went over every mile of the river by water. He did not make any stump speech, did not rate himself a great discoverer, did not call his lake, 'Lake Chambers,' was not greeted by brass-bands, and did not finally receive the freedom of the city of New Orleans."

can easily believe that this is the course he describes as " two or three miles in length. . . ."

But lake *C* is not the source at the present time from which Nicollet's stream draws its principal supply of water. To find this source, after considerable exploration, we were obliged to go to a lake which has its head in the north-western quarter of section 34. This is the utmost source and fountain-head of the water flowing north into Lake Itasca. The lake itself is fed by numerous springs along its borders, and its surface is 92 feet above the level of Lake Itasca. The small inlet from the lake marked *I* was dry when we visited it, but water runs through it in the wet season. The hills south rise from 20 to 160 feet high, and water never has flowed over them, north-ward. It might be interesting to know how far it flows under them. It is certain that it does, but there is no way to trace the course or distance. All the streams in this part of the basin rise in springs in tamarack swamps, which are undoubtedly fed by water percolating under the hills from lakes and swamps beyond; and, no doubt, the group of lakes *U, B, W,* and *X,* in the southern part of sections 33, 34, and 35, which spread out to a considerable extent in sections 3, 4, and 5 of the townships next south, are the reservoirs that feed a number of these streams. Beginning with the lake marked *H,* it spreads northward nearly half a mile. At its northern end, the water flows out of this lake in a stream 1½ feet wide, and 1 foot deep, and, running west about 200 feet, empties into a small lake about 2 acres in extent, marked *G.* This lake connects with another of the same size about 20 feet to the west of it.

At the time we were there, both ponds were full of moss and bogs, and almost dried up, the abundant inflow of water running out by underground passages as fast as it came in; but both lakes show that at some seasons of the year they contain 4 feet more of water, caused by the increased flow in the springt me and in the rainy season. At that time the underground passages are not large enough to carry the water off, and so it accumulates and the ponds fill up. Apparently they once had a surface outlet which is now closed by a beaver

9

dam. The water flowing from the two lakes feeds the two springs numbered 3 and 5.

Proceeding to the spring marked 5, we find the water bubbling up and flowing away in a rapid, lively stream, in a direction generally northward. It is fed by springs along its course until it reaches the extreme south-western corner of section 22, where it is 2½ feet wide and 8 inches deep, and discharges into a small pond of about 5 acres in extent. This pond is the most remarkable one in the course of the stream; *it has no surface outlet,* and, from the formation of the land about it, apparently has never been any larger than it now is; but, with the large volume of water flowing into it, we perceive that it must, of course, have a steady and sufficient outlet underground. This we found to be toward the west, where it bursts forth in an immense spring or pool, marked 2, in the extreme south-eastern quarter of section 21. The lowest point on the hill between the pond and the spring is 12 feet above the level of the pond; and the water, dropping underground, bubbles up in the swamp 200 feet away and 33 feet below that level. The stream passes underground from section 22 into section 21, and is therefore invisible to one following up the course of the section line.

Proceeding from the spring marked 2, the water flows in a north-westerly direction, and empties into the lake marked *B,*—the second one of Nicollet's chain of lakes. The outlet of this lake is on the west side, a stream 3 feet wide and a foot deep, joined at a short distance by another from the south. Following up the stream, which joins the main one on section 21, we find it rises on section 28 at a spring marked 3, evidently fed by an underground passage from the pond *F.* These streams are re-enforced throughout their course by springs which ooze from the bases of the hills that line the tamarack swamps; so that, when the creek leaves lake *A,* it flows with a brisk current 12 feet wide and 1 foot deep, which is further re-enforced by numerous springs all the way to Lake Itasca. At the point of its discharge into the lake, it is a broad, well-defined stream, 16 feet wide, and 2½ feet deep at its deepest point.

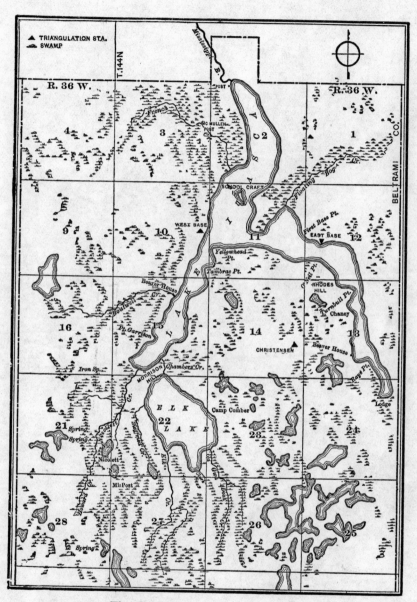

The Sources of the Mississippi.
First Official Survey Map, 1875, by Edwin S. Hall.

The Sources of the Mississippi.
First Official Survey Map, 1875, by Edwin S. Hall.

CHAPTER X

Elk Lake to South-west Pass

"SCHOOLCRAFT in 1832 and Nicollet in 1836, —nobody of record since that time!" exclaimed a New York newspaper correspondent in the Congressional Library, at Washington, one day, after an examination of all reports, official and otherwise, of exploration at the head-waters of the Mississippi River. The time was January, 1872. Forty years had elapsed since Schoolcraft had visited and named Itasca Lake, as " the true source " of the " Father of Waters."

Mr. Schoolcraft's official report showed that he had merely paddled from the southern end of the eastern arm of Itasca to the only island in the lake and thence direct to the outlet. That he had overlooked important features was proved by Nicollet's visit, four years later. This capable and scholarly Frenchman had passed four days at Itasca and had examined the west arm of the lake, which Schoolcraft had wholly neglected.

Plans for a trip to the sources of the Mississippi took form in the correspondent's mind, which were subsequently carried out. Three months in the open air had been ordered by a physician, to supplement recovery from serious illness, and such an outing afforded opportunity to obey that command. The correspondent financed the expedition himself, although he arranged to send letters to the New York *Herald*.

The best map that Colton, New York's cartographist of the time, could supply, showed the Itasca region as a blank! A journey was made to Troy, and a canoe was ordered from Waters, Balch & Co., to be delivered at Saint Paul the first week in May.

When the correspondent arrived at the capital of Minnesota, he visited the State Land Office, in hope that the large Colton map could be supplemented with details sufficiently clear to lay out a route to Itasca Lake. Not a single profitable addition was made to the chart! It was desirable to go by some other route than that of Leech Lake, which Nicollet had followed. Greatly disappointed, the would-be canoeist sent his boat by rail to Brainerd, but personally stopped in Duluth, still intent upon obtaining needed information. This " City of the Unsalted Seas " was then a small nest of white frame houses, clinging to a rocky hillside, with not enough scrubby pines to shelter its brood from the keen winds of Lake Superior. Its streets were sloughs and its hotel was something memorable. A photograph, secured that day, is veritable.

The Northern Pacific Railroad was slowly progressing across Minnesota toward the Red River of the North. Possessing a personal letter from Jay Cooke, the directing mind in that enterprise, the writer of this narrative went to Brainerd and sought information at " Headquarters," as the combined hotel and offices of the corporation were described. There, Dr. Day, then Indian Commissioner, was encountered. He was on his way to White Earth. Acting upon his advice, the correspondent resumed the journey westward by rail. Leaving the train at Oak Lake station, not far from the present town of Detroit Lake, the night was passed

Saint Paul, Looking Southwest.
From a photograph taken in 1872.

The City of Duluth in 1872.

in a log tavern, and on the following day a waggon carried the Commissioner and the correspondent twenty miles across the prairie to White Earth, seat of the Chippewa Indian Reservation of that name, where, at Morrison's trading post, the expedition to Itasca Lake was outfitted.

I—AT WHITE EARTH MISSION

The "hotel" was chiefly of logs and its partitions were of straw-board. Its mistress was a daughter of "Hole in the Day," a Chippewa chief whose name was national. A church and a school were the only evidences of civilisation, although a few small plots of ground were devoted to agriculture. "Graves in the air," bodies of the dead supported by poles, were seen. One of the best guides in the North-west, Henry Beaulieu, of a famous French-Canadian family at Mackinaw, and a packman were engaged; word was sent by runner to another Chippewa carrier to meet the party at the first long portage.

The people at the Mission were gravely anxious, just then, regarding the fate of a missing man. One of the most widely known "timber-cruisers" in Minnesota, Peter Kelly, had set out, more than a month before, to locate land-scrip in the Itasca wilderness, but had not returned.

Frontiersmen are united by a brotherhood of common, ever-present danger. Men belonging to the White Earth Mission had vainly tried to follow Kelly's trail into the brush and through a broad belt of fallen timber. The lost man was not familiar with the Itasca region. He was a servant of foreign monopolists, that, in local belief, were stealing timber lands from the government: nevertheless, these natural philanthropists could not permit Kelly to die in the woods, unsought. The second search party had returned, unsuccessful and hopeless. The pioneers at White Earth agreed that the "timber-cruiser" had been maimed in crossing a tornado path and had died of starvation in the woods.

"Cruising for timber" is a livelihood of the forest primeval. The simile is apt. A woodman who seeks new lumber regions amid the pathless wilderness, where the sun is hidden by day and the stars by night, is as bold a navigator as is the sailor on the trackless waste of the deep.

The "timber-cruiser" is a child of the woods, as was the *coureur de bois* who preceded him; and, like his precursor, he is an advance agent of civilisation. Scientifically, he knows little of astronomy beyond the sun's course and the polar star. In the forest primeval, the heaven-lit constellations can rarely be seen; but the secrets of terrestrial nature, sacred possessions of pathfinders gone before, guide him on his way. His trained eye will detect the deflection of tender twigs toward the south. The gray moss of the tree-trunks is always on the side toward the north; the bark is more supple and smoother on the east than on the west; southward the mildew never comes. On the prairie, he knows that the tips of the grass incline toward the south, and are less green on the northward side. Thus does an unlettered savant box the compass in the wilderness.

The "timber-cruiser" is a forest king! The wealth of the woods is his. Here he reigns alone,—he dares not have a confidant! His is the task of locating the land-scrip that capitalists or corporations have pur-

chased from government. He precedes the woodman,
the axe, and the saw. He undertakes arduous jour-
neys, equipped only with a blanket, a gun, a compass,
and salted provisions. He relies upon his weapon to
provide fresh meat and protection. His acts of
courage, endurance, and skill never are witnessed,—
never are discussed by himself. His success or failure
is known only to the directors of the lumber companies
that employ him and to whom he makes a detailed
report. So retentive is his memory that at the end of
a two months' " cruise " he can indicate upon a map the
tracts of valuable woodland among a hundred square
miles of worthless tamarack: but the exact location of
the treasure is a secret to be guarded with his life.
Months may pass before the lands can be " taken up "
and entered upon the records at Washington.

The pathless forest is the " timber-cruiser's " home.
Solitude is his companion; and, like his brother on " the
multitudinous seas," he often dies alone, his unburied
body becoming part of the elements he so intimately
courts. He is unknown to song or story.

A waggon carried our boat and provisions through
six miles of morass, briars, and pine woods to White
Earth Lake. Crossing this, the route followed the
White Earth River for two miles to a portage around
a fall. Seven miles farther, against a sluggish current,
through another reed-encircled lake, brought us to a
portage of one mile to the Twin Lakes. These bodies
of water are prettily located amid pine-covered hills.
We crossed the first one and encamped on the narrow
strip of land that separates the two lakes. A wretched
night among wood ticks and mosquitoes followed.

After crossing the second lake, we were met by an

aged Chippewa, engaged for the long carry of ten miles across a desolate tract of red sand and charred stumps, due north by the compass, to the Wild Rice River. The soil was a-bloom with purple moss, its only vegetation. Late in the day, this river was reached. It is twenty-five feet in width at this point, although on Colton's map it did not extend more than ten miles east of the Red River. We camped for the night.

At four o'clock, sunrise, the ascent of the river began. Wild Rice Lake, six miles long, was traversed. It is an immense field of rice, nowhere more than five feet deep, and supplies grain for a vast region. After leaving the lake, the stream became so tortuous that the compass "boxed" itself; thence, through a dense forest of pine, from which the river emerged into a grassy meadow, strewn with trunks and branches of large trees,—carried thither by tornado from a nearby tract of woods, across which it had passed. Several hemlocks and oaks were noticed standing on their tops, with trunks skyward! This was not a "windfall" in the accepted sense, which is a tornado track through a forest. Two of the real sort, of different ages, were encountered on the following day, when a long portage (five miles), chiefly through tamaracks, had to be undertaken to reach a chain of three lakes, in the Wild Rice watercourse, the river course turning too far northward to be followed.

Amid the fallen timber, the guide wielded a hand axe with surprising effectiveness, often leading the path up an inclined trunk of a fallen forest-monarch and chopping a path for descent along a similar bridge, equally slimy and treacherous. Within half a mile of this portage, we entered a fine grove of oak and basswood.

A Typical Chippewa.

A small stream of clear water, that separated it from a tamarack morass, drew the line of demarkation.

The methods of native guides have not changed since the days of St. Cosme or of Father Gravier, for my Chippewas frequently said: "Up this stream so many days," or "so many carries to such and such a place."

The first of the three lakes mentioned charmed the eye. A mile and a half long, with a beach of sparkling sand, it seemed a harbinger of civilisation; but not a house or wigwam was visible upon its shores. Although early in the afternoon, this marked the end of the day's work, because the aged packman, who had followed afoot, must be awaited. While the chief of the expedition was enjoying a bath in the cool water, the guide speared several large pickerel. The carrier came into camp about sunset. We decided to take him as far as the Mississippi.

Two trips across the lake next morning were necessary to carry over our party and stores. The creek had become very shallow and clogged with grass, and the way to the third lake was most tortuous. Two of us walked along the banks of the first and second lakes.

The last of the pretty lakelets is known to Sioux and Chippewa as "Kak-sha-boor-cow-mond." In its centre is a grass-covered islet, revered as a "spirit isle" by the Chippewas. Like the Puritan forefathers, Chippewas and Sioux believe in witchcraft: the Sioux tell tales of "were-wolves" encountered or heard in the forests. This is probably due to the fact that Chippewas can imitate a wolf's howl to perfection. It is the cry they use on a trail to acquaint their companions of their whereabouts.

II—AT SPIRIT ISLAND

Under strong protest from the two packmen, the guide and I crossed to the green island.   After our return, the young Chippewa, learned in the traditions of his people, spoke:

You were on holy ground.   There dwelt a great-great-granddaughter of the first pale-faced woman.   Her hair, white as the birch tree's bark, floated like a frosty mist about her head.   On "Me-ne-do-me-nis," as we name that isle, is one of every species of tree between here and O-mus-kose [Itasca Lake], brought here and planted by that gentle spirit's hands. Thus rose a sacred grove.   Across these waters the warpath often led, but Sioux or Chippewa never profaned this hallowed spot,—as you have done.

To which, Ka-ba-be-zen, aged carrier, did comment, in utmost seriousness: "A white spirit dwelt here, beyond dispute.   Men, known to me, have seen her standing on yon hill, whence she watched them cross the lake.   In later years, *voyageurs* profanely landed on her isle and found her lodge in ruins.   The gentle spirit of that grove had gone away."

Henry Beaulieu, guide, then said:

There is some historic basis for this tradition.   The story of such a woman was told at Mackinaw when I was a boy.   Her name was Temple.   She came to the Straits, in the summer of 1835, with her father, a Major in the British service, long stationed at Quebec.   When retired for age, he visited Mackinaw, intending thereafter to return to England.   The old soldier was a widower; his wife, who had shared his active life in the barracks of the Château Saint Louis, was at rest in the lofty cemetery at Quebec, near the tall monument raised to both Montcalm and Wolfe.

The population at the Straits was then composed of French-

Canadians, rather than English, and half-breeds of a dozen tribal affiliations. Instead of a fortnight's stay, the visit lengthened into weeks. The girl was young and of exalted imagination. She was fascinated by the romantic side of savage life. The Indian dances diverted her: she heard, again and again, tales of the *coureurs de bois*,—knights-errant of the wilderness. Their leader was an expatriated Frenchman, young and handsome as a picture, Henri Sainte-Ange. His name was chief passport to Major Temple's favour and brought to him acquaintance with the daughter. The young man was born to inspire admiration in the heart of a girl whose imagination was aglow with the weirdness of border life. The soldier's daughter allowed herself to be overcome by infatuation for this handsome boy of the woods and fled with him. The music of the name, " Sainte-Ange," dulled her conscience, no doubt.

The lovers, with two strong men at the paddles, had been gone two hours when their flight was made known to Major Temple. The father's rage was terrible.

" One hundred guineas to the crew that overtakes them ! " he shouted; and, at the shore, he added: " A guinea to every man who joins the hunt ! "

A score of canoes were manned. The pursuit began. Its course was out the Straits, eastward, toward Lake Huron, where, late in the day, the fugitives were descried. In the leading boat knelt the girl's father, toiling, like a maniac, at his paddle. The chase grew furious, for the sun was low: all had fear that, after dark, the guilty pair might escape and the reward be lost.

The lovers beheld the vengeance that pursued. Crouching in the *coureur's* canoe, repentant and in tears, was she. As soon as his voice would carry to the hunted, the soldier's threat to the abductor was heard.

" You die, you dog ! " he shouted.

The evening breeze bore the challenge to Sainte-Ange; he acted under the forest code. At a sign from him, his paddlers stopped. He stood to his full height and awaited the onset of the guinea-grabbing pack. When distance served, he brought his rifle to his eye, and, with sure aim, shot Major Temple dead! The veteran's body tumbled out the boat! The game had rendered the hunter!

The daughter's horror was too deep for tears. The panting crews from Mackinaw, kneeling at their places, were silent. All prospect of reward was gone and, in the twilight, the paddlers turned their faces homeward.

The rest of this history [continued Beaulieu] I had from Monsieur Boulonger, who lives on the eastern bay of Winnebagoshish Lake, in our direct route to Pokegama Falls:

Sainte-Ange dared not return to Mackinaw, fearing trial and punishment; so he carried his prize to the Chippewa country, at the head of Lake Superior. This meant fifteen days under paddle, through the Sault Ste. Marie and along the southern shore of the great lake to the present site of Duluth. The ascent of the river Saint Louis, with its foaming rapids and tiresome portages, consumed another week. Thence to Sandy Lake, on the Mississippi.

Sainte-Ange was no longer a hero to the soldier's daughter: she covered him with maledictions. Neglect, reproach, and ill-usage were encompassed in the winter and spring that succeeded. Then came another grief,—a child was born.

Before the river froze, Sainte-Ange descended the Mississippi, through the French Rapids, and passed the winter at a Chippewa village where Crow Wing now stands. His " white squaw," hopeless and remorseful, was shunned by all women of the tribe. The curse of her father's death was said to be upon her.

In the spring of 1836, Sainte-Ange set out for Pembina [continued the guide]. Ascending the St. Peter's, he portaged over the familiar trail into a branch of the Red River of the North. Several stages were made toward Greater Winnipeg. His party camped one night at the mouth of the Wild Rice River. There the craven adventurer deserted the woman and his child. Frantic in her despair, Madame Sainte-Ange gathered provisions and set out alone in a small canoe which had been left for her. She turned its prow up the Wild Rice River, only because it led eastward: after days of hardship, she reached this lake. She did not know that she was within five miles of "The Father of all Running Waters" that would have carried her to the sea. That island, over there, became an abode of penitence. She built a lodge, no doubt, as she had seen them built; she had learned to call a spark from the flint, and lived upon roots and fish. The child probably succumbed during the first winter. The mother's end could not have been long deferred.

Word for word, as the guide spoke, less tersely than above, the younger Chippewa, beneficiary of a mission school, translated the story to his companion. When he had finished, the aged carrier shook his head.

"It is a white man's tale; and false," said he, " for spirits never die! "

III—THE MISSISSIPPI

Crossing the Spirit Lake in relays, the final five-mile tramp to the bank of the stream I was to follow to the Gulf of Mexico began. This is the famous A-ze-wa-wa-say-ta-gen portage, a route between the Upper Mississippi and the Red River of the North known to the Dakotas and Chippewas for generations. A clearly marked trail led for two miles through dense pine woods, thence into a tamarack swamp,— a dreary journey. We could not cover more than one mile an hour in the swamp.

About five o'clock, we emerged from a tangled mass of hazel and willow bushes into a pretty meadow a mile wide, through which meandered a sluggish stream eighteen feet in breadth,—the Mississippi!

While pitching camp, we were overtaken by a young man and woman, brother and sister. They came from White Earth. The girl, sweetheart of the missing

Kelly, was typical mate for a " timber-cruiser." When
the people at the Mission abandoned the search, she
set out.   There was n't any romance in her nature.
Compelling her brother's co-operation, they started a
day after us, but less encumbered, travelled more
rapidly.   They made their camp for the night near
ours and shared our supper of " slugs,"—dough boiled
in water in which bacon had been prepared. Excellent,
if hungry! When we separated, after breakfast, the
girl held out a small, brown hand and asked:

" You 'll look for him, I 'm sure? "

" Indeed, we shall," I promised, little thinking how
real that pledge would become.

" We shall go down-stream to Lake Pemidji; then
we shall return to the Itasca region by the east
branch and ' do up ' these hills. I 'll stay till I find
him."

We watched that brother and sister launch their
bark canoe, and we waved a farewell as they disappeared, down-stream, round the first bend of the young
Mississippi.

Until a survey fixes upon a map the exact location
at which the A-ze-wa-wa-say-ta-gen portage terminates
on the Mississippi's bank, one has difficulty in estimat-
ing its distance below the outlet of Itasca Lake. The
aged carrier, before he left us, reckoned it at sixteen
miles; but almost three days' struggle with nature that
followed led me to think the distance twice that much.
Nicollet locates this point forty miles down-stream from
Itasca,—as good a guess as any. After we had reached
the goal, my guide calculated the journey at twenty-six
miles. Personally, I have n't an opinion.

The general direction was south. After the first

Sample of Cedar Forest in the Itasca Country.
(Minnesota Historical Society Collection.)

The Mississippi River—Thirty Miles below Itasca Lake.
(Minnesota Historical Society Collection.)

day's paddling up-stream, rapids were encountered, around which the boat had to be carried. Stretches of canoeable water were rare. We often had to tramp for hours in the bed of the stream because progress along its banks was impossible. This journey was attended with many hardships. Among the hills, on the third day, the stream was strewn with boulders; our supplies had to be packed in relays. The guide laid out a new trail along what appeared to have been a former bed of the river, carrying our route across a strip of tamarack and through a birch forest. This "cut-off" saved a detour in the bed of the rock-and-tree-gorged creek.

Beaulieu was master of his trade, a true *coureur de bois*. He "blazed" this trail so that it was as plain to him as Broadway. It was, nevertheless, a lonesome forest path. During these days, not an animal of the squirrel kind was seen: not a bird sang at dawn or a cicada chirped at nightfall. We found plenty of game lower down the long river, but in the Itasca wilderness, we absolutely saw nothing to shoot and must have starved had we depended upon hunting. Fish are not plenty in Itasca Lake although the Chippewa did succeed in spearing a few pickerel during our stay. His method was to go out after dark, with a roll of birch bark ablaze upon a pole of green wood projected over the bow of the canoe.

When heart-breaking climbing over boulders and fallen timber in the channel, and slow, discouraging tramps through quagmires and pathless underbrush along the river banks brought us to the crest of the hills, gravelly stretches of water were met and ultimately a depth in which the canoe could be floated. The ascent of that eight or ten miles of the Mississippi is not a job for " a quitter "!

When the trees broke away and the last rays of an afternoon sun were discernible ahead, in the open, we felt that a large lake was not far away. It could not be anything else than Itasca. The Mississippi not far below Itasca is very picturesque, as the frontispiece to this volume proves.

IV—ITASCA

The boat was dragged through what proved to be the last rapid, and in great expectancy we climbed in. Rounding a bend in the almost currentless stream, which had broadened to forty feet and bore every evidence of back-water from a large pond, we emerged into the north arm of Itasca Lake. We had arrived!

The prospect from the outlet, looking eastward (as shown by a recent photograph) is not thrilling. The north arm of Itasca is half a mile broad and its eastern shore rises to a bluff of twenty-five feet. At the time of my visit, it had a background of soft-wood trees, with a few pines. The loneliness of the entire landscape was appalling.

Below the outlet, on a grassy slope, we camped for the first night, preferring to select a better site on the following morning. We were worn out and hungry after a day spent in climbing the hills,—probably not more than seven or ten miles. While the guide was preparing supper, the Chippewa and I paddled a short distance down the lake and selected a camping site to which we could move on the following day. It was a

The Outlet of Itasca Lake, 1904.
(Minnesota Historical Society Collection.)

The Mouth of Boutwell Creek, West Shore of Itasca Lake.
(Minnesota Historical Society Collection.)

dry knoll on the western shore, reached through a fringe
of grass.

As this trip occurred before the introduction of the
kodak, recent pictures of the scenery of the Itasca region and of the Mississippi have been made by special
photographers or supplied by Commissioner Brower
and by the Minnesota Historical Society. The recent
death of J. V. Brower is most lamentable. At the
time of my visit to Itasca, the landscape did not contain a house or wigwam, or any evidence of human
visitation. There were no clearings, as shown in recent
photographs. A government survey was not attempted
until three years later,—probably ordered by an official
of the United States Land Office, after the indifference
shown toward the region had been set forth in my
correspondence.

Leaving the Chippewa with directions to move camp
down the western shore of Itasca about three quarters
of a mile, to the place selected the previous evening,
the guide and the writer began the first real excursion
on Itasca Lake. Out in the north arm, my first thought
was to look for the island mentioned by Schoolcraft
and Nicollet. At first, it could not be separated from
the background; but in a little time the reason was explained. A headland shut it from view. When that
had been turned, Schoolcraft Island came plainly into
sight; but, as we were looking at its narrow end, it
appeared insignificant in size. Some stiff paddling,
against a strong breeze, blowing up the lake, landed
us upon its rocky shore. It does not exceed five hundred feet in length and I walked over its area, despite
underbrush and its rock-strewn surface. The guide
thought the season too early for snakes, but he agreed

10

with me that it was promising snake-land. These two acres of rocky ledge contain many fine trees; but the surface is grown with thorns and brush. No evidences of camp-fires were visible; there was not a sign of recent visitation. Nicollet, I remembered, had camped elsewhere. The exact location of the island is shown in the first government survey, made by Edwin S. Hall, in 1875, and published in 1876.

In shape, Itasca Lake most nearly resembles a three-pronged starfish,—the eastern arm slightly longer than the other two. Its extreme length is three and one sixth miles. Mr. Brower " chained " it upon the ice. The most picturesque view of the sparkling water is had from Schoolcraft Island, looking south-west.

M. Nicollet fixed the altitude of the surface of Itasca Lake at one thousand five hundred and seventy-eight feet; but Mr. Brower, in 1891, corrected these figures to one thousand four hundred and fifty-seven feet. The elevation was confirmed by heavy frosts on the June mornings during our stay. One expects to find Nature at her best in that merry month; but in the Itasca region April weather continues through May and June. Although it does not impress a visitor as a land suited to tender sprouts, some of the vegetation has tropical rankness. The days are noticeably longer than in lower latitudes; but the sun shines in such half-hearted fashion that the waters of the lake retain the chill with which they come from the springs.

The first day was devoted to an exploration of the eastern arm of Itasca Lake. Passing through the channel on the eastern side of Schoolcraft Island, we paddled round a grass-lined promontory, jutting from the north-eastward, into a reedy bay of considerable

The East Arm of Itasca Lake.
(Looking North from the Southern End.)

size, which terminated in a morass of wild rice. A small stream enters this bay.

From this estuary, the east coast line was examined southward. The beach is gravelly, always grassy, and the forest comes down to the shore. Its tall trees are well shown in the photograph. Three landings were made at gullies that might have been mouths of small streams; but hills rose from the shore and a few rods of tramping in each instance dispelled any supposition that permanent bodies of water existed above. I sought in vain for evidences of continued use of the two trails by which Schoolcraft and Nicollet had portaged to Itasca from the eastern branch and from Leech Lake, respectively. Forty years of disuse had obliterated all traces of them.

Not a rivulet enters the eastern arm of Itasca, except at the extreme south-eastern end. There a small stream comes down a gully. Disembarking, I walked up that ravine to the top of a rise, at which point the brooklet became insignificant. I saw no signs of a pond beyond; but recent official surveys show a small one half a mile to the southward. I did not " discover " it. Hopewell Clarke's experience was similar to mine. In the rainy season, this creek doubtless sends considerable water into Itasca.

The coast line of the promontory that obtrudes itself from the southward into Itasca was laboriously scrutinised. It does not contain an inflowing creek. The west shore of this east arm occupied much of the afternoon: it is generally reed-grown. Here was seen the finest timber between Itasca and Pemidji Lake, —where the right bank of the Mississippi, amid its Ten Rapids, is absolutely superb in its woodland.

A tired party returned to camp that evening.

V—A NEW LAKE

The second day, June 9th, was devoted to the west arm of Itasca. During the forenoon, the real find of the trip was made. In paddling southward from the new camp, we deviated from the direct course to make a brief second visit to Schoolcraft Island; but it lay in shadow, because the sun had not yet climbed above the tree tops on the eastern hills. In going thence toward the west arm, we must have passed in close proximity to a submerged, rocky shoal, discovered by a government surveying party in after years, but we did not detect it. Its presence, however, accounts for surprisingly shallow soundings obtained in that part of Itasca.

We began the day's work at the western point of the promontory,—recently christened by Commissioner Brower "Ozawintib Point,"—and found the eastern shore of the west arm to possess reed-grown characteristics similar to those of the western beach of the east arm. The bluff is the same height, but large trees appeared to be fewer. At the southern end, however, the land back of the rushes sloped down to a swamp,—one of the same old tamarack quagmires we knew so well. Crowding our way along the edge of the grass, in a reedy cove, I saw an unmistakable current entering Itasca. A clogged watercourse was distinguishable in the rank sod of the tamarack bog beyond the grass: it had the distinctive character of a perennial stream,— the outlet of a storage reservoir.

The canoe had been lightened of all luggage, except the gun, and carried only provisions for the mid-

The Shore of Itasca Lake, East Arm, near Nicollet's Portage.

day meal: nevertheless, fallen saplings and shallow water rendered progress slow. The boat had to be lifted over logs and much brush had to be dragged out the watery path. After a half-hour's tedious progress up this crooked stream, we found unmistakable back-water and, climbing into the boat, soon paddled from the shade of overhanging boughs into a charming lake-let. It is more than a mile long and nearly as broad, although it did not look so large in the bright morning sunlight. Here is a sizable lake certainly not seen by Schoolcraft, who never entered the west arm and only spent a few hours at Itasca. Nor is this deep reservoir mentioned by Nicollet, even after the most liberal interpretation is given to his language.

This charming body of clear water lies in a deep bowl, formed by low hills on the east, a ridge on the west ending in a swamp. Southward are two swamps, but into the lake from that direction projects a prong of dry land, dividing the sheet of water, somewhat like Itasca, into two bays. Crossing to the western bay, the canoe was pushed up a large creek that entered at that point. Although the swampy valley was narrow, obstructions were such that I soon left the boat and tramped or waded a considerable distance, probably a mile, without finding any other lake. The forest in that locality is so thick that I could not see the " Heights of Land " lying to the southward. Returning to the canoe and to the lake, we paddled into the eastward of the two bays, which had been clearly noticeable while crossing the water. Among the rushes at its extreme end, we found a smaller stream than the one before visited and a short tramp along the eastern edge of the marsh soon brought me to a little pond. Further examination of the south-eastern shore disclosed only an inconsequential creek. Some tentative soundings were taken with a trolling-line but the depths found along the eastern shore were not great. Subsequent investigation has shown this lake to be much deeper than Itasca, proving it to be a separate bowl. Soundings of sixty-five feet, made by the Mississippi Commission, are frequent. Of the streams flowing into the lake, the one entering the west bay appeared to the writer the most important, although Mr. Clarke differs with this opinion. A small brook on the west side has since been named after A. H. Siegfried.

Without consciousness of important achievement, I playfully called this lakelet " Dolly Varden," intending at a future time to rechristen it " Lake Lincoln," in honour of the martyred President; but, although the Minnesota Historical Society conceded the original discovery to me, General James H. Baker, then Surveyor-General of the State, was directed from Washington, wisely, no doubt, to transfer to the newly discovered lake the name originally borne by Itasca, namely, " Omoskos," or " Elk." Such act might be assumed to indicate that the government authorities, at Washington, believed the lakelet to be the " true source." [1] J. V. Brower, Itasca Park Commissioner and official representative of the Minnesota Historical Society, set

[1] Regarding the choice of this name, Henry D. Harrower, of Ivison, Blakeman, Taylor & Co., who sent Mr. Clarke to make a special survey, after the Glazier fiasco of 1881, says in the preface to the Clarke report: " The former surveyor-general of Minnesota, who had charge of the government land-office at St. Paul, states that, acting in accordance with general instructions from the government, he transferred the name from the larger lake, which Schoolcraft had called ' Itasca,' to the smaller in order to retain the designation originally used by the Indians."

Chambers Creek, Connecting Itasca with Elk Lake. (Elk Lake
in the Distance.)
(Copyright, 1909, by H. D. Ayer.)

forth the Society's decision on page 98, volume xi., *Minnesota Historical Society Collections:*

Discoveries at the Source

EARLIEST PROBABLE OCCUPANTS, ...	Prehistoric.
EARLIEST KNOWN OCCUPANTS, ...	Aboriginal.
FIRST KNOWN OF WHITE MEN, . .	William Morrison, 1803.
FIRST AUTHENTIC DISCOVERY, Lake Itasca, ...	H. R. Schoolcraft, 1832.
SECOND AUTHENTIC DISCOVERY, Principal Stream, ...	J. N. Nicollet, 1836.
THIRD AUTHENTIC DISCOVERY, Elk Lake, ...	Julius Chambers, 1872.
FOURTH AUTHENTIC DISCOVERY, United States Survey, ...	Edwin S. Hall, 1875.
FIFTH AUTHENTIC DISCOVERY, Special Survey, ...	Hopewell Clarke, 1886.

Returning to the outlet of the lake, I disembarked and ascended a hill thirty feet high, from which the waters of Itasca were visible through trees along its shore. Hardly four hundred feet separated the two bodies of water, indicating that the stream connecting them was tortuous. The presence of a bluff on each side of the narrow outlet of the smaller lake—hardly a rod separating the two—precludes the assumption that the two bodies of water were united in 1836, otherwise than by the present stream. Hopewell Clarke, C. E., has authorised me to quote from his report and to reproduce his sketch map, made in 1886, fourteen years after my visit. Incidentally, the map explains why I originally described the stream, since named " Chambers Creek " by Commissioner Brower, as traversing a tamarack swamp its entire distance from Itasca

Lake. First, I reproduce Mr. Clarke's survey of the locality, as found in his report (page 11):

One of the most interesting parts of our work was the survey and examination of the narrow strip of land between Lake Itasca and Elk Lake. We found it to be 350 feet wide at the narrowest point between the lakes, and 520 feet measuring along the crooked trail at the base of the knoll. The lakes run nearly parallel for 1020 feet, and the strip of land contains in all about 10 acres.

The portion shown as hilly on the plat is a small mound-like elevation, nearly devoid of all timber, which rises with a gradual slope south from Lake Itasca to a height of 33 feet, and descends abruptly to the shore of Elk Lake. Its direction between the lakes is nearly east and west. Its height above Lake Itasca at its western base is 10 feet, where it is less than 100 feet wide; and thus, if each lake were a little higher in elevation, they would at this point be within 100 feet of each other. The highest point on the trail between the two lakes is 12 feet. The ridge extends to the outlet of Elk Lake, from which point Lake Itasca is in full view. Another hill rises to the east of the outlet, leaving an opening 12 feet wide, through which the stream flows with a rapid current, in a channel 6 feet wide and 6 inches deep. The balance of the land between the two lakes, on either side of the creek, is a tamarack swamp.

The outlet of Elk Lake flows nearly north-east 80 feet, and enters the tamarack swamp, where its general direction is north for 600 feet, until it reaches a point within 110 feet of Lake Itasca. It then curves back toward Elk Lake, and finally enters Lake Itasca, its whole course from Elk Lake measuring 1084 feet. Where it debouches into Lake Itasca, it is 7 feet wide and 8 inches deep. We noted its width at numerous places in its course, and found it to vary from 6 to 12 feet, and its depth from 2 to 8 inches. It gains nothing from springs along its route, and its increased width and depth are caused by back water from Lake Itasca. It is a very pretty little stream, and has been cleared out by the Indians. The dif-

Elk Lake, Looking South from Morrison Hill.

ference in elevation between the two lakes is 1 foot and 1 inch. The stream between the lakes falls 6 inches between Elk Lake and a point where it enters the tamarack swamp, in the first hundred feet of its course; the balance, 7 inches, measures the fall in its course through the tamarack swamp of nearly 1000 feet.

A sketch map, by Mr. Clarke, is on opposite page.

One thing particularly noticeable about Elk Lake, namely, its great depth, has been mentioned. In Itasca, soundings rarely exceed twenty-five or thirty feet, while in Elk Lake they are generally twice as deep. The aged tamaracks in the swamp between Itasca and Elk, as well as the two points of land, confirm a belief that the lakes have never been one since the original subsidence of the waters,—as special pleaders for Nicollet argue. One of the streams emptying into Elk Lake extends southward therefrom two miles to the region of the shallow ponds on higher ground, so clearly shown in the map of the Itasca State Park. The most accurate charts recently made do not show communicating watercourses between many of these lakes and ponds. The writer of this volume has not any personal jealousies to exploit. To him, the Elk Lake trip is a delightful memory, unmarred by a single unfriendly thought. He was in search of health, not glory.

When camp was regained, after most of a day spent in sight of the sparkling lakelet to the southward, including a refreshing splash in its waters, Itasca looked, after sundown, as forbidding as Lethe's stream. Sleep, but not a bath therein, brought forgetfulness to a tired canoeman.

VI—NICOLLET'S CREEK

Great honour belongs to Jean N. Nicollet for researches he made in the narrow valley west of Elk Lake. The writer of this volume had read Nicollet's official report, also his preliminary one, before starting on this trip. "The Cradled Hercules" had not inspired the enthusiasm with which its discoverer had endowed it. An inspection of its mouth, on the morning following the day spent at Elk Lake, sufficed to dampen such ardour as he might have felt. That creek belongs to M. Nicollet! When expert civil engineers, like Hopewell Clarke and J. V. Brower, cannot reconcile vital features in Nicollet's survey, special correspondents would best keep off. The mouth of the creek was insignificant in 1872, compared with its aspect since a lumber dam has been built at the outlet of Itasca (1903).

Its present appearance, from a recent photograph, is shown in the picture.

The work of M. Nicollet, in 1836, has been so thoroughly followed up by Hopewell Clarke, in 1886, and J. V. Brower, in 1891-96 and 1901, that their reports have been given precedence, out of chronological order, in the chapter on M. Nicollet (IX.). These gentlemen make out a better case for the French explorer than he does for himself. This may have been due to unfamiliarity with our language, although that explanation never has been offered.

Coasting the west beach of the west arm of Itasca, after leaving the mouth of "The Cradled Hercules," a thousand yards of paddling brings one to an estuary, into which a small stream flows from a tamarack

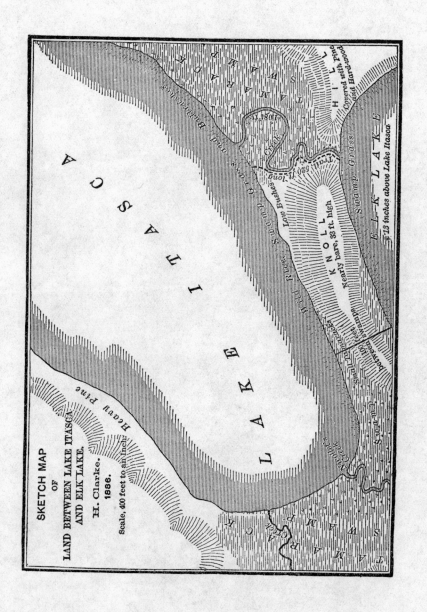

SKETCH MAP
OF
LAND BETWEEN LAKE ITASCA
AND ELK LAKE.
H. Clarke.
1886.

Scale, 400 feet to an inch.

LAKE ITASCA

Heavy Pine

TAMARACK SWAMP

TAMARACK SWAMP

Beaver Dams

Small tamarack swamp

3 to 20 ft. wide

Swamp

KNOLL
Nearly bare, 38 ft. high

Swamp Grass

Creek
1081 ft.

low Bushes

Source of Red River

Trail 660 ft. long

HILL
Covered with pine
and Hardwood

ELK LAKE

13 inches above Lake Itasca

forest, having its sources in springs at the base of the
bluffs, half a mile back from the lake. (Commissioner
Brower named it "Boutwell Creek," after the guest of
the Schoolcraft party.) This is the last feeder to
Itasca Lake.

VII—DOWN THE YOUNG MISSISSIPPI

The descent of the river to the A-ze-wa-wa-say-ta-
gen portage is play compared with the ascent. The
canoe was readily dropped through the Kakáb-ikans
Rapids by the guide and Chippewa walking in the
stream, each holding an end. The first affluent of the
Mississippi enters it from the west. In the series of dismal gorges, where the river tumbles over huge boulders,
darts around sharp, rocky corners, and gurgles over
fallen logs, boat and provisions were packed. It is a
region of evil omen.

Much lighter in equipment than when we ascended
the hills, I had only my knapsack to carry. At the
end of a toilsome afternoon, we encountered the guide's
newly made trail, which left the river to our right-hand
and traversed a defile into a region of tamarack. Near
its northern end, we had left a cache of provisions, of
which we were now in need. Cache is hardly the word,
because a bag of flour and of salt fish had been fastened to a sapling, "ridden down" by the native and
then allowed to return to its natural position with our
stores at its top. The guide insisted that we push ahead
to that point before camping for supper. Much fa-
tigued, I demurred; but, in the woods, a guide speaks
by authority. He explained that a young bear, able
to climb a sapling, might get our provisions. The sun

was above the horizon, as I sat down to rest. Guide and Chippewa were told to go ahead; I was confident of my ability to overtake them. I fell asleep instantly: when I awoke, twilight had begun. I transcribe my experiences, as written that night in the log-book:

Hurrying along the new trail, I cover half its length before darkness renders invisible the axe-cuts upon the trees. Very soon, I am wandering among scrubby pines and tamaracks, out of sound of the river. Turning eastward to regain the stream, I stumble over entangling roots and sink into bog-holes. Dry wood for a fire is not to be had; I am not woodsman enough to light a strip of birch-bark. Not an echo returns my shouts. One cartridge remains in my revolver; but I dare not use it to fire a signal of distress. Climbing the hills, the guide had pointed out trees torn by bears' claws, a trivial incident in his company.

A shower bursts, accompanied by lightning and thunder. Camp lay north-west, from one to three miles, —dependent upon my wanderings. The shadow of a hill looms up and I follow its base, hoping to reach the river bank. I ask no greater boon than to hear its waters again. Into the tamaracks, over treacherous sod that hides bog-holes,—doubling on my tracks! Dangerous to go forward: equally so to remain where I am. My companions may not find me, and that means starvation!

Exhausted with fatigue and anxiety, under dripping boughs, I stand stock still and listen. In all my world, the only sound is rain! In indescribable loneliness, I shiver with nervousness, or chill. I remember the lost timber-cruiser. What if I meet him, crazed with hunger! In growing dread, I dare not shout for aid.

A Minnesota Forest.
(Minnesota Historical Society Collection.)

A new sound! Not rain, although the drip, drip, drip from the water-laden boughs goes on. Not the movement of man or animal; surely, not the rustling of leaves? 'T is running water I hear: the way to the river is mine!

A few yards distant is the tiniest of brooklets, hailing me in Nature's own sweet language of hope. Its voice is low at the brush-formed cascade from which it calls, but its word is—" Thoroughfare! "

Into the channel of that tiny creek, lest it elude me in the dark: a physical contest with tangled boughs and bushes soon brings me to the Mississippi. Here, also, the river bed is easiest route. At a bend in the watery path, the glare of my camp-fire flashes up.

I find it deserted: guide and packman, alarmed at my non-arrival, are seeking me, in true chivalry of the forest.

VIII—PEMIDJI, CASS, AND WINNEBAGOSHISH

The descent of the Mississippi through the three large lakes of the watershed above Pokegama Fall is crowded with sensational incidents. When the meadow land is reached, the river becomes tortuous but amply deep for paddling. During forenoon of the third day after leaving Itasca, we passed our camp site at the end of the White Earth route. Only a short distance farther, a real mystery of our voyage was met. A new, birch-bark canoe was found overturned in the stream. It had been fitted for a single occupant. The inside was blackened, as by an explosion of powder. It had caught in roots at the riverside. Instinctively, we thought of the missing timber-cruiser.

The guide gave as his opinion that a gun or powder flask had exploded in that boat.

We camped that night upon a smooth bit of sod, under a sheltering maple tree. Next morning we entered a broader prairie and passed two short bits of very rapid water. On the left bank, a creek of considerable size joined the river. It drains a lake not far inland and is known as "Pinnididiwin,"—an abbreviation of *Jah-pinuniddiwin,* "place of violent deaths." "Once upon a time," the people of a Chippewa village on the shores of the lakelet were massacred by their ancient enemies, the Sioux. Age and youth were not respected: captives were put to death with tortures. Our Chippewa, responsible for this statement, pointed out a tree into which a squaw of his people had climbed, to hide among the foliage. She was the only woman that escaped. My informant said the Chippewas thought the ability of a squaw to climb a tree so wonderful that this woman had been deified. Tree climbing is utterly unnatural to an Indian, he explained. The importance of this lake outlet is due to the fact that it is reckoned to be one hundred miles from Itasca.

We camped that night in a forest of pine and birch. The duty of making "smudges," or smouldering fires to smoke out mosquitoes, fell to me: the guide soon had a roaring fire and supper. It was chiefly of "slugs,"—dough, roughly torn into pieces and boiled in water with the last piece of our salt bacon. The product was tough as rubber and heavy as lead; but when one is hungry, "slugs" are highly edible.

We started at four o'clock next morning, in dense fog and raw weather until the sun got high. The Mis-

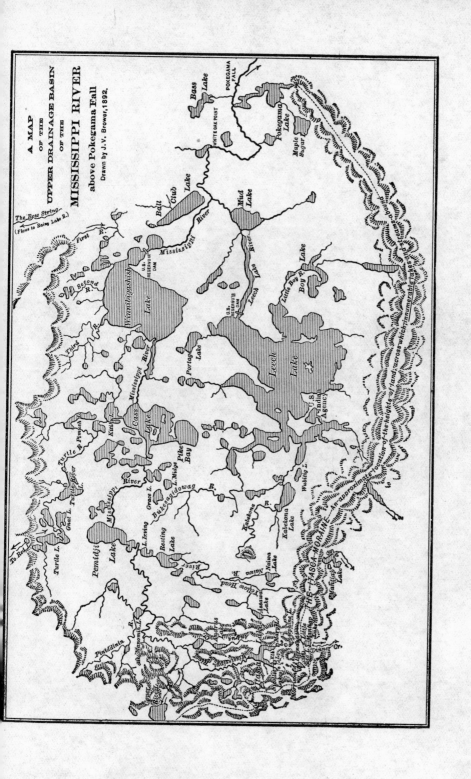

A MAP
OF THE
UPPER DRAINAGE BASIN
OF THE
MISSISSIPPI RIVER
above Pokegama Fall
Drawn by J. V. Brower, 1892.

sissippi kept in the forest; the scenery was of exceeding picturesqueness. Sometimes, the river encroached upon hills and created bluffs fifty feet in height. In such cases, a broad, sandy bank formed upon the opposite side. No noticeable increase in the size of the Mississippi occurs until junction with the eastern branch, coming from lakes Marquette, La Salle, Plantagenet, Assawe, and other small ponds. Each branch is about forty-five feet wide. The volume of water from this stream is larger than that of the main river, and more than doubles it in size. (This opinion differs from Schoolcraft's.) Below the junction, the right bank becomes a beautiful grove of maple, oak, and beech. On the left, the land rises to a knoll and stray hemlocks are seen. The river has a straight stretch of about half a mile at this point. Woodland shifts to the left bank; the right merges into a swamp of reeds, cat-tails, hazel bushes, and scrub poplars. The stream soon enters a marsh and a sharp turn to the right landed us in the smaller, or southern, section of *Lac Travers* (Pemidji [1] Lake).

Little Pemidji is a handsome sheet of water. Dark forests of pine are seen to the east, but the soft woods on the western hills are of inferior character. Our course across this lakelet to the channel into the larger body was N. one point E., and the distance is one and one quarter miles. These two lakes were probably connected by a brook, but they are to-day practically one sheet of water, separated only by a narrow strip

[1] Since this region has been invaded by railroads, Pemidji is often spelled Bemidji. A town of that name, on the Great Northern Railroad, has been established. The writer prefers to retain the original Chippewa spelling, without any philological discussion.

of low land, covered with a thick growth of beech and poplar. The view of Greater Pemidji, as one enters from the inlet, is impressive. The lake is probably seven miles long by four in breadth and has every sign of being deep. In the distance, the north shore appeared to be a high bluff, surmounted by fine forests. The north-eastern beach is swampy, but the land soon rises into a wooded plateau, pines predominating. The western shore is of yellow clay. We dined on the northern bank of the Mississippi, just where it leaves Pemidji; a hemlock there bears the Greek letter "delta."

The Mississippi flows placidly out Pemidji, through a grove of towering hemlocks on the right: so clear is the water that the pebbly bottom can be seen at a depth of eight or ten feet. Fish are plentiful and our Chippewa speared many of them. At the end of a mile comes a change. A series of dangerous rapids follows one another so closely that there is not breathing space between them. They are called the Metoswa, or Ten, Rapids: we counted seven. The river has now increased to such volume as to render rapids dangerous to the craft that carries us. The destruction of one's canoe in the wilderness is almost as serious as loss of musket or cartridges. In the third rapid, where the roaring stream makes a sharp turn to the right and tears downward among rocks for fifteen hundred yards, the Chippewa steered us into the wrong channel and our boat was so seriously broken that we got ashore with difficulty, for repairs. An hour sufficed to cure the leaks.

The remaining rapids were less troublesome. At one of them, the river expanded to such width that the water was too shallow for our heavily loaded canoe. Chippewa and guide stepped overboard and directed the course of the boat. At the foot of this rocky stair-way, the Mississippi resumes its placidity and, after winding through a fine forest of poplar, oak, and pine, expands into a lake,—the first of three. The scenery at times is wild and picturesque. The three lakelets are in a vast meadow and their shores are reedy. The smallest is one mile in width. In the largest, which is twice as broad, we were treated to a hail-storm that badly battered us. The icy balls were large as filberts. Some were an inch in diameter; all were of milky whiteness. They fell in such quantities that the lake seemed a bubbling cauldron. Severe as were bruises upon wrists and shoulders, the scene was both curious and interesting. Our Chippewa insisted that many ducks, quail, and pigeons would be killed by the hail, but we looked for feathered victims in vain. The storm was followed by a double rainbow of resplendent charm.

Cass Lake looks like a large body of water upon the map; but islands are so numerous therein that it can be navigated without hazard in canoes in all weathers. We stopped for a brief space at a Pillager *teepee* on Grand Island; then proceeded to the mouth of Turtle River, where we arrived at dark. This is the point at which David Thompson, the English trader, and Beltrami, the Italian *voyageur,* encountered the Mississippi.

Turtle River is a large stream, and Governor Cass can hardly be blamed for thinking it the continuation of the Mississippi. He stopped at the mouth of Turtle River. There is a village of twenty lodges on the west-ern side of the river's mouth, but at the time of our visit all the men were away, hunting. The women were sociable. In return for a pair of moccasins, bestowed upon a young native woman, I was invited to go fire-fishing that night at a small lake a few miles northward on Turtle River. The courtesy was declined; but the art of attracting fish by a flambeau and spearing them as they come to the surface to look at the torch has attained a high degree of perfection among the Pillager women. This tribe of the Chippewa nation was at one time larger than any other. In Schoolcraft's day, there were eight hundred families about Leech and Cass lakes. When I visited the village at the mouth of Turtle River, there were less than one hundred bucks, squaws, and pappooses attached to that settlement. The Chippewa nation gave to the Red Cedar (Cass) Lake tribe the name Muk-im-dua-win-in-e-wug ("men who take by force"), of which "Pillager" is an admirable translation. They were named by the natives, but the philologist who Anglicised their title understood the English language. My fishing-tackle and cooking utensils disappeared, as by magic. Whenever we served a meal, a bunch of old women sat down to eat with us. But these Cass Lake Pillagers were the first living people we had seen since parting with the "timber-cruiser's" mate, many days before, and, for that, we forgave much.

That was Minnesota in 1872.

After the natives had partaken of three meals on our provisions, all served before noon, I ordered a start. We first moved across to the eastern bank of Turtle River's mouth; but in fifteen minutes ten squaws and three times as many boys and girls rejoined us. The river is forty feet broad and the current very swift. There must be a ford somewhere. My visitors had taken off their single garments and carried them on their heads, because their clothing was not wet. We bade farewell to Turtle River in the middle of the afternoon. The outlet of the lake was attained at four o'clock.

The Mississippi is one hundred and seventy feet wide where it leaves Cass Lake, and has become a majestic stream. This stretch of the river, almost to Lake Winnebagoshish, will always be remembered with great delight: it is a succession of handsome villa sites, without villas. The banks rise in gentle slopes to a plateau forty feet high; a sod of lawn-like smoothness is underfoot; the giant Norway pines do not keep out the sunlight and not a shrub of underbrush is seen. Each bend in the river develops a charming, grassy knoll; all that is lacking are houses and people.

One mile of the Mississippi, before it enters Lake Winnebagoshish,—the Victoria Nyanza of the American river,—can be saved by a portage directly into the lake at a point where the stream approaches within a hundred yards of the large body of water; but darkness admonished us to remain in the boat.

As we emerged from the river's mouth upon the broad expanse of the lake, moon and stars were reflected in the water. The weather was clear and cool. We hugged the west coast and very nearly suffered disaster by running ashore, under full headway. A tall tree, silhouetted against the sky, was assumed to be upon an island, but it marked the extremity of a narrow spit of land that runs a quarter mile into the lake. Rounding that point, we landed at the mouth of a small stream, and passed the night in an abandoned trading post. The memorable feature of that house was its wall-paper.   Two sides of the interior were covered with pages from a folio Bible!

Mr. Schoolcraft says he found pelicans on this lake; we did not see any.   Our first daylight look at the great lake and its ten miles of open water, which must be crossed in a frail canoe, was almost terrifying.   A gale was blowing from the eastward, which continued for forty-eight hours.   Heavy surf dashed upon the beach and the broad expanse of this miniature sea was white with foam.   We were " wind bound " two days.   On the third morning, we crossed Winnebagoshish,—a very unpleasant experience and probably the most dangerous incident in my entire trip on the river.   A squall occurred near the middle of the lake and a heavy swell developed.   Constant bailing, which duty fell to me, alone prevented the boat from swamping.   With much relief, we ran into smooth water in a narrow estuary that extends to the south-eastward,—a small replica of Green Bay, Wisconsin.   On the shore, at this point, stood the hut of an aged French trader, Boulanger.

Three miles of paddling down the river after leaving the bay brought us to a smaller lake, surrounded on all sides by reeds.   (At this point the United States Government has recently built a dam, shown in the picture.)   A portage exists at the south-eastern shore of this lake, leading to the Ball-club Lake.   The saving of distance would have been considerable, but we followed the river, intending to make White Oak Point trading post before dark.

We were soon in The Eagle's Nest Savannah, thirty square miles of meadow, covered by a foot of water. A novice might readily get lost in this vast shallow lake of waving grass, because the river channel is difficult

The Winnebagoshish Reservoir Dam.
(Minnesota Historical Society Collection.)

to follow. Stalks of wild rice, resembling wheat, rise six feet above the water and as a canoeist pushes them aside to effect passage they envelop him in their writhing embrace. A compass is necessary, for the only visible outlook is the sky. Despite the best of guidance, we got astray among the grass and sacrificed much time in regaining the channel. Leech Lake River enters the Mississippi from the westward through this meadow and, for that reason, the volume of water it supplies is difficult to estimate.

Darkness had fallen when we landed at White Oak Point, where the progress of a lively game of " Moccasin " was made manifest by a dirge-like chant, issuing from a wigwam.[1]

The scenery between White Oak Point and Pokegama Fall is truly picturesque. Hills rise abruptly from the river and forests crown them. Alternately traversing dense woodland and pretty valleys, the half day's paddling to the lumber camp at the mouth of Pokegama Lake remains a pleasant memory. The group of huts, where dwelt the Maine lumbermen, seemed a return to civilisation,—the first habitation of white men encountered since leaving White Earth. We were soon enjoying salt pork, which is exceedingly appetising after a long diet on fresh fish, pigeons and ducks. Two nights and a whole day were passed with these genial hosts; the only return I could make was

[1] Hennepin, *Description de la Louisiane*, Paris, 1693 (Shea's translation, 301), gives a clear account of the Indian game of " Plum Stone." It was played as craps are thrown to-day with dice. The plum pits were marked and the better had an even chance at guessing which side fell upward. The game of " Moccasin," which I found to be the Chippewa gambling game, is not mentioned in any of the Jesuit " Relations " so far as noticed.

to act as bearer of mail to the nearest post-office, at Muddy River, or Aikin, about three hundred miles down-stream.

The morning we left, the young woman with whom we had parted in the Itasca foot-hills paddled into camp, attended by her brother. They were much emaciated and worn; but the girl appeared glad to have overtaken us. In simple language, she told how they two had hurried down-stream from the A-ze-wa-wa-say-ta-gen landing to the mouth of the Marquette River and, examining every timber tract, had ascended it to the dividing ridge between Leech and Itasca lakes. Crossing to the latter, they had followed us along the rocky river bed. They had seen many trees blazed by me with the Greek letter "delta," for "Delta Kappa Epsilon,"—although the girl called it "a triangle,"—and had used our camp sites on more than one occasion. Among the Itasca hills, they had found the body of the timber-cruiser. Records of his discoveries were in his rubber tobacco-pouch, placed there by this faithful servant, in face of death.

"We found him, as I said we would," were her words, with a long sigh, "but dead."

IX—POKEGAMA TO ST. ANTHONY

The Mississippi above Pokegama Fall narrows to sixty feet in width. Restricted to these limits by a rocky bluff on the northern side, the river slides down the face of a limestone ledge, over twenty feet in height and standing at an angle of thirty-five degrees. It is not a "fall," in strict sense. Where the water takes

Pokegama Fall.

Photograph by C. H. Dickinson.

the "toboggan," the stream was divided at the time of my visit by a mass of rock, upon which a few spruce pines clung with surprising tenacity; not an ounce of soil was visible,—the trees doubtless drew their sustenance from the river. This obstructing rock has been removed. Rapid water at the top of the fall had to be crossed to reach the portage; the prospect of involuntarily "shooting the chute" was not pleasant. Why the carry was not made on the right bank was not explained.

The Pokegama portage is less than two hundred yards and easy. This fall is an impenetrable barrier to navigation by small steamers, until the government builds a series of locks around it. Thrice each summer, in my day, a stern-wheeler of the type that "runs in a heavy dew" came up from Aiken with supplies for the lumber camps and trading posts; but to-day railroads have penetrated to the locality. A prosperous town has developed at Grand Rapids, four miles below Pokegama, at the "Thundering Rapids." The United States Government has erected a barrage near that point, for the control of the river.

Pokegama Lake, five miles long, having its outlet at the head of the fall, was the site of one of the missions located in the Mississippi lake region during the first half of the nineteenth century. Hither came Rev. Frederick Ayer, from Massachusetts, in 1836, and upon the natives that gathered about this sanctuary the Sioux fell, in 1840, to avenge wrongs they claimed had been inflicted upon them by the Chippewas. Their principal complaint was that two of Little Crow's sons had been murdered. The Chippewas insisted that the young men had been killed in self-defence. When the

Sioux were known to be in the neighbourhood, the Chippewas sent their women and children to an island in Pokegama Lake and beat off their ancient enemies. The winter of 1850-51 at Cass, Leech, Pokegama, and Sandy lakes was one of great suffering. The crop of wild rice had been very poor the preceding fall and starvation existed in all native villages. Chippewas ate their children.

Experienced woodmen, who had made the trip, estimated the distance from Pokegama to Sandy Lake at one hundred and fifty miles: we easily traversed it in two days, camping the first night at Split-Hand River, after a run of sixty-eight miles. We ran through the " Thundering," or " Grand," rapids and the river maintains a strong current all the distance. It was a long, uninteresting trip, through an alluvial region, its timber worthless for any purpose except fuel.

Starting from Split-Hand camp at five o'clock, under a blue sky, we soon entered a region of pine forest. Flocks of pigeons rose at every bend of the river; we bagged a large mess. A few ducks were overtaken, but they were of the " hell-diver " variety and difficult to shoot.

An entirely new danger menaced us. The river abounded in floating logs on their way to the saw-mills at Minneapolis. Landing for breakfast, at the mouth of Swan River, our Chippewa stepped upon a nest of small snakes, the first we had encountered. His fright was surprising; one would have supposed that, raised in the forest, an Indian would not entertain unfriendly feelings for fellow-citizens of the wilderness. A charge of shot put the snakes out of suspense, but the native belaboured the nest for several minutes. We break-

The Second Government Dam on the Mississippi, below Grand Rapids.

fasted sumptuously upon pigeons and biscuits, with salt pork, brought from the lumber camp.

Swan River is a large stream, entering the Mississippi on the eastern bank and is navigable for canoes ninety miles, due north to Swan Lake. During the forenoon's progress, the track of a tornado, locally described as " a windfall," was passed.

We slept that night at the mouth of Sandy Lake River, upon the floor of Mr. Libby's historic trading post. " Libby's " has been known for three generations as the point of portage for the " Big Sea Water " (Lake Superior), reached by descending the turbulent St. Louis River. The eastward trip is made in two days; the westward in three, owing to the dalles of the St. Louis. Sandy Lake is a body of water three miles across and contains many small islands.

From Sandy Lake to Muddy River was an easy day's run. Two stretches of rapid water were encountered between the mouths of Cypress and Willow rivers. The latter stream, about forty miles below Libby's, possesses historical importance because Lieutenant Zebulon M. Pike ascended it when he visited Leech Lake in 1805. The forests are dense, but their timber is worthless for lumber. Muddy River to Brainerd occupied one day. The River of the Pines, two hundred feet wide, enters the Mississippi from the north and an island divides its waters at the mouth. Pine ridges are supplanted by bottom-land, growing elm, ash, oak, and maple. Tall, slender trees, recalling the cypress but really Lombardy poplars, that have been numerous, become more and more scarce until they disappear from the landscape. Five miles below Pine River are six islands. Beltrami, always classical, named

the centre one " Cythrea." He says, in describing the
place, " Only a temple is wanting to make of it another
Cythrea "—the island of Venus. The French Rapids
were hardly noticeable, owing to high water. This
swift spot is about twenty miles above Brainerd and
marks the northern limit of that tract of primitive rock
described as *" petites roches."* The mouth of a stream
known as the Nokassippi enters the Mississippi at the
end of those rapids. Twilight was settling over Brainerd as a landing was made under the Northern Pacific
railroad bridge.

We had returned to civilisation. There my Troy-
built Baden-Powell canoe awaited me. The guide and
Chippewa carrier were paid off and sent by rail to Oak
Lake station. Next afternoon, I paddled alone to Fort
Ripley, where I became the guest of its Commandant,
Captain McCaskey.

Next day was a strenuous one, during which I parted
with my long-while companions, the pines. Little Falls,
jammed with logs, was portaged. A waggon carried
the trim canoe through the village to a point below the
rough water. Pike Rapids were " run," owing to wil-
ful misinformation regarding landmarks of the approaches to that dangerous stretch of river. I had
been advised to watch for an island with two trees upon
it, and to go ashore on the western bank: but when
I passed the island, the speed of the current precluded
all possibility of making a landing. If attempted, I
would be drawn, side on, into the foaming rapid. The
" falls " are caused by ledges of rock, many sharp points
serving to tear the stream into ribbons. Safety lay in
a try at the deepest looking watery chute. Sitting
astride the canoe, behind the cock-pit,—as I remembered

St. Anthony Fall.
From a photograph taken in 1872.

A View of Fort Snelling, Showing the Round House
and the Original Stockade.
Photo. in 1872.

MacGregor did on the *Rob Roy,*—to raise the bow, I steered straight for the crest of a big roller that, apparently, hid a smooth-topped boulder. Fortunately, the canoe's keel bore a strip of steel, for, at railroad speed, it struck. The shock was tremendous, but the crew clung by his heels, as he would have done to a bare-back horse. A barrel of water was taken aboard; but as there was a recurrence of rapids for half a mile, bailing was impossible. There was not any danger, but an upset would have entailed loss of property. Great sport!

The land became prairie. I camped on a small island, only separated from the west bank by a narrow channel; but, hearing the bark of a dog, I launched the boat in search of a human habitation. It was found near Brockway and I slept on a feather bed that night. I got under way early, and as a stiff breeze was blowing down-stream, sailed at single reef for ten miles. Coming out from the end of an island, a squall struck me, jibed the boom, and an upset was narrowly averted. Handling a main sheet and steering with a double-bladed paddle is not as easy as it looks. Then came rough water above Wautab, and sail had to be taken in. This was done by unstepping the mainmast. The rapids were child's play. There is a three-mile bend in the river at this point at which a cut-off of a hundred feet would save the entire distance. As I was alone, I could not portage, although the point had been clearly indicated. Reaching Sauk Rapids, I contracted with a teamster to carry me around the bad water; but a riverman assured me I could run through if I implicitly followed his advice, owing to the height of the stream. He drew a rough map. I removed from the

canoe the sails, the gun, and everything portable and
kept faith with the waggoner by having him carry these
articles to a point below the village. I then walked
to a landing from which the rapids could be closely
studied. My adviser, the riverman, pointed out a
place near the centre of the stream where the water
went through a depression in the rocky ledge. It
looked safe, provided I could reach the middle of the
river, without being carried abeam into the foaming
waters. He advised that I pull up-stream for a short
distance.

This having been done, the canoe was headed direct
for the big chute in midstream. The noise of the
water was terrifying; but I went through without striking. Considerable water was taken aboard, and I fear
my cheeks were a trifle pale when I pulled ashore to
get the traps from the waggon. Half a dozen men
who had accompanied the teamster made remarks about
my adviser that were not complimentary. But they
overlooked the fact that I had been running through
rapids all way down-stream.

St. Cloud, on a bluff to the westward, presented a
charming appearance. Its tall church spires shone
beautifully in the sun.

The country became an elevated plateau and the
banks increased in height. Prairie still exists on the
eastern bank but on the west, where the land slopes down
to the shore, is a continuous fringe of maples and poplars. These trees shade the western bank from Sauk
Rapids to Anoka. The river swarmed with logs and
lumbermen were met at every village. I stopped for
luncheon at Bailey's at the mouth of Elk River,—important as marking the northern limits of Hennepin's

Roman Catholic "Basilica of Saint Paul," Built by Father
Gaultier in 1841, after which the City was Named.
Painted by H. W. Wack, after a Drawing by R. O. Sweeney
of Saint Paul, 1852.

and Carver's explorations. Between that village and Anoka rapid water is constantly encountered.

Anoka is a snug town on the eastern side, at the mouth of Rum River, a stream one hundred and sixty feet wide and the outlet of *Les Mille Lacs,* or Thousand Lakes, as the large, island-studded pond south of Aikin is known. Canoes can ascend Rum River one hundred and ten miles. Mille Lacs was discovered by Du Luth, and by him named Lac Buade in honour of Frontenac, Governor of Canada, whose family name was Buade.

Every mile developed a larger quantity of floating logs and in rapid water these are not agreeable companions. At such time, one recalls the fable of Æsop about the drifting jars of earthenware and brass. Already the stream seemed gathering strength for its mad plunge at St. Anthony and about four miles above the cataract, I took a train into Minneapolis. The *Dolly* and her crew were soon resting at the Nicollet House.

The picture shows how St. Anthony looked at that time.

Professor Winchell, a physicist who has made a study of the geology of the Upper Mississippi, concludes that the cataract at St. Anthony has worked back from Fort Snelling, eight miles, since the glacial period, or five thousand years, and that the time required to cut the Mississippi channel from Cape Girardeau to St. Anthony was four hundred thousand years. The rock from the fall down to the mouth of the Wisconsin River is St. Lawrence limestone, and the stratum averages two hundred feet in thickness. According to John Arnold Keyes, St. Anthony is " the remnant of the most stupendous cataract the world ever saw, having a perpendicular descent of six hundred feet." There is a fall in the Yosemite Valley with a perpendicular drop of fifteen hundred feet but the volume of water is insignificant. The Victoria, on the Zambesi, is one thousand yards wide and has a sheer descent of three hundred and sixty feet. Therefore, " if his [Mr. Keyes's] theory be correct, his statement is not exaggerated." The Sioux called the fall *Ha-ha,* the " loud laughing " or " roaring." The Mississippi they described, according to Gordon, as the *Ha-ha-Wâ-kpa,* " River of the Falls." The Chippewa name for the fall was *Ka-kâ-bik-kung.*

The cities of Minneapolis and Saint Paul are one in interest, and ultimately will be united under one corporate title,—just as are Brooklyn and Manhattan. Opposition to such union is shared equally by the two cities. For nearly a generation, Brooklyn balked at uniting with New York. " The Twin-Cities," as they describe themselves, are the immediate market for the largest wheat growing section of this country. The centre of Minneapolis is only seven miles in a straight line from that of Saint Paul.

Minnesota is larger in area than all New England. It is the watershed of the continent. The great rivers that drain it have their rise only a few miles apart and radiate east, north, and south. The St. Lawrence drains the eastern slope, the Red River of the North the northern, and the Mississippi the middle and southern sections. The highest elevation is one thousand six hundred and eighty feet above the sea level. Minnesota is the Land of Lakes. Dr. Day, of Saint Paul, calculated that three and one half acres of every one hundred acres, or one million six hundred and one thou-

View from Red Wing, Looking South.

View from Barn Bluff.

sand eight hundred and forty acres, are of inland lake surface.

After reposing upon cushions in the hotel parlour during the night, the *Dolly* was taken in a waggon to the river front at the southern end of Minneapolis and launched. Passing the mouth of Minnehaha Creek, I was able to paddle nearly up to the fall; a short walk was necessary. Returning to the Mississippi, the frowning and picturesque heights of Fort Snelling dominated the landscape. This imposing and romantic fortress, sole reminder of the long struggle with man and nature for possession of the North-west, is still calculated to cause a heart-thrill. Its white stone walls cling to the brink of a precipitous cliff, and over all, upon a tall staff, floats the flag of our country. The entrance of the Minnesota River, at Mendota, a Dakota word for " meeting of the waters," is very imposing; the mouths of the Missouri and Ohio surpass the Minnesota in volume but not in scenic effect. Finding a favouring breeze, the mast was stepped and a speedy sail to Saint Paul followed.[1] One of the rowing clubs offered the hospitality of its boat-house and the crew rested at a hotel for two days.

The Mississippi scenery between Saint Paul and Keokuk is as beautiful as that of any river in the world. The Hudson has higher mountains, the Rhine its historic ruins, the Seine its artistic châteaux, the Danube its " Iron Gates," and the Colorado its cañon; but, for

[1] Carver's cave, at Saint Paul, was known to the Dakotas as " the sacred lodge " (Neill, 207). It is now a beer cellar.

five hundred miles, our own greatest river passes
through a variety of scenery attractive to the eye and
romantically associated with the early development of
our republic. The river banks below Saint Paul are
high bluffs on the east and beautiful lowlands on the
west.

Leaving the club, where my canoe had been housed
most hospitably, I sailed and paddled to Hastings,
thirty-two miles, by one o'clock. Finding a breeze, I
sailed about two miles below Prescott where the wind
died out. The beauty of the landscape to the eastward grew with each bend of the river. Diamond
Bluff, the end of the day's run, has for background a
charming, rocky precipice.

In the absence of any breeze next morning, I
tugged at the paddle as far as Red Wing, famous in
song and story as the site of the village of a tribe having a chief of that name. The town is prettily located
on the western bank; the view therefrom, shown in
the photograph, is one with which the eye does n't tire.

Then comes the grand expansion of the river known
as Lake Pepin, twenty-five miles long by three to five
in width. Not an island in it. High looms the bare
front of the Maiden Rock, grand in nature and fasci-
nating in romance. Every passenger upon steamers
and trains is told the tale anew. I heard it at every
hamlet upon the lake: it represents tourist capital.
Ever since the time of the Tarpeian Rock, precipitous
cliffs have served for the immolation of real or mythical
maidens. The story of Winona's self-destruction generally takes this form: The Dakotas and Chippewas
were engaged in bloody warfare about the close of the
eighteenth century. Red Wing, chief of the Dakota

The Maiden Rock, Lake Pepin.

The Author's "Baden-Powell" Canoe.

tribe on Lake Pepin, had for daughter Winona, traditionally beautiful. She had many suitors but she rejected all the braves of her own people, having secretly pledged herself to a son of Wahnabozah, chief of the Chippewas and the hereditary foe of her father. With the opening of spring, Red Wing called a council of war and asked the aid of all tribes among the Dakotas. The most powerful young chief, who had come from far up the Mississippi, Wazikoota by name, demanded Winona for wife as the price of his assistance and Red Wing acceded to the conditions.

The Indian girl had a stolen interview with her Chippewa lover, informed him of her father's plans, and they agreed that as soon as the decisive battle had been fought they would meet atop this rock and flee to the Red River country. The lovers were spied upon, the Chippewa brave was pursued and killed. When Wazikoota turned to claim Winona, she ran to the edge of the cliff and with a despairing shriek cast herself headlong upon the rocks below. The Indian legend asserts that the angry Spirit of the Lake caused a great wave to sweep to the base of the hill which, returning, bore the bodies of the lovers to a grave beneath the waters.[1]

A delightful sail across the lake to the pretty village of Frontenac followed. Pepin is an enlargement of the Mississippi twenty-five miles in length and no-

[1] Col. John W. Bliss, son of Major John Bliss, U. S. A., who passed his boyhood at Fort Snelling, tells of having to tie up for two days in Lake Pepin, at the base of "Maiden Rock" (then called "The Lovers' Leap"). He was travelling with his parents to the post to which his father had been assigned, on the stern-wheeler *Warrior*, which made two trips each summer from Saint Louis to Fort Snelling.

12

where more than five miles in width. Its general direction is towards the south-east and its form is that of an extended line of beauty. A range of low hills extends into the lake from the west which the steamboat men call "Point No Point," for the reason that, hour after hour, it looks like a headland but proves to be only a continuous bluff. Frontenac, called a watering place, is just below Point No Point. The French, under M. Frontenac, drove the Reynards from the Wisconsin up the Mississippi and built a stockade on the west bank near Point de Sable. Lake Pepin, as seen from the rocky hill above Frontenac, is shown in the photograph.

From Frontenac, I again crossed the lake to a small hamlet about one mile above Reed's Landing where I spent the night. In the morning, against a head wind, I pulled ten miles to Wabashaw for breakfast.

"Wah-pah-sah" was the hereditary name of a long and illustrious line of Dakota (Sioux) chiefs. "Wabashaw" is the white man's pronunciation. The name is descriptive of the pole used in the Sioux dances, upon which, like a May pole, feathers and coloured cloths were fastened. Therefore, Wapasa meant "The Standard," not "The Leaf Shaker," as has been suggested. The principal village of these aboriginal forest barons was Ke-uk-sa, the present site of Winona. Stephen R. Riggs, author of *The Dakota Grammar*, says, "Ke-uk-sa means 'Village of Law Breakers,' so described because this band disregarded the custom of the Dakota nation against marrying blood relations of any degree." Wapasa, grandfather of the last chief of that name, was a friend of the British during the American Revolution.[1]

[1] Neill's *History of Minnesota*, 225–229.

Lake Pepin, from Top of Maiden Rock.
Photo. by E. J. Hall, Oak Park, Ill.

Here was beautiful prairie, still within the Minnesota border. Here was the capital of " The Standard " tribe of the Sioux.

A strong wind blew against the current all day, making the paddling laborious. The water was so rough that I could not land at Almy but proceeded to Buffalo, remembered solely as the site of a saw-mill and a beer-garden. As the wind increased, so did the blisters upon my hands. Mount Vernon, eighteen miles, was passed at one o'clock and a luncheon of cove oysters, hard bread, and coffee was eaten on the river side. After waiting in vain for the wind to moderate, I paddled eleven miles to Fountain City.

The scenery on both sides of the river is magnificent, but the heaviness of the work at the paddle prevented its entire enjoyment. The little German town of Fountain City nestles at the foot of a hill and seemed very comfortable in the warmth of the afternoon's sun. Although I had hoped to reach Winona before dark, I spent the night there and the beer tasted as good that night as any I subsequently have drunk in Munich. The hospitality of the Wisconsin town was agreeable. My boat was carried from the warehouse, where it had been kept under lock during the night, and I started down the river at nine o'clock.

Not far from Winona is the picturesque " Sugar Loaf." It casts a very heavy shadow across the river in the early morning, as will be seen from the photograph. A sandy beach runs along its base. A brief stop was made at Winona to mail letters, after which I paddled to Trempealeau.

At half-past five, I stepped ashore at La Crosse, at the end of a dashing sail, carrying all canvas, and

the much admired canoe was taken to the parlour of the
International Hotel.   The river is almost four miles
wide at La Crosse owing to innumerable islands and
channels.   A start was made at six o'clock next morning.   Brownsville was reached at ten and a stop for
the night was made at Lansing, after paying a visit
to the supposed grave of Minnehaha at De Soto on
the Wisconsin bank.

Lansing, on the Iowa side, lies at the foot of the
usual range of bluffs.   The day was fine and hugging
the Iowa bank to avoid numerous channels made by
countless islands, I paddled all the way to McGregor,
opposite Prairie du Chien.   The upper town of McGregor first came in sight to the south of a long stretch
of water.   The levee was found very rocky.   After
luncheon at the Evans House, I crossed the river to
Prairie du Chien, the oldest town on the Mississippi,
dating back to the time of Père Marquette.   The
modern city is not exactly where Father Marquette
saw the prairie dogs.   At Fort Crawford,—" Prairie-
Dogtown," as described in a report on file at the War
Department,—Colonel Zachary Taylor, then a recognised Indian fighter and afterwards to carve his way
to the Presidency by success in the Mexican War, was
in command for several years, dating from 1833.   He
had then served in the Sauk and Fox campaigns.

The Wisconsin, where it joins the Mississippi, is
imposing, but historical associations give to it pre-
eminent importance.   Very little imagination was
necessary to see, in mind's eye, the figures of grave-
visaged missionaries and the strong, daring counte-
nances of French traders in canoes emerging from the
river's mouth.

Lake Pepin, Looking North from Point No Point.

Below Prairie du Chien, the scenery becomes of picturesque grandeur. Lofty bluffs appear on each side, some of rock, others alluvial, having similitude to ruined castles, Saracen watch-towers like those seen upon the Sardinian and Spanish shores of the Mediterranean, and grotesque figures of gigantic size. In places, these bluffs attain a height of six hundred feet; many of them are coloured by various mineral deposits and are often crowned with clumps of chestnut and oak.

I paddled into Guttenberg, Iowa, at dark and spent the night at the Crawford House,—the day's voyage being forty-six miles. Next day was the Sabbath but there did not seem to be any observance thereof, so, after breakfast, I decided to proceed to Dubuque. The scenery began to lose many of its charms. The bluffs, cheerful companions since leaving Minneapolis, began to melt into the prairie. A light breeze springing up, sail was set and the fifteen-mile run from Cassville to Wells' Landing was made in two hours. After a stop for luncheon, the voyage was resumed without incident to Dubuque. In the afternoon sun, the church spires and pretty villas of this flourishing city could be seen on rising ground far inland. The water-side part of the town appeared common enough. I proceeded down-stream and passed the night at a white frame cottage on the Illinois bank where I was hospitably received. My canoe was stored in the carriage-house.

Next day, being overcast, with a fair wind downstream, I paddled and sailed to Sabula, forty-eight miles, without incident. The following day, I proceeded as far as Le Claire, forty-seven miles. An early

start was made next morning, because I expected to
enjoy running the Rock Island Rapids. I arrived at
the head of the rapid water about nine o'clock and had
passed through several miles of it before I realised its
character. The length of the rapid is fourteen miles,
or from Rock Island to Port Byron on the Illinois
side. According to Captain R. E. Lee, U. S. Engineers, the fall in the river is 25.74 feet. The Mississippi flows over a bed of limestone, the ledges of
which sometimes reach quite across the river. In times
of very shallow water, one might possibly incur some
danger in running the Rock Island Rapids; but I had
followed the spring freshet down and had a thoroughly
enjoyable hour among the swift currents.

The shores are generally prairie above Rock Island
and the background well timbered. Davenport, with
a charming range of sloping hills behind it, formed a
fine landscape. Muscatine was the halting place for
the night. The next day was intolerably warm and
the trip to Burlington, sixty-two miles, was very
arduous.

Here followed one of the red letter days of the
voyage. Starting from Burlington at nine o'clock, I
followed the Iowa shore hoping to secure a sailing breeze,
but the wind was blowing up-stream and this made the
heat more endurable. Bluffs reappeared on the west
and soon grew to almost the magnitude they had possessed about Lake Pepin. Charming little green islands
were scattered in the stream. As the meal hour approached, I came to a little town, the water front of
which was lined with rafts. Upon one of these, I saw
a frame boarding-house and immediately applied for
entertainment. The landlord was an Irishman and fed

Great Spirit Bluff, near Alma, Wisconsin.
Photo. by E. J. Hall, Oak Park, Ill.

me on boiled beef and dried peaches. The meat was tough, but the appetite was indulgent.

I set out for Nauvoo. The imposing site had been described to me, but its beauty far exceeded expectations. I beached my canoe under the bluff about five o'clock, at a point from which a path led up the slope to a red brick hotel. There I found a hale and refined old lady, Mrs. Joseph Smith, widow of the founder of Mormonism. She was mistress of the tavern. After supper, she and I sat upon the brow of the bluff, with the mighty Mississippi flowing between us and the Iowa shore, while I listened to her narrative of the terrible privations and persecutions of early Mormon days. Mrs. Smith's conversation is very memorable, due to the romantic surroundings and especially to the excellence of its English. Nauvoo cannot be dismissed in a few words. It belongs to the history of religion in the Mississippi Valley, and its romantic features equal those of the missionary priests who devoted their lives to the dissemination of doctrines in which they devoutly believed.

Nauvoo is the sacred town of Mormonism: to true believers, it is what Benares is to Buddhism and Mecca to Islam. The Mormon idea—older than Joseph Smith, who gave to it form and direction—was a product of several communistic movements that began between 1820 and 1830, in various parts of the Eastern States. This farmer's son, living at different periods of his boyhood near Palmyra and Manchester, in western New York, saw visions, had dreams, and practised healing by faith. His father, mother, and maternal grandfather had asserted similar unusual powers. There is a quaint " chap-book " in the Berrian Collection, published by one Solomon Mack (Windsor, Canada, 1810), which foreshadows the neurotic conditions that developed in Joseph Smith.

Solomon Mack was an illiterate, shiftless man who described himself as "a wild ass's colt," and his daughter, Lucy Mack, became the mother of Joseph Smith. The boy grew up in an atmosphere of unreality and probably inherited a taint of epilepsy. Solomon Mack confessed to "frequent fits." Smith's mother was a mental freak. She implicitly believed in dreams. Thus, the founder of Mormonism was a product of atavism; his erratic temperament was inherited. Journals left by Mrs. Lucy Smith foreshadow the recent work of Mrs. Mary Baker-Eddy. They were published in Liverpool (1853), and are of undeniable authenticity.

Joseph Smith, Senior, came as a colonist from New England to the property of the Holland Land Company, owners of a large tract west of Seneca Lake, in New York. Palmyra had only four log houses. In this environment, Lucy Smith raised her children. For a brief period, the Smiths lived at Manchester, a place equally desolate: but at Palmyra, the son, Joseph, began to argue and to exhort whenever he could secure hearers. On day, he announced the finding of a set of golden plates, upon which were inscribed "The teachings of Nephi, his reign and ministry."

"The Book of Mormon" appeared in 1830, printed by E. B. Grandin, for the author, at Palmyra.

After Smith's followers had migrated to Kirtland, Ohio; thence (1838) to the town of Far West, Missouri, where relentless persecution culminated in the massacre of twenty people at Haun's Mill, we find

Fountain City.

Photo. by E. J. Hall, Oak Park, Ill.

them at Nauvoo, on the Illinois bank of the Mississippi.
Already Orson Pratt was preaching the faith in England and sending to America a constantly increasing
stream of converts.

The site of Nauvoo probably is the most beautiful
on " the Father of Waters." A majestic bluff, overlooking the broad river, and a vast stretch of level
country behind it, affords ample room for a city of
vast proportions. Had the Mormons not been ruth-
lessly driven to the Great Salt Lake, a city equal in
beauty, wealth, and industry to the capital of Utah
would stand upon this commanding eminence to-day,
adding to the pride of the State and nation. Here the
sect thoroughly organised for the first time. The original title of the boat-landing had been " Commerce ";
but Smith renamed it " Nauvoo," or " The beautiful."
A large tract of land was purchased for $14,000, and
broad streets were laid out, crossing each other at right
angles. A busy, thriving town developed. Two hundred houses and many public edifices were built. In
1841, Smith had a revelation, directing that a great
temple be built. Underneath the land a fine quality
of limestone had been discovered and quarries were
opened, from which material was procured to build the
temple. The corner-stone was laid with much ceremony in 1841. The structure was of polished stone,
one hundred and thirty-eight feet long, eighty-eight
feet wide, and sufficiently capacious to accommodate
three thousand people. It was surmounted by a tower
rising one hundred and seventy-five feet, and its interior decorations were costly. The total expenditures
exceeded $500,000.

Nauvoo soon had a population of ten thousand

people, and Joseph Smith was supreme in authority. With prosperity came internal dissensions among the Mormons and many malicious reports were circulated regarding Smith's moral character. He was accused of having "spiritual wives," although that part of the Mormon doctrine had not been propounded. The entire population of Illinois eventually divided on Mormon and anti-Mormon sentiment. Smith's bitterest opponents and critics were Dr. Foster and Mr. Law, editors of *The Nauvoo Expositor:* they published so many attacks upon Smith that he ordered their printing-office burned. These editors got warrants for the arrest of Joseph and Hiram Smith, but the constable was driven out of town when he tried to serve the papers. Conditions became so strained that Governor Ford sent a demand from Springfield for the surrender of the Smith brothers. He feared to call out the militia, knowing that bloodshed would ensue.

Joseph Smith expressed a willingness to submit to the authority of the State government, at the same time declaring that he believed he would be a victim of mob fury. The Governor promised protection and the two men surrendered themselves at Carthage. They were incarcerated in the jail at that place. On June 27, 1844, a mob gathered which broke into the prison and shot the two men to death. It was a very brutal outrage.

The assassination of Joseph Smith strengthened Mormonism. Alive, he may have been an imposter; dead, he became a martyr. His biographers have found many difficulties in arriving at a correct estimate of Joseph Smith. He was a remarkable man, possessed of superior natural talent and of much executive

The City of Winona, Minnesota.
Photo. by E. J. Hall, Oak Park, Ill.

ability. Under unceasing persecutions and constant hardships, he established a combination of thrift and religion that has endured in Utah unto this day.

At the time of his first alleged revelation, there were forty-three separate sects of the Christian religion in this country. The land resounded with the hysterical cry, " What must we do to be saved? " Appeal for salvation was so general that Smith found hundreds of followers, when, at any other period, he would not have secured scores. Smith was either a sincere religious fanatic, or a remarkable imposter.

The grave and imposing stone temple at Nauvoo, upon which the faithful had laboured so devotedly, was burned by anti-Mormons in 1848. With Brigham Young as their leader, the Mormons trekked across the plains to the Great Salt Lake and established, at "Deseret," a new home, which their energies have caused to bloom. Their new city was laid out upon lines similar to those adopted at Nauvoo.

After the exodus of the main body of the " Latter Day Saints," Nauvoo became the seat of a sect of French Socialists calling themselves " Icarians." Repudiating the new leader, Brigham Young, the widow of Joseph Smith remained behind, to end her days at the scene of her beloved husband's preaching and only a few miles from the place of his murder. She remarried, when past middle life, and I was introduced to her husband.

" Joseph Smith never suggested or practised polygamy," said the aged lady, with a directness born of sincere belief. " He was a devoted and faithful husband. The blemish of polygamy was engrafted upon Mormonism, which was a pure, gentle, trusting faith,

—beautiful as the beliefs of the ancient Greeks,—by Brigham Young and Orson Pratt, after my husband's cruel assassination."

"You love this place and his memory so deeply that you would not trek to far-away Utah?" I asked.

"Not altogether that. I was a devout believer in the faith as disclosed by Joseph Smith; but I would not follow false prophets."

After breakfast, next morning, I visited the site of the great temple, a ploughed field. Not a villager appeared to realise a lost opportunity. Wayfarer as I was, I could have lingered for hours watching the grand river that I had seen grow from a brook.

The pull to Keokuk, nineteen miles, was made through rapid water; but I would not have known I was descending a fall had I not noticed a steamer ascending through a lock on the Iowa side. The distance was covered in about ninety minutes. Although the heat was intense I pushed on to Canton, twenty-four miles farther. I landed on the Iowa shore at half-past two, utterly fagged. I was twenty miles from Quincy and after waiting until the sun got low, I easily made the distance before dark. The following day was uneventful. To avoid getting into chutes and ponds along the route required watchfulness. I went miles out of my way on two occasions. I intended to stop at Hannibal for luncheon, but had run by it before the error was detected. I stopped three hours at Saverton, on account of the intolerable heat, and then proceeded to Louisiana, Mo., opposite Quincy junction, and spent the night.

As I was getting ready to start, next morning, the steamboat *Belle of La Crosse* ran on the levee. This

"The Sugar Loaf," near Winona.

Trempealeau.

was the second time she had met me since I had left
Saint Paul.   Realising that she would reach Saint
Louis, a round one hundred miles distant, before dark,
I decided to dodge sunstroke and take her.   My canoe
was carried aboard and I received a warm welcome from
the captain.   We passed the mouth of the Illinois River,
sacred to the memories of the early explorers and missionaries, at four o'clock, and, after a brief stop at Alton,
saw the coffee-coloured flood of the Missouri add itself
to the clear waters of the Mississippi.   As far as Saint
Louis, the western third of the broad river remained
café au lait in hue.   Putting the canoe in a warehouse
near the wharf, I went to the Southern.

XI—BY STEAMBOAT TO NEW ORLEANS

The voyage from Saint Louis to New Orleans on
the steamboat *James Howard* developed sufficient incidents to fatten a story book.   The boat was only
partially loaded, because the chief part of the cargo for
New Orleans was to be received at Cairo, from Ohio
River craft.   This would necessitate a stay at the little
town in "Egypt," Illinois, and many passengers for
the lower river preferred to wait in Saint Louis and
overtake the boat by train.

Any narrative of a week's life upon a Mississippi
steamboat without gambling experiences would not
possess the flavour of reality: but the run to Cairo was
uneventful.   The captain was an interesting man who
had spent forty years on the river.   He mentioned the
suicide of Captain Durkin, of the *Minotaur,* who lost
all his earthly possessions in a game of poker, aboard
his own boat.   The spell of the terrible name borne by

the craft did not impress the captain; but he was very
sure that ill luck attended all steamers christened with
names beginning with " M." The same fatality applied to the Missouri River as well as to the Mississippi.
He cited the cases of the *Magnolia*, which took fire and
burned two hundred and twenty-five of her three hundred passengers; of the *Metamora*, sunk above Choctaw
Island; of the *Midas*, snagged at the bend above Island
No. 16; of the *Mayflower*, burnt at Memphis, and of
several others. He then recurred to Captain Durkin
and said:

On a down trip, two well-dressed passengers came aboard
at Memphis and announced themselves as Louisiana planters.
That evening, one of these strangers suggested a game of
poker to the captain. Durkin was fond of " draw " and
agreed. After play with varying fortune, he was dealt four
kings. Then he bet all his money and his quarter interest
in the *Minotaur*. His opponent showed four aces. Durkin
signed a bill of sale for his share in the boat, went to his
stateroom, and shot himself. He left a note, saying: " A
man who would bet his last dollar on four kings does n't
deserve standing-room on earth."

As an exception to popular superstition among
Mississippi steamboat captains, it may be stated that
the *James Howard* was burned soon after the trip that
served to continue my voyage as far as the Crescent
City. The explosion of the *Sultana's* boilers, in 1864,
had caused a sacrifice of six hundred and forty-seven
lives, and the *Saluda*, ending her career in similar
fashion, destroyed one hundred human beings.

Train from Saint Louis brought fifty passengers
for our boat, among whom was a collector for a New

Minnehaha's Grave, near De Soto.
(Tumulus upon the Crest of the Hill.)
Photo. by E. J. Hall, Oak Park, Ill.

York house known to me.   That afternoon, as we were passing Island No. 10 and New Madrid, historically interesting, owing to the places they occupy in the records of the Civil War, I listened to a gambling episode that had occurred to the narrator while ascending the Mississippi during the previous winter:

I never shall touch a card again [he began].   I have had my lesson.   I arrived at New Orleans from a collection tour in Texas, with quite a bunch of money in certified checks and cash.   Coming too late for banking hours, I carried this money aboard the boat, which was to leave at nine o'clock, intending to secure a draft at Memphis to the credit of my house.   I scheduled the checks and mailed them to New York; then I made the bills into a bundle, which I deposited with the purser of the steamboat.   He was in collusion with gamblers aboard, and before supper, I had been introduced to several sleek but respectable-appearing men.   A game of poker was proposed after the boat got under way, and having several hundred dollars of money of my own, I had no objections. I thought I could take care of myself.   I met a Cincinnati salesman aboard, Whitney by name, and persuaded him to join us.   We adjourned to a stateroom from which a four-poster bed had been removed and six of us " sat in."

The game ran along quietly for half an hour, nobody making any suggestion to increase the modest five-dollar limit. I was ahead about $80.   Whitney was a small loser.   No amount of money worth talking about had changed hands.   I had my eyes about me, but had failed to detect evidences of collusion or cheating on the part of my new acquaintances. I played with a feeling of increased confidence, and under pretext of getting some cigars from my stateroom, dropped out long enough to secure the wad of money from the purser's safe.

There was a " jack pot " soon after my return.   The player at my left, one of the strangers, was dealing.   The first man said, " No."   The second player " declined to open."

The third, Whitney, tossed a blue chip into the centre of the table, with the statement: "I open, for the limit!" The fourth man, at my right, "chipped along."

I had a pair of kings and a pair of jacks; so I "hiked it." The dealer quit, as did the chap next to him. The second player stayed for the $10, as did Whitney. Fourth man saw my raise and raised back. I "chipped along," but was surprised to find strength develop at Number Two, who "tilted the pot," as if he meant to stay. Whitney would n't quit. When Number Four's turn came, he "made good" and raised! I merely chipped, feeling that I was over-playing two pairs. Surely enough, Two "bumped it"; Whitney quit; Four merely "stayed"; I decided to "linger" and take cards. This is what the draw revealed:

Number Two asked for two cards. The logic of that act was that he had declined to "open" on threes, or, quite improbably, was holding "a kicker" to a pair. I "read him" for threes.

Number Four's draw was interesting. He took one card, ostentatiously placing his discard before him and covering it with a chip. Although he had n't "broken the jack," he intended to give the impression that he had split a pair and was about to draw to a straight or flush. I reasoned that if he had been given fours "to go in" he would have "stood pat," in order to indicate a smaller hand than he actually possessed. With the probability of having threes to beat at Number Two, and a completed flush at Number Four, I made a freak draw. I had a pair of kings, therefore nobody else could get four kings. I tossed them away, with the three spot of hearts, and drew to the jacks. To my surprise, I was given a king and two jacks! That ought to have made me wise; for, don't you see, on the assumption that I would draw only one card, the intention of the dealer was that I should have a king full,—a very respectable hand. Four jacks, however, were different. I would have played a "full" with caution: but f-o-u-r-s! I did n't worry about a straight flush; as for fours, only aces or queens could beat me. I tried to look unconcerned, as I awaited the first bet. Whitney being

The City of Dubuque, Iowa.
Photo. by E. J. Hall, Oak Park, Ill.

out, that distinction fell to Number Four. I raised him, heard
Two raise me and saw Four "hike" it, again,—as he spoke
of the folly of over-playing a flush.

Here is where the usual thing occurred. Somebody suggested "taking off the limit." The passion was on me; I was
glad to agree. All the avaricious traits of my character were
in evidence. I was a different man from the one who had
entered the game,—a soulless thing, money-mad.

When Two topped my re-raise of Four's raise by a hundred
dollars, I was delighted. I was doubly glad when Four added
another hundred. I pushed two bills across the table to
"make good" and taking all the rest of my own cash, raised
$250. I had expected a show-down at this point; but in the
half minute of silence that followed, I decided to use the
money of my firm, if necessary to force a conclusion. Em-
bezzlement? Yes; but at that moment my dying mother could
not have convinced me I was doing wrong. After unusual
deliberation, the gamester at my left "saw" Four's hundred,
my $250, making $350, and added five crisp hundred dollar
bills to the stake. Cold perspiration appeared on my fore-
head; the only choice lay between jail or victory. "Mine are
as good as they were," commented Four, as he again raised
another $500.

A glance at my hand showed that none of the jacks had
got away; I still held five cards, with the king. My hand
was n't foul, whether it won or lost. The possibility of a
straight flush in Four's hand froze the marrow in my bones.
What could I do but go on?

It is well enough to say I could have retired with the loss
of a few hundred dollars and remained honest. Persons who
reason thus fail to comprehend the passion that swayed me.
I opened the bulging envelope and spread the bills across a
knee. It cost me $1000 to "call," but I did so. As I had
feared, Number Two "saw" his friend's $500 raise and "went
up" an equal amount. Without an instant's hesitation, Four
"made good" and raised a plumb thousand.

I saw two things clearly. First, I was being "saw-bucked"
by the players alternately raising on either side of me;

13

second, I had probably over-played my fours and could not win on a " show-down." I had already embezzled $1000 of my employers' funds. Suicide suggested itself, in case I failed to win; but I did not have the slightest impulse to quit. Meanwhile, Four tossed in $1500, meaning an increase of $1000.

With swimming eyes, I " saw " the $1500 promptly, fortunately counting the money in my lap. That meant $2500 of the money entrusted to my keeping. But, I made a discovery! Upon the back of the envelope, I had written " $3260." I had overlooked several sums, and still had $3000 left. I could win, if my antagonists had n't that much between them. After my " call," Number Two " made good " Four's raise and added $500. Instantly, Four counted out precisely $760, meaning a " raise " of $260!

My eyes were opened by that bet. I glanced at the back of the envelope I had given to the purser,—" 3260." Exactly the amount! The fellow wanted my last dollar and was n't afraid of a " show-down."

Here 's where the catastrophe was to have occurred. I detected an expression of sarcastic glee on the face of the dealer, —who had not joined in the betting but was to be sharer in the spoils. Number Two had only a few bills on the table, but he appeared to know that he would n't need more. Four acted as if he already had my cash in his clutches. He was contentedly swinging upon the gate of hell! The satanic leer of joy in that man's eyes decided me: I " made good " and raised him $2240!

Consternation appeared upon the faces of the three professional gamblers. Number Two leaned over to Whitney and, showing to him four aces, begged for enough money to " call." Number Four in a low voice asked to have the bet reduced to $800,—all the funds he had with him.

" Never! " I fairly screamed.

Four then asked to leave the room to secure money; but, at a motion from me, Whitney stepped to the door, and, making sure it was locked, put the key in his pocket. I was armed and meant to die rather than let that gang of scoun-

A View of Nauvoo, Illinois, from a Photograph Taken from Bluff Park. Showing Government Canal.

(Copyright by Goulty, Nauvoo, Ill.)

drels do me. Number Four, the dean of the trio, rose, throwing down his cards, faces upward. He bowed and said:

"It is a dead 'freeze-out': but your nerve and your money
win."

As Whitney showed a pair of queens, his "openers," I saw
that Number Four had laid down a ten-high, straight flush.

The *James Howard* chugged away throughout the
night and ran her bow upon the levee at Memphis
shortly after noon of the following day. The city had
not fully recovered from the effects of the Civil War.
It was far from being the beautiful place it is to-day.

Several stops, notably at Helena, were made during
the night and all the next day was spent " rounding the
bends " in this crookedest of American rivers. The
Jordan, in Palestine, is probably the only stream on
earth containing more convolutions. Although the distance from the Lake of Tiberias to the Dead Sea is
hardly sixty miles, the Jordan uses full two hundred
miles in making the steep descent. The point of greatest interest during that long day's steaming was the
mouth of the Arkansas River, where is the defunct
village of Napoleon. Visions of La Salle, Tonty, and
other early explorers came before my eyes as we steamed
smoothly past the outlet of this great river. Lost towns
are scattered along the entire made-lands of the Mississippi's delta; but the most notable is this one of
Napoleon, which from 1844 to 1874 was county seat
of Desha County, Arkansas, and had eight hundred inhabitants in 1860; but, since my visit, the Mississippi
took a dislike to it and washed away its streets and
houses. I am assured that to-day the site of this
ambitious town cannot be identified.

Amidst the sunlight of the following morning, I

caught sight of Vicksburg. Standing at the wheel-house, an obliging ex-Confederate pointed out the strategic features of the landscape. Especially did he indicate the locality near the mouth of the Yazoo, at which General Sherman suffered defeat. Our steamer carried a great deal of merchandise for Vicksburg, and passengers spent until four o'clock visiting places of historic interest. Many of the cave dwellings, cut into the hard-clay hillsides and occupied during the bombardment, were still in existence and some of them were in use as beer cellars.

At daylight the following morning, we were at Natchez-under-the-Hill: five hours were spent in rambling about the upper town. Memories of the Spanish, French, and English pioneers were awakened by the names of many of the streets. I would have liked to have seen a few streets or squares bearing the titles of the wonderful native chieftains described in the Jesuit "Relations." John Hay, an associate on the *Tribune,* had not published *Jim Bludso of the Prairie Belle,* who "had one wife at Natchez and another here in Pike." Having read Châteaubriand's *René* and *Atala,* I sought for a monument to Chactas.

Baton Rouge was announced at breakfast and I drove over much of the desolated city. Deserted houses were numerous. Like Natchez, the streets were paved with square, red tiles. Dwellings of the poor were crowded among the business houses. The really impressive object of the then former capital of Louisiana was its ruined State House, standing as evidence of the ravages of the terrible conflict so recently ended. (In 1880, this city was again made the capital of the State.)

The roofless capitol stood upon an eminence at the

A Cypress Swamp on the Mississippi, near New Orleans.

southern end of town, overlooking the broad and placid
river I had followed for weeks and watched its growth
from a brooklet to a thing of majesty. It stood in
grounds filled with blooming shrubs: banana, plantain,
palmetto, magnolia, and box trees spread their foliage
over the paths. The stucco with which the brick structure was covered gave to the ruin the effect of white
marble. It belonged to a school of architecture the examples of which are more beautiful as ruins than
as habitations of men. Not a hillock appears below
Baton Rouge: the bluffs that shone so grandly at
Vicksburg and Natchez have dwindled to nothing.
Sugar plantations are well-nigh continuous from the
mouth of the Red River on the western and Baton
Rouge on the eastern banks, as far south as Pointe-à-la-
Hache, fifty miles below New Orleans. In their rear
are the vast cypress swamps of Louisiana, with their
moss and vine-laden trees of most funereal aspect.

During the night, the *James Howard* tied up at
her wharf, not far from the foot of Canal Street, New
Orleans, but most of her passengers remained aboard
until next day, when, going ashore, I drank water of
Elk Lake, iced for a mint julep of New Orleans.

XII—TO THE SEA AND TO NEW YORK

The steamship *George Cromwell,* Captain Samuel
L. Clapp, did not sail for New York until the following Saturday, leaving four days in which to visit many
interesting places identified with the early history of
the Mississippi's development. Canal Street is as
indelibly associated with the " Crescent City " as
Broadway is with " Gotham." It is a broad, open thor-

oughfare into which a visitor inevitably drifts, no matter
at what point he enters the city. Thereon are its fash-
ionable clubs and one of the best restaurants in all
creation,—the place at which one can obtain real gombo
soup and eat the Creole *papabotte,* or marsh-fed plover.
But the visitor who knows his New Orleans does not
linger on Canal Street: he seeks the French quarter
through Royal Street. Within a few squares of the
busy modern thoroughfare, crowded with all forms of
traffic, he enters a region wherein is yet the eighteenth
century. He has revealed to him the New Orleans of
the Provincial period. Without any stretch of imagination, he can easily fancy himself in the older streets
of Bordeaux. Quaint depots of antiquarians, little
absinthe and wine shops; tobacco factories in hallways
(where one can have a cigar rolled while waiting) ; tiny
furniture warerooms having mysterious yellow or red
paper slips pasted in a corner of their front windows
which mean that lottery tickets are sold " on the side."
There, too, are many quaint Spanish houses, a single
story in height, with their red-tile roofs. The
" quarter " is honeycombed with courtyards that might
be in Southern France or in Spain, veritable *patios*
that lack nothing of Andalusian glamour, even to sparkling fountains. Royal Street was the Faubourg St.
Germain of the Orleans of the Louisiana Province.

Especially did I visit the old St. Louis Hotel
around which all social activities of the Franco-
American city revolved during the first half of the nineteenth century. There duels were arranged; the great
ball of each winter was given there. It was the central
point of " Acadia," as the merry French-Creoles, as late
as the Fifties, understood it. The interior of its cen-

Old State House at Baton Rouge, Burned
during the Civil War.

Old Absinthe House, New Orleans.

tral cupola was frescoed by a nephew and pupil of
Canova; but far more curious to me, as existing evidence of a barbarism from which the Civil War had
so recently freed my country, I walked to the corner
of the rotunda and stepped upon the raised block of
stone between two massive columns that had served
for a generation as an auction-block from which human
beings were sold to the highest bidder! Years afterward, when shown into a slave market at Tangier, a
city of the most debased survival of medieval barbarism, the mental picture of this auction-block at New
Orleans recurred to me. There was the stone, with the
auctioneer's name cut thereon. One had only to close
his eyes to find around him the gilded youths of the
Forties and Fifties, bidding against one another for
this pretty slave or that sinewy field-hand. How easy
to see a graceful octoroon, standing upon that grey
stone, her scantily-clothed, coppery-hued figure framed
between the fluted Corinthian columns, an object of
jibes and rivalry between the members of a group of
brandy-heated libertines!

I strolled into Charles Street, a corridor of balconies,
and to the "*rendezvous des amies de l'art culi-
naire*," an unincorporated organisation that assembles
about four o'clock, every afternoon, at "The Old
Absinthe House," to discuss the latest thought in cooking and, incidentally, to imbibe uncounted glasses of
pale, amber-hued drink,—properly dripped into a gob-
let with a pointed bottom. Not far distant, in Chartres
Street and upon a corner, I was shown the house that
the " pure-blooded " Creoles built for the Exile at St.
Helena, the great Napoleon who had given their land
and themselves to the young Republic. Instead of

effecting the intended rescue and building his house when they had " their Emperor " to occupy it, the hero-worshippers were celebrating their intended benefaction in a noisy revel when word of Napoleon's death, months before, at " Longwood," on his lonely island prison, reached New Orleans.

A visit of reverent sympathy was made to the tomb of Dominique You, the Baratarian pirate who rendered such heroic service to General Jackson on the Plain of Chalmette. It is in need of repair and if the city of New Orleans does not attend to the task, Congress should appropriate money for the purpose.

At eight o'clock on the morning of August 3d, the steamship *George Cromwell* swung from her wharf and headed for the Gulf of Mexico,—the last stage of the Mississippi journey. In mid-stream, aboard an ocean-going craft, the majesty of the great river was felt as not before. Every eye was watching for the Plain of Chalmette, the field upon which the squirrel-hunters of the woods and the smugglers of Barataria defeated British veterans of the Peninsular war. Its site was indicated by an uncompleted shaft. Between Pointe-à-la-Hache,—where a clumsy carpenter is said to have dropped overboard an axe,—and Forts St. Philip and Jackson, the river banks are lined with orange groves. Across the narrow strip of land that restrains the river in its channel below the forts, rarely a mile in width, the Gulf can be plainly seen. Here and throughout lower Louisiana, the people speak of " the coast " of the Mississippi; it is quite improper to say " banks." A panorama of splendid plantations unrolled before us. Reaching the head of the passes, we took the south-west channel to the sea. The bar, one hundred and twenty

The House Built for the Emperor Napoleon.

miles from the " Crescent City," was crossed at 4.30 in the afternoon; the three-pronged delta, having mysterious place upon the famous " Admiral's Map " of unknown authorship, came clearly into view as the mouths of south and north-east passes were reached.

The red-sandstone walls of the frowning but worthless fortress upon the Dry Tortugas were sighted at five o'clock of August 6th, and Key West light appeared at ten the same night. We went through Florida Strait with the onrush of the Gulf Stream at its most constricted point. Along the east coast of the Peninsula, we had the dainty flying-fish and bright-hued nautilus with us as far as Canaveral light. The Gulf Stream, veritable " river in the ocean " and greater in volume than the mighty flood from which I had parted company, was hurrying us northward at a speed of five miles an hour. It was bound for that Haven of Missing Ships, the Sargasso Sea; we for that Port of the Living, New York.

Cape Hatteras, with its resplendent, companionable light, amid the loneliness of that generally storm-tossed part of the Atlantic, was sighted at 8.58 P.M., of the 9th. Thirty hours later, we were at our pier in New York. A trip of more than six thousand miles at an end, the writer was at once asked to and did volunteer for an undertaking far more hazardous than that in which he had been engaged.

CHAPTER XI

The Itasca State Park

THE preservation of the sources of the Mississippi probably grew out of a suggestion made by the late Alfred J. Hill, of Saint Paul, in March, 1889, that the Itasca region be secured by the State of Minnesota and converted into a park. Joseph A. Wheelock, in the Saint Paul *Pioneer Press,* warmly advocated the measure and it was formally brought before the Minnesota Historical Society in 1890 by Emil Geist, of Saint Paul. General John B. Sanborn, a member of the State Senate, was asked to prepare and submit a bill to the Legislature. This act, which met with hearty approval, created " The Itasca State Park, composed of thirty-five square miles of territory at Itasca Lake, for ever dedicated to the public." Under the provisions of the act, Governor William R. Merriam appointed J. V. Brower, First Commissioner of the Itasca State Park. Although Mr. Brower had visited the region in October of 1888, he had not been equipped at that time with instruments for charting the lake. He returned, however, in March, 1889, and measured Itasca on the ice. In 1891, he made a topographical survey, as directed by the special act, and the results of the hydrographic survey of 1889 and of the topographical examination of 1891 were combined in a chart that afterwards became known as a map of the Itasca

The Itasca State Park.

(Map Supplied by the Minnesota Historical Society.)

Strip.   Act of April 14, 1903.

State Park. It is herewith given. Representative J. N. Castle, of Minnesota, introduced a bill in Congress giving to the State of Minnesota all government lands lying within the limits of the park; but despite the promptitude with which the bill became a law, timber-cruisers and lumber companies "located" vast tracts of the territory. These they have largely denuded of timber and some of the splendid forests along the shores of Itasca Lake have been destroyed.

The name of J. V. Brower will always be associated with sturdy efforts made to retain the natural beauties of the Itasca Lake region. He had performed the task for which he was commissioned by his State and the Governor thereof, before the Mississippi Commission took cognisance of the sources of the mighty river. Of great value were the calculations he compiled regarding the elevations of the points upon the river and especially of the large lakes in the Minnesota watershed. He computed the elevation in feet above sea level, at the surface of the stream, to be as follows:

Gulf of Mexico	0.0	Prairie du Chien	597.5
City of Saint Louis	384.8	La Crosse	621.2
Mouth of the Illinois	399.4	Saint Paul	680.5
Hannibal	444.9	Above St. Anthony Fall	782.0
Quincy	453.8	Below Pokegama Fall.	1248.0
Keokuk	472.3	Above Pokegama Fall.	1269.8
Burlington	505.1	Winnebagoshish Lake .	1292.8
Rock Island	533.7	Cass Lake	1302.8
Dubuque	578.2	Itasca Lake	1457.0

Taken in connection with the distances between the localities mentioned, the changes in altitude unmistakably indicate rapid water in many places. The height

of Pokegama Fall is established at 21.8 feet. Mr.
Brower and his assistants gave more than five months
to their work, and the survey made by them would
appear to have been more thorough and satisfactory
than that of Edwin S. Hall, C. E., for the United States
Government, in 1875, when, for the first time, the Itasca
country had any lines run.

Mr. Brower spent many months in compiling his
report. It gives a topographical description of Itasca
Lake, but states that the soundings made were inadequate for an accurate calculation of the cubic gal-
lons of water contained in the lake. Depths of twenty
to thirty-five feet were found in numerous places and
some as great as fifty. The deepest water is off Turn-
bull Point,—the cape that divides the two southern
arms. Mr. Brower's measurement of Itasca Lake upon
the ice gives the following figures: " From the centre
of the channel at the outlet of Itasca, on the surface
of the ice, to the mouth of Chambers Creek, 16,727
feet,"— 3 miles, 887 feet, or about three and one sixth
miles. This is the first actual measurement and is defin-
itive. Mr. Brower adds, on the same page: " There
is no doubt whatever that Elk Lake is supplied to some
extent by waters from the greater ultimate reservoir
bowl by tortuous channels through the ways which
nature in her grandeur has provided." [1]

Itasca Lake varies in width from one sixth to three
quarters of a mile. " Many precipitous hills, covered
with pine timber, nearly surround it," continues the
Commissioner's report.

Among them it is deeply embedded. In places, the shores
are lined with boulders, thickly bordered with overhanging

[1] *Minnesota Historical Society Collections*, vol. vii., p. 259.

flora. At occasional points along the shore, springs of clear, cold water appear, around which cluster balsam, fir, spruce, the native tamarack, willow, aspen, ash, and birch, with pine groves at higher elevations. Drought does not greatly affect the outflow of the lake. The following streams of running water supply the lake with an inflow equalling the outflow; Nicollet's Creek [called by him "the Cradled Hercules"] at the extreme south-west angle; Chambers Creek, the outlet of Elk Lake, at east side of west arm; Mary Creek, at extreme south-east angle; Boutwell Creek, at west side of west arm; Island Creek, on west side, opposite Schoolcraft Island; and Floating Bog Creek, at Floating Bog Bay. The area of Schoolcraft Island is 2.62 acres. A shoal of boulders exists in the main body of the lake, a short distance west by south from the island. There are a series of small lakes extending southward through Mary Valley, from the eastern arm as far as Deming Lake.

Stanley A. McKay, of Owatonna, Minnesota, contributes a statement regarding the outflow of Itasca, which Commissioner Brower has deemed worthy to be included in his report. It is as follows:

It seemed to me beyond question that the volume of water flowing out Itasca Lake was far greater than the combined volume of all its four streams and inlets. If actual measurement prove this to be true,—and it seems to me probable, thus showing that the added volume of the outlet comes from springs in the lake,—would not that leave Itasca as the real source of the Mississippi?

The answer to Mr. McKay's query is that everything depends upon the facts; his theory is based upon an assumption. A decision in the matter ought to be easy of attainment.

Commissioner Brower's latest exploration of the Nicollet Valley and of Nicollet Creek is given herewith in his own words:

Where the stream becomes a part of Itasca Lake, it is forty feet in width and two feet in depth; narrowing as ascended, it was found to be three feet in depth, twenty feet in width, with a brisk current, a short distance from the lake. The character of the locality is a deep valley, somewhat swampy along the stream, with prominent hills on either side, heavily timbered with the native pine. These hills also appear in detached groups in the tamarack and fir thickets, sometimes a hundred feet in height and the pines a hundred feet higher than the hills beneath their stately branches, making the locality easy of access and not difficult to closely examine. Passing up the stream, the explorer is impressed with its importance, as compared with all the other streams found there, by its sharply defined banks, its winding, meandering channel, deeply cut into the stratum to a sandy, gravelly bed, with the appearance and characteristics of the Mississippi below Itasca Lake. It has sandbars, sharp angles in its channel, deep and shallowing currents, and all the striking features of a river. Trees have been felled in several places across its banks to permit of passage on foot (1904). Upon the removal of these trees, canoes might be propelled nearly two miles up this channel from Itasca Lake.

The lines of measurement were extended throughout the entire locality, thereby securing the distances and elevations; lakes were sounded for depth, the streams were measured for width, depth, and flowage, and the topography was carefully taken, even to the extent, when found necessary, of opening passages through the thickets around Nicollet Valley. A line penetrating the wilderness from Morrison Hill, directly to the north shore of Hernando de Soto Lake, discovered the existence and continuance of a spur of the *Hauteurs de Terre*, sharply separating the waters of Nicollet Valley from those of Elk Lake. The lines of measurement, extended to every locality, gave the following results:

From the centre of the channel at the outlet of Itasca Lake to the mouth of Nicollet's Creek, 17,926 feet; thence up the channel to mouth of Demaray Creek, 3797; to Nicollet's lower lake, 2760; to Nicollet's middle lake, 1956; to Nicollet Springs,

Itasca Park Lodge.

A Birdseye View of Itasca Basin.
(Minnesota Historical Society Collection.)

690; to Nicollet's upper lake, 315; to centre of Mississippi Springs, 5265; to north end of Whipple Lake, 1320; and thence to inner flank of the *Hauteurs de Terre* at south shore of Hernando de Soto Lake, 12,060: or a total of 46,089 feet.

Due almost wholly to the enthusiasm, energy, and persistence of the late J. V. Brower, the Itasca State Park is now an established institution. Its area is 19,701.69 acres. Of this, the United States granted 6956.92 acres; the Northern Pacific Railroad Company, 2452.96; two school sections 1280; purchased of Weyerhauser 3191.90; swamp lands 82.67; Great Northern selections 210.16, and acreage in unsuccessful negotiation 5527.08. Since the locality has become easy of access, many tourists visit the Park every summer. A lodge for the entertainment of guests has been built south of the east arm of Itasca, in a fine forest.

CHAPTER XII

Delta of the Mississippi

NO other river delta in the world compares with that of the Mississippi. Geologists assure us that an arm of the Gulf originally extended as far north as Cape Girardeau, Missouri, and that the creation of the present frontier line has been " the slow, calm toil of Nature." This gives to it a stretch across eight and one half degrees of latitude, say one thousand miles!

The Nile delta extends southward from the Mediterranean,—the Sea of All Antiquity,—as far as Helouan, a village ten miles south of Cairo, principally memorable for its fossilised forests. This is one hundred and forty miles distant from the sea. Standing by the great obelisk at Heliopolis,—and the tall monolith is the only evidence extant that a city of a million people once was there,—the writer of this volume realised, recently, that the surface of the Nile delta, in which Heliopolis stands, had been raised twenty-five feet since Sesostris set up the shaft, four thousand years ago. The delta of the Ganges is not so large as that of the Nile.

The made land of the Mississippi's delta averages sixty miles in width, narrowing in places to thirty and expanding at other times to ninety miles. It is widest at the mouth of the Arkansas River, where is the dead

town of Napoleon; and narrowest at Natchez and at
Helena.   Interlocking bayous and channels, navigable
for light-draft steamboats, parallel the Mississippi's
entire course through these thousand miles of soft, alluvial bed.   Every available acre of land is thus brought
into close proximity to navigation,—a characteristic
that renders the mighty American river different from
any other in the world.

Before the completion of the present dyke system,
Colonel Caleb G. Forshay, a distinguished engineer
who devoted many years to the problem of controlling
the waters of the Lower Mississippi, estimated that one
tenth of the delta area was consumed by channels or
water spaces: yet, such was their importance, as means
of inter-communication, that they added assessable
value to the real estate in every State along that part
of the river.

The part of the delta bordering the Gulf of Mexico
contains seven thousand two hundred and thirty-two
square miles of marsh lands.   The fertility of the soil
is apparently inexhaustible.   In the last two latitudinal
degrees of the river's course, rice and sugar are grown
in an abundance and quality not equalled in any other
part of North America.   Sugar-cane is cultivated only
in the Mississippi delta, south of latitude 31 degrees
and 30 minutes.   From that point, northward, for five
degrees, cotton grows in double quantities as compared
with the uplands. Oranges, figs, grapes, apples,
peaches, and other fruits of the semi-tropics and of the
temperate zones are grown in various parts of the delta.
Pecans, most valuable because most marketable of all
nuts, abound over the entire alluvial basin.

This productiveness is universally applicable to all

14

unsubmerged alluvial lands of the Mississippi delta and does not apply exclusively to chosen areas.

Colonel Forshay calculates the productive lands in the basin at 22,920,320 acres. "It is the largest body of equal fertility known to geography," he adds. It is fully twice as large as Egypt, as represented by the Nile valley, delta and the Fayum. In the Mississippi valley, a loss of one crop in five from overflow (a large estimate) leaves to the agriculturist double the product of continuous half crops upon the uplands.

The forests of the delta are remarkable for the large size of their trees and the exuberance of foliage: cypress and oak are the chief varieties, but many other kinds abound. Great festoons of parasitic moss and climbing vines cling to the branches of the trees. While ships were built of wood, live oaks, at the southern section of the delta, supplied angles and braces for the marine of the world. Some cypress swamps have produced as much as fifty thousand feet of lumber to the acre,—not mentioning several hundred yards of moccasin snakes.

I—ITS LEVEES

Prior to the building of levees, the Mississippi always overflowed at 38° 30′ N., and passed into the White Water lakes and swamps connecting with the St. Francis and the Black rivers, whence the flood pursued its course to the White River and Arkansas valleys, through Macon Bayou, thence by the Red and Atchafalaya rivers into the Gulf of Mexico. Often, this overflow did not find its way back into the Mississippi, but formed a parallel, although shallow, channel a thousand miles long. This peculiar geographical feature is only to be likened to the annual overflow of the Amazon and Orinoco rivers, by which they are temporarily united. When Sir Charles Lyell, an English geologist, examined the Mississippi delta, he limited its northern boundary to the head of the Atchafalaya and gave to it an area of thirteen thousand six hundred square miles: but Colonel Forshay fixed its northern limit at three miles below Cape Girardeau, and gave to it an area of thirty-eight thousand seven hundred and thirty-six square miles.

The Nile has subsided every season before the Mississippi begins to run aflood. What is a supreme blessing in Egypt, is in Louisiana gravest of calamities. Millions have been spent at Assuan, at Assiut, and below Cairo to *distribute* the fertilising floods far and wide; in Louisiana, Mississippi, and Arkansas money has been poured out to *restrain* the angry river within its banks.

The fertility of the Mississippi delta is so extraordinary and its climate so salubrious that the rescue of its cultivable lands from submergence by annual floods has engaged the attention of the best engineering ability since an early period in the history of the Republic. During the last half-century, the subject has become a matter of supreme importance to American commercial growth, has commanded the attention of Congress, and has warranted a constant expenditure of enormous sums of money by the States along its banks, as well as by the general government.

The first systematic attempt to control the great river was undertaken at New Orleans in the year 1717, when De la Tour, who had laid out the city, ordered a

dyke built along its river front from Canal Street to
the Esplanade to protect the citizens from overflow.
Planters then began continuing levees along the river.
This constant struggle of man against the elements
continued in a desultory way for a hundred years
and, especially in Louisiana, during three changes of
government. The defence of man against the relentless encroachment lacked organisation. Its weakness
at some points amounted to incapacity; the strength
of the defence was gauged only by the weakest point
and the river proved its might whenever it chose. In
1828, however, the assaulting force grappled the problem seriously. The levees then reached from Pointe-
à-la-Hache below New Orleans to the Red River's
mouth on the west side, a total of four hundred
miles of dykes. The young State of Louisiana had
been aroused to activity by the disastrous flood of that
year. After ten years' continuous labour, the outlets of
the largest bayous were closed. Bayou l'Argent, a
few miles above Natchez and opening into Lake St.
John, and Bullet's Bayou, opening into Lake Concordia, were closed by a parish tax, not by riparian
proprietors. The filling up of these two bayou con-
nections with the river marks the beginning of State
and national reclamation.

The rescue of the Concordia plantations from the
grasp of the Mississippi River is a historical event,
remembered and celebrated from one end of the delta
to the other.

One by one, Bryan's Bayou, Alligator Bayou, and
River Styx, leading into Lake St. Joseph; Bayou Vidal
leading to Tensas; and Providence Bayou, communicating with Lake Providence, were sealed up. Before

the advent of the great flood of 1844, every old river
lake for six hundred miles up the right bank of the
Mississippi was cut off from the river's overflow. No
braver struggle between man and nature ever was made.

The next step was an effort on the part of the
Louisiana Legislature to secure aid from the general
government. This took the form of a memorial from
the former body in the winter of 1849 praying the
Congress of the United States for aid to protect the
people and property of the Mississippi delta against
inundations. The government had many thousand
acres of unsold land in the delta and Congress acted
with promptitude. A survey of the delta by United
States engineers was ordered. To assist the States, the
unsold government swamp lands were given to the
various States. In 1853, after the several States in
interest had formed a combination for mutual protection, the national government practically took charge
of the work.

According to Humphreys and Abbott, the levee
line was completed on the eastern bank from Pointe-à-
la-Hache to Baton Rouge; thence for two hundred
miles, until Vicksburg is reached, the mighty river im-
pinges upon bluffs which serve as nature's own dykes.
The line was finished from Vicksburg north to Horn
Lake at the Mississippi State line, in which section the
largest outlet grappled with anywhere along the river
up to that time, Yazoo Pass, was closed. From that
point to the northern end of the delta only short
stretches of dykes were required.

The problem on the western bank was an almost
equally serious one. Before the government took hold,
the line of the defence against floods had been com-

pleted through Louisiana and along the Arkansas shore nearly to the mouth of the Arkansas River. Above that point, the river front of Arkansas and Missouri required only forty miles of levee,—due to high banks.

When this work was thoroughly in hand, the Civil War burst upon the country in 1861. All work stopped. Spades were laid aside for muskets. Instead of using sand bags for stopping crevasses in the levees, men piled them into breastworks for protection from bullets. The amount of levee destruction due to military necessity during the four years of conflict never can be accurately calculated. Within a few weeks of the surrender at Appomattox, the States of Louisiana and Mississippi began repairing the most important breaks in levees along their banks. In many places, due to changes in the river's course, levees have been destroyed and rebuilt thrice since 1865. In Louisiana alone, the amount of filling necessary to stay the encroachments of the river, for the five years immediately following the close of the war, amounted to 8,135,656 cubic yards and cost $4,881,936. Louisiana issued during that time,—according to O. D. Bragdon,—$8,134,000 in Levee Bonds.

The Mississippi has tributaries that surpass the greatest rivers of Europe. It discharges into the Gulf of Mexico one half more water than do the Rhine, Loire, Po, Elbe, Vistula, Danube, Dnieper, Don, and Volga into the ocean and lake front of Europe. Its flow past New Orleans is equal to that of the Indus, Euphrates and Ganges combined; about twice as much as the Nile; equals that of the Rio de la Plata, and is surpassed by the Amazon. Unlike the floods of the Nile and the Ganges, which occur annually and with chronological precision, the Mississippi risings are irregular as to time and magnitude. The flood of 1882 exceeded all previous ones and still holds the high-water record. Theoretically, the Missouri ought to be the determining factor and generally does supply the greatest volume of superfluous water; but the freaks of the Ohio, assisted by the Cumberland and Tennessee rivers, are very curious. When floods of large proportions arrive simultaneously from the north and east at the meeting point, Cairo, a rise of forty to fifty feet has occurred and the mighty river expands to a width of ten to sixty miles. "It would seem as if the sea had again returned to its own," comments Robert Stewart Taylor, a student of flood phenomena. He has prepared exhaustive data on the levee system of the Mississippi from which we arrive at an estimate of the menace to agriculture by these floods. The area of rich, tillable land so threatened, he places at 10,000,000 acres. Of this area, 2,000,000 acres belong to the corn belt, extending from Commerce to the Washita River; 6,000,000 acres are in the cotton belt, between the Red and Washita rivers; and 2,000,000 acres are in the sugar and rice belts, extending from the Red River to the Gulf. Were these lands secure from overflow, they have a productive capacity of 60,000,000 bushels of corn, 4,000,000 bales of cotton (500 pounds each), 2,000,000,000 pounds of sugar, and 1,000,000,000 pounds of rice. "Up to date," says Mr. Taylor in a recent article on this subject, "less than one third of these possibilities have been realised." This would indicate that the general government and the States of the Mississippi Valley cannot expend too much money for the construction and maintenance of levees.

The Mississippi Commission was created by an act of Congress three years before the disastrous flood of 1882, but it did not bestir itself until after that calamity had aroused the energies of the entire country, looking to the protection of the lowlands of Mississippi, Arkansas, and Louisiana.   The Commission consists of three United States engineers, two officers of the Coast and Geodetic Survey, and three civilians, eight members. It has expended from one to four million dollars annually in maintaining the dykes.   Since 1882, the States bordering upon the mighty flood route to the sea have spent $18,000,000 and the government $16,000,000, in fending off the Mississippi along 1300 miles of levees. A continuous system to-day extends from New Madrid to St. Francis, 200 miles; an unbroken dyke incloses the Yazoo Basin, north of Vicksburg, 300 miles; another line from Arkansas City to the mouth of the Red River, 331 miles; another from the Red River to Fort Jackson, 274 miles; and, on the east bank, another from Baton Rouge to Fort St. Philip, 193 miles.   There are many smaller sections, especially at the mouths of tributaries.   Chief success has been attained in the lowest third of the river.

" There was a time, ages ago, when an estuary extended from the Gulf of Mexico to the hills above Cairo," says Robert Stewart Taylor, specialist on the levee problem.[1]

If the relative elevations of sea and land were as they are now, the Mississippi River ended in a waterfall three hundred feet high, at the head of that bay and near the site of the present town site of Commerce. A few miles eastward, the Ohio, the Cumberland, and the Tennessee leaped from similar

[1] " The Levee Problem," *Forum*, vol. xxiv., 325.

elevations into the same abyss. With this enormous down-pour came the sand, clay, and loam, scoured from a million square miles of watershed,—with which the estuary of the Mississippi has been filled and from which has been formed its present alluvial delta. Into this basin has been gathered the cream of the Continent, a hundred feet deep and having an area of twenty-nine thousand square miles.

Generals Humphreys and Abbott have made elabo-rate calculations as to the annual soil-waste caused by the Mississippi and its tributaries, which show that the river carries into the Gulf over 400,000,000 tons of solid matter, in addition to large quantities of earth salts, in solution, and of sand, or other coarse material swept along its bottom. In a recent article [1] intended to ex-plain why the riches of American farms take wings, Emerson Hough comments on the Humphreys and Abbott conclusions:

At the time of these determinations [he says], settlement in the Mississippi Valley was comparatively limited, and, as shown by local observations on different rivers, the effect of extending agriculture has been to *increase* the soil-matter car-ried by the Mississippi *fully twenty-five per cent.* Ninety per cent. of the matter transported by the waters consists of rich soil-stuff washed from the surface or leached from the subsurface of fields and pastures and (in less degree) of woodlands. Reckoned on the basis of value as fertiliser, the material could hardly be appraised at less than one dollar per ton; so that the annual loss to the agricultural interests of the country can hardly fall short of a billion dollars—equivalent to an impost as great as most other taxes com-bined, and one yielding *absolutely no return.*

The watery inhabitants of the Lower Mississippi

[1] "The Waste in Mud," by Emerson Hough, *Saturday Evening Post*, March 27, 1909.

possess marked peculiarities. The alligator is not found north of the Yazoo. He frequents the bayous of Arkansas and Louisiana,—especially those of Plaquemines parish,—in preference to the main channel. His fear of man, dread of the porpoise, curious night trips ashore, the toughness of his hide, the tremendous strength of his tail, the ease with which the saurian is called to the surface by an imitation of the bark of a dog or squeal of a pig, his slow growth and longevity of three hundred years are noteworthy. The bellow of the alligator is heard only in stormy nights.[1]

Land crabs, or "fiddlers," are the foes of levee builders. The banks are sometimes covered with these crustaceans. They possess a single claw, instead of two, sometimes upon the right and sometimes upon the left side, which they throw up as a menace.

In the Mississippi is the garpike, which Hugh Miller declares "has remained to unlock the marvels of the ichthyology of the remotest periods of geologic history appropriated to the fish dynasty." It is half fish and half reptile. A coat of mail, composed of bony plates, from which a steel will strike fire, covers it. It has two rows of teeth, one reptilian and one piscatorial, and an air bladder upon which it can draw when out of water. Lyell says of the garpike: "He can hurt anything and nothing can hurt him."

II—THE JETTIES

For more than two generations, there has been open war between man and nature at the outlets

[1] See an article on this subject by James A. Noyes, *Putnam's Magazine*, 1868.

The Mississippi River at the Head of the Passes.

of the Mississippi. The Gulf Stream sweeps past the three mouths of the mighty river and phenomena not found elsewhere on the globe exist there. Of these, the most remarkable are the mud lumps that often rose in front of a navigator while he was waiting at the bar for high tide. These mud volcanoes were the dread of pilots, ancient and modern: they were " the evil genii of the Passes."

Soon after the close of the Civil War, Captain James B. Eads began a study of conditions at the mouths of the Mississippi. His first great undertaking associated with that river was the building of a steel and iron bridge at Saint Louis; but when that enterprise was fairly under way, he turned his attention to providing an assured depth of thirty feet at the outlet of the river. Three distinguished government engineers, Gen. A. A. Humphreys, Capt. H. L. Abbott, and Major C. W. Howell, strenuously opposed Eads. Major Howell had proposed a canal from the Mississippi, at a point three miles below Fort St. Philip, to Breton Sound, whence a five-fathom channel, running southward to deep water, already existed. The canal would have had to have a lock, the capacity of which would not exceed twenty-four vessels per day. Captain Eads contended that jetties could be built for one half the cost of the canal. He maintained the contest for several years and finally won. He contracted to build jetties at South Pass for $11,000,000 and to maintain them for nine years, payment to be made when success was assured.

In 1875, Congress authorised the late James B. Eads to construct jetties at South Pass, by which the fourteen miles of channel was to be straightened and increased to a depth of twenty-six feet of water. The work was placed under the immediate direction of E. L. Corthell, C. E., and was completed with entire success. The actual cost was $8,021,740.87.

In one of his memorials to Congress, Captain Eads stated his theory about the delta problem. " The Mississippi is simply a transporter of solid matter to the sea, chiefly sand and alluvion held in suspension by the mechanical effect of the current," says Captain Eads. " A certain velocity gives to the stream ability of holding in suspension a proportionate quantity of solid matter; and when thus charged, the stream can sustain no more,—hence will carry off no more,—and therefore cannot wear away its bottom or banks, no matter how directly the current may impinge against them." This was new hydraulics; it flew in the face of accepted theories.

" The Gulf does not present a barrier to the outward flow because less friction exists in walls of water than between banks of earth," argued Captain Eads.

At the bar, the river flows between banks of salt water and over a bottom of brine instead of mud. No longer having a descent of a few inches to the mile, it must maintain its current in the Gulf simply by acquired momentum. Friction finally brings it to a state of rest, when a spreading out movement begins. The tides in the Gulf are feeble, averaging less than fourteen inches in height.

Jetties are simply dykes or levees under water, and act as banks to the river to prevent its expansion and diffusion as it enters the sea. Where the banks of a river extend boldly into the ocean a bar never exists. In delta forming rivers, they are always found.

Captain Eads reasoned that if bars result from the

The Mouth of South Pass, Showing Eads Jetties.

diffusion of the alluvium-laden river water, fan-like, after entering the sea, the remedy was to prevent such diffusion. An examination of the passes showed a narrow and uniform width of channel until a point within seven miles of the bar, the latter being three miles beyond land's end. The Mississippi was extending its own banks into the Gulf "at the rate of eight to nine inches per day"! Eads decided that the bar would not continue to advance seaward if jetties were constructed. The river averaged sixty feet in depth between the bar and the city of New Orleans; but on the bar, it rapidly shoaled to twelve and seventeen feet. This was the problem Captain Eads grappled at South Pass. He tried for a deep, open, permanent outlet, without locks, agreed to maintain the jetties for nine years, and they were not to be paid for then unless entirely successful. The terms of the contract showed the confidence of the engineer in his theories. The achievement was one of the most brilliant in modern engineering.

The jetties were formed by layers of brush mattresses, weighted with forty to fifty pounds of broken stone to the square foot and capped with a heavy concrete wall. Up to the level of mean high water, the jetty-structure consisted of tiers of mattresses two feet in thickness, made of willow brush, held together by a top and bottom framework of yellow pine, and braced at the sides with three-by-six-inch timber. These mattresses were in two hundred feet lengths and varied in width from ninety-five feet for bottom layers to thirty-five feet at the top. The isolated position of the work necessitated the construction of quarters for the workmen, and thus the town of Port Eads came into existence. A flotilla of tugs and barges was employed in bringing materials and provisions from New Orleans.

Although the initial experiment of the Eads system of improving the Mississippi's entrance to the sea was tried at South Pass,—primarily because official influence was strong enough to prevent the test at South-west Pass—complete success of the concessionaire compelled the adoption of the same methods for the latter. Increase in the draft of ocean steamships and the prospective completion of the Panama Canal, which will bring New Orleans into direct communication with the commerce of the Far East, counselled the creation of a channel of thirty-five feet depth. The contract for the improvement of South-west Pass was awarded to Christie & Lowe of Chicago. Mr. Cornelius Donovan, United States Assistant Engineer, supervised the construction. The Eads system of willow mattresses and broken stone, with concrete capping, was employed. The two jetties, 17,000 feet long on the eastern bank and 11,000 feet on the western, were completed in the spring of 1908. The quantities of materials used in the construction were 1,085,830 square yards of mattress, 337,426 tons of rip-rap stone—brought from Birmingham, Alabama,—and 44,511 cubic yards of concrete. The contractors were paid $2,629,360.35.

This achievement converted New Orleans into one of the deep-water ports of the world.

North-east Pass is in the hands of United States engineers, not with a view to rendering it navigable for ocean steamships but as a chute for carrying off surplus water during floods. It had a formidable crevasse, opening directly into the Gulf. Into this was dumped thousands of tons of concrete blocks and broken stone.

A ditch, three feet wide in 1872, afterwards widened to 2230 feet! A closure was made in 1898 by a dam 6600 feet long; but on the night of its completion, one of the worst storms known to the coast carried away 170 feet of the dam, which breach had widened by June, 1907, to 1029 feet. The break has since been closed and is under permanent control.

CHAPTER XIII

Joining the Great River to the Great Lakes

AGITATION for the creation of a deep-water route from the Great Lakes to the Mississippi and thence to the Gulf of Mexico has taken definite shape since the completion of the Chicago Drainage Canal, uniting Lake Michigan with the Illinois River. That enterprise was carried through solely by the city of Chicago, at an expense of $50,000,000, and that populous and enterprising municipality is willing to contribute its canal if the national government will guarantee the maintenance of a fourteen-foot channel from Chicago to the sea.

The Chicago Drainage Canal extends from the mouth of Chicago River to within sight of Joliet Lake, below Lockport: it is navigable the entire distance of thirty-six miles by vessels drawing twenty feet of water. Much of the distance was through solid rock, a soft limestone. In offering this splendid improvement to the government, Chicago stipulates that a fourteen-foot channel be maintained in the Illinois and Mississippi rivers to Saint Louis. Army engineers report that such a channel which will be easy of maintenance can be constructed for $31,000,000. Congress has instructed the Mississippi River Commission to make a survey and estimate of the cost for continuing the channel from Saint Louis to New Orleans. This plan to connect the Great Lakes with the Mississippi, through which the sea can be reached, is equal in importance to the construction of the Panama Canal. Better internal water communication is imperative to meet the growing demands for more prompt transportation at periods of railroad congestion. Proof of the value and earning capacity of such a deep water canal as proposed is seen in the splendid success of the Sault Ste. Marie Canal, connecting Lakes Superior and Huron, the freight traffic through which exceeds fifty-five million tons annually. According to Representative Joseph E. Ransdell, of Louisiana, " The total cost of government improvements on the Great Lakes has been about $70,000,000, and the saving on the commerce through the ' Soo ' alone in one year (1905) was nearly two and one half times as much as the entire cost of all our improvements on the lake system." [1]

The total cost of the projected improvements that will enable steamships of fourteen-foot draught to deliver grain loaded at Duluth or Chicago at Havana, Colon, or Liverpool will exceed $100,000,000,—a sum which the State of New York is expending to provide a barge canal from Lake Erie through the Hudson to the metropolis. The problem from Lockport to the mouth of the Missouri, which enters the Mississippi twenty odd miles below the confluence of the Illinois River, is comparatively simple; but the route below that point presents many difficulties. The Missouri carries so much soil that fifteen feet of silt are often deposited in one place during a year. The channel below Saint Louis has an average depth of eight to nine feet, but

[1] Speech of Joseph E. Ransdell in House of Representatives, Jan. 31, 1907.

it is constantly shifting. Sand-bars created in a year are often carried away in a week's time. Dredging in such places is useless. Therefore, it is evident that the difficulties of maintaining a deep waterway between Saint Louis and Natchez, at which point the river becomes deep enough for battleships (as recently shown by a visit of the *Mississippi* to that city), surpass those presented by the Panama Canal. They are not insurmountable, however, if we may believe statements of competent engineers.

While President of the United States, Theodore Roosevelt took an active interest in all plans to improve transportation facilities throughout the Mississippi Valley. In one of his memorable addresses, during his triumphant trip down the mighty river, he said:

The valley of the Mississippi is politically and commercially more important than any other valley on the face of the globe. Here, more than anywhere else, will be determined the future of the United States, and, indeed, of the whole western world; and the type of civilisation reached in this mighty valley, in this vast stretch of country lying between the Alleghanies and the Rockies, the Great Lakes and the Gulf, will largely fix the type of civilisation for the whole western hemisphere.

Twenty-two States are included in the Mississippi Basin. They comprise forty per cent. of the total area of the United States and produce seventy-five per cent. of its exports. The bulk of our agricultural products, nearly two thirds of our manufacturing industries, and about ten billion dollars' worth of finished merchandise come from its valley. Until recently, railroads have been able to keep pace with its transportation demands, but such has been the development during

Cotton Staves and Steamboats at the Levee, New
Orleans.

(Courtesy of M. B. Trezevant.)

the past decade that traffic must again seek the water-ways belonging to the arterial system of this mammoth river. A fourteen-foot channel from Saint Louis to New Orleans would go farther to relieve the entire Middle West and South-west than any other national improvement that could be undertaken. With such a depth of water a single powerful towboat would carry from thirty to forty train-loads.

Systematic plans for improving the navigation of the upper Mississippi by deepening its channels were inaugurated in 1902 at Quincy, Illinois. A convention of representatives from every city and town between Saint Paul and Saint Louis was held and " The Upper Mississippi River Improvement Association " took form. The second meeting was held at Dubuque. The River and Harbour Committee of the House of Repre-sentatives is asked at each session of Congress to appro-priate money to procure and maintain a navigable channel of six feet, at low water. Excessive railroad freights will restore the steamboat to pre-eminence. The lumber business of the North is almost at an end: lumber is now shipped North from southern pine dis-tricts, and the consumers on the upper river are clamorous to bring it by water. Opinion is that the Mississippi must at no distant day again bear the burden of a mighty internal commerce. Precedent is found in France, where hundreds of millions of francs have been spent in internal waterways. Commerce that uses these improvements is created by them. Al-though it exceeds in volume the maritime commerce of the Republic, railway traffic has steadily grown, de-spite competition. Americans must remember that the areas of the five States preaching this propaganda for

Mississippi improvement are almost twice that of France.

The Mississippi steamboat traffic of to-day is largely coal from the Ohio River and its tributaries. There was a period in the history of the West when the great river from New Orleans to Saint Paul was crowded with steamboats carrying thousands of passengers and many thousand tons of freight. The railroads have destroyed that industry.

The first steamboat to plough the waters of the Mississippi was built at Pittsburg in 1810, by Nicholas J. Roosevelt, great-great-granduncle of ex-President Roosevelt, backed by Robert R. Livingston and Robert Fulton. She was a stern-wheeler, one hundred and sixteen feet long and twenty feet beam, named *New Orleans.* She had two masts and was painted sky blue! She cost $38,000. Starting from Pittsburg, September 24, 1811, she reached Natchez on December 24th and New Orleans on January 10, 1812. The actual running time was two hundred and fifty-nine hours, the speed being seven and one half miles an hour, with the current. This boat never attempted to ascend the river farther than Natchez. After use as a packet between New Orleans and that city, she ran on a snag and sank.

Fifty-nine steamboats were engaged in traffic on the Mississippi and Ohio by 1819, most of them built at Ohio River towns. The *Zebulon M. Pike,* a boat of thirty-seven tons, was first to ascend the Mississippi above the mouth of the Ohio, touching at Saint Louis on August 2, 1817. The *Independence,* built at Pittsburg in 1818, was the first steamboat to stem the strong current of the Missouri, ascending it to Boonsville, two hundred miles above the river's mouth, in May, 1819. In the same year, the *Western Engineer,* seventy-five feet long, ascended the Missouri to Council Bluffs, six hundred and fifty miles from Saint Louis by the river course. In 1823, the *Virginia* first ascended by steam to Fort St. Anthony (afterwards known as Fort Snelling).

Steamboating on the Mississippi reached its culminating point a short time before the Civil War. On the upper river, the maximum was attained in 1857, with ninety-nine steamboats landing at Saint Paul: but they chiefly carried freight, as the passenger arrivals at the outpost of civilisation were only nine hundred and sixty-five, or less than ten passengers to a trip. The maximum of steamboat traffic on the lower river is found in New Orleans records for the year ending August, 1860, which show 3245 arrivals from river ports, 785 from sea ports; $289,565,000 in value of the river commerce received and despatched, and $183,-725,000 of ocean imports and exports. The Ohio River was always the largest traffic feeder.

Any account of Mississippi steamboat traffic would be incomplete without mention of the historic race from New Orleans to Saint Louis, between the *Robert E. Lee* and the *Natchez* in 1870. I heard the story thus:

Captain T. P. Leathers, of the *Natchez,* a Cincinnati built boat, made the trip from New Orleans to Saint Louis, one thousand two hundred and seventy-eight miles up-stream, in three days, twenty-one hours and fifty-eight minutes. He arrived on June 24, 1870, and wired the fact to Captain John W. Cannon, commander of the *Robert E. Lee,* a New Albany built craft and rival of the *Natchez.* Cannon knew it was a

challenge and began to prepare for the return of the *Natchez*.
He lightened the *Lee* in every possible way and arranged for
coal barges to be anchored in mid-stream at various points
along the river. He refused all freight or passengers.

The *Natchez* returned to the Crescent City, took several
hundred tons of freight and a few passengers, and started for
Saint Louis at five o'clock, June 30th. The *Lee* swung into
the stream at the same moment. Captain Leathers had been
informed of the preparations of the *Lee's* commander. It was
a race from the start! At first, only the people of the Mississippi Valley looked on; but before the end of twenty-four
hours, the entire population of the United States was following telegraphic accounts of the contest. The *Lee* gained
slightly every hundred miles. At Natchez, three hundred
miles from the starting point, she was ten minutes ahead,
because the *Natchez* had made two landings for coal and
wood.

At the Vicksburg bend, although the two boats were ten
miles apart by the river's course, their smoke commingled.
More people stood upon the shore at Helena than at any time
since De Soto was there! Forty thousand men, women, and
children watched the steamers pass Memphis without making
a landing. The *Natchez* had cut down the *Lee's* lead, because Leathers had adopted Cannon's method of taking fuel;
but in the bend near Island No. 10 she ran aground and
lost six hours! The *Lee* arrived at Saint Louis only thirty-
three minutes ahead of the previous record of the *Natchez!*
Captain Cannon was "lionised," although opinion ever will
be divided regarding the relative speeds of the two boats.
The South was not rich in those days; but more than
$1,000,000 changed hands in the Mississippi Valley on the
result of that race.

CHAPTER XIV

The Age of Water

STEAMBOAT traffic upon the Mississippi and its tributaries almost disappeared toward the end of the nineteenth century. Railroads paralleled these great rivers, reached the towns upon their banks, and, until the extraordinary crops of 1906, were able to carry the products of the earth from farmer to consumer and to return to the former such merchandise, machinery, or food as he needed. Suddenly, as appeared, the utter inadequacy of the railroads for the purpose of moving that great crop was demonstrated. Congestion existed in every part of the country. It was not confined to any particular locality. There were not cars enough upon which to load the mountains of accumulated freight; there were not locomotives sufficient to draw the miles of cars filled to their utmost carrying capacity; there were not new rails in existence, adequate for doubling the trackage of existing lines; men were not to be spared from other activities to mine the iron ore, to smelt it, or to lay the steel rails after they were rolled. Terminals for the proper handling of the enormous quantities of freight were utterly inadequate. The amount of capital invested in the railroad systems of the United States had grown to $17,000,000,000, and every dollar so invested had added ten dollars to the wealth of the country. "More

railroads, more engines, more cars, more terminal area!"
was the cry; but as wise a man as James J. Hill at
once showed that the money necessary to provide present relief—at least $5,000,000,000—could not be de-
voted to that work without paralysing other branches
of business. He further demonstrated that were the
rails ready, the men at hand to lay them, and the engines and cars built, the relief would only be temporary.
Therefore, the master minds in railroad transportation
were among the first to point to a necessary resumption
of river traffic. H_2O again came to the fore!

The agitation broke out sporadically in various parts
of the country. New York State was digging a barge
canal from the Hudson to Lake Erie. Chicago had
completed a drainage canal, primarily to carry the almost stagnant waters of Chicago Creek into the Illinois
River and thence to the Mississippi, in order that the
sewerage-laden stream should not flow into Lake Michigan and infect the city's drinking water. Consideration
for the health of the people of Saint Louis, who took
their water from the Mississippi, was overlooked in the
enthusiasm of those who prosecuted the splendid enterprise. But the size and efficiency of the canal, when
water began to flow through its broad channel, suggested a deep-water highway from the Great Lakes
to the Mississippi and thence to the Gulf of Mexico.

Delegates and representative business men from all
parts of the Middle West assembled in convention at
Saint Louis in November, 1906, and formed the Lakes-
to-Gulf Deep Waterway Association. This organisation sent a representative committee to Washington
in December of the same year, urging upon the President and members of both Houses of Congress the

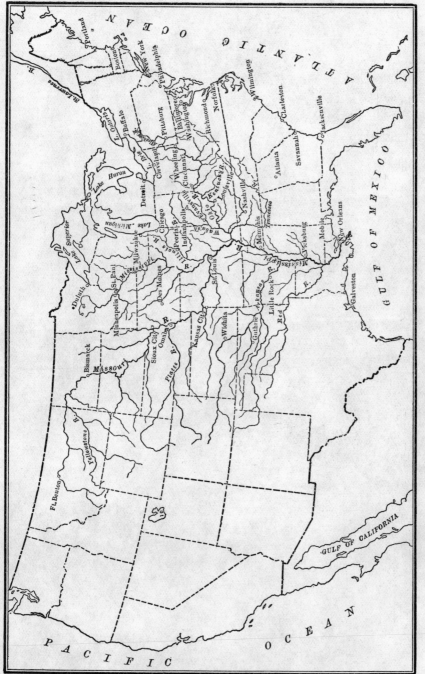

Outline Map of the United States, Showing the Mississippi and its Watershed.

creation of a Commission " to prepare and to report a comprehensive plan for the improvement and control of the Mississippi River system and other inland waterways in such manner that the rivers of the country may be fully utilised for navigation and other industrial purposes." Every city of importance in the Mississippi Valley memorialised the President or Congress and on March 14, 1907, Theodore Roosevelt created the present Inland Waterways Commission of nine members. He said, in part:

In creating this Commission, I am influenced by broad considerations of national policy. Our inland waterways, as a whole, have thus far received scant attention. It is becoming clear that our streams should be considered and conserved as great natural resources. The time has come for merging local projects and uses of the inland waters in a comprehensive plan designed for the benefit of the entire country. The task is a great one, yet it is certainly not too great for us to approach. The results which it seems to promise are even greater. The present congestion affects chiefly the people of the Mississippi Valley, and they demand relief. When the congestion of which they complain is relieved, the whole country will share the good results. . . . It is not possible to frame so large a plan for the control of our rivers without taking account of the orderly development of other natural resources. The cost necessarily will be large, but it will be small in comparison with the billions of capital now invested in steam railways.

The Commission began active work in the spring of 1908, by inspection trips through the Great Lakes and down the Mississippi, being accompanied from Keokuk to Memphis by President Roosevelt, in what proved to be one of the most triumphal pageants ever seen in this country.

Previously, in May of the same year, had occurred the memorable Conference of Governors at the White House. This convocation had grown out of a suggestion made by William George Jordan, a young New York newspaper man. Its influence in awakening the American people to the importance of conserving the natural resources of the broad territory was momentous. Another step was the creation of a National Conservation Commission which prepared a three-volume report, that is by far the most complete summary of the resources of the United States ever collected.

Such were the beginnings of the campaign that signalises the entrance upon an Age of Water. Great steamers will reappear upon our broad rivers and an industry that seemed dead for ever will be revived in more than original splendour.

Mr. W J McGee, Secretary of the Inland Waterways Commission, has compiled some startling figures to show the immensity of the transportation problem, as it exists at present in the United States. There are in the United States 26,200 miles of navigable rivers, Mr. McGee estimates, and 2800 miles of canals in operation (with nearly as much more inoperative or abandoned), which in 1904 carried respectively, 127,000,000 and 5,000,000 tons of freight. There are 222,500 miles of railway which, during 1906, carried 1,631,374,219 tons.

That is to say, although the United States has a more extensive and better distributed natural system of inland waterways than any other country, and despite the fact that water carriage costs on the average only a third or a fourth as much as rail carriage, less than one ninth of our freight lines are waterways, and only one twelfth of our commodities are carried by water. And of our aggregate assets of say $107,000,-000,000, our steam railways have risen to $18,000,000,000, or about one sixth, which even at first sight seems out of proportion; and the disproportion becomes still more glaring when current production is compared with railway earnings—the former in 1906 reaching $7,000,000,000 to $10,000,000,000 (according to mode of estimate of farm products) and the latter $2,325,765,167, or fully one fourth as much. The case is clear; we are employing extravagant agencies and paying exorbitant rates for transportation; the prices of our staples depend too little on cost of production, too largely on cost of carriage.[1]

According to careful estimates, two hundred trillion cubic feet of rain descends annually upon the two billion acres of " Uncle Sam's " mainland farm. Again quoting Commissioner McGee, than whom no better authority on this subject exists, " Nominally, land sells by the acre or front foot; but, actually, the price, within ten per cent., is fixed by the associated water." Of course, the statist refers, primarily, to land used for agricultural purposes; but his statement is quite correct, even when applied to the greatest of our cities. New York, for example, owes everything it is to the sea. Without the hydrosphere that surrounds the earth, there would not be any ocean or rivers. Therefore, there would not be any New York, with some of its land selling as high as $400 a square foot. "The two hundred trillion cubic feet, or ten Mississippis, of annual rainfall is, in verity, the sole effective capital of the country," continues the Commissioner.

Without it, the land would be desert, devoid of tree or shrub or other living thing. Say five eights of this rainfall is evaporated to temper climate, form dews, and redescend

[1] Commissioner W J McGee, in *Popular Science Monthly*, April, 1908.

elsewhere. A fifth goes down to the sea in rivers. An eighth is stored for a time as ground water. The remaining twentieth, or half a Mississippi's volume, is stored or used in the onto-sphere,—meaning in the living structures and functions of animals and plants. The time of storage is short: an animal may survive a week, a humid-land annual plant six weeks, or a tree six months, without renewed supply. Springs fail, and brooks run dry under a three months' drought. Had we a rainless year, half the lesser rivers of America would dry up. At the end of seven such successive years, the Mississippi would cease to flow; within ten years, the lake-fed St. Law-rence would be no more. The days of witchcraft and mystery, about water are ended. Science has risen to show that the sources of spring and well and brook and river, of flowing sap and pulsing blood are the life-giving benediction of the clouds.

There is found the " true source " of the Mississippi.

Keokuk.
(From a Daguerreotype, 1847.)

CHAPTER XV

The Mississippi in War

PRACTICALLY, every mile of " The Father of Waters," from Itasca Lake to Natchez, has been fought over by antagonistic aboriginal tribes. Except near the Mississippi's mouth and in Minnesota, conflicts between natives and white men have been of small importance. Early Spanish adventurers, seeking gold and finding it not, vented their disappointments upon the natives; their inhuman conduct is chiefly responsible for the deadly hatred displayed by the Indian toward the invaders of his hunting grounds and the destroyers of his villages. Pledges of good faith made by the strangers were generally broken, and in nearly every way the white man fixed the standard for treachery that the red man adopted. Tales of Spanish brutalities passed from tongue to tongue, through many different native languages and dialects, losing nothing in repetition, up the length of the mighty river and thence, through the Red River of the North, as far as the ice-bound coast of Hudson Bay.

The anthropoid of the copper-hued countenance devoted three centuries, a brief space according to his spare mind, to " getting even " with the pale-faced intruder.

I—STRUGGLES WITH THE INDIANS

The French in the North-west tried the blandishments of religion and of cajolery. The effect of the great feast given by Radisson in the country of the Illinois endured for several generations. The example of patience under such afflictions as famine and pestilence was most salutary. Crude, untutored minds comprehended that bravery was not entirely confined to the war-path and battle-field. The savages saw pale, thin-visaged priests come among them, alone and unarmed, and they recognised the sublimity of a faith that sustained them. They marked the difference between the religion of the Spaniard and that of the French-Canadian.

Largely due to the Spaniards who had preceded him, Iberville, a French-Canadian military and naval commander, sent to Louisiana in 1699, built Fort Biloxi and a fort upon the Mississippi; but he paid a visit to the Natchez with Tonty and left the country without taking the life of a single native. Bienville, who succeeded him, and was in turn followed by Cadillac, was sent by the latter to attack the same tribe. This developed what is known in history as the first Natchez war. The pretext for the expedition was the murder of four Frenchmen by the Natchez, and Bienville started with less than sixty soldiers and boatmen to make reprisal on a tribe of eight hundred warriors! Cadillac hoped for Bienville's defeat, for he had refused to marry the Governor's daughter,—he, a Canadian adventurer, although for a time Governor of Louisiana province, had rejected an alliance with the proud French family of Cadillac! Bienville employed diplomacy, which is another word for falsehood. He went to an island occupied by the Tunicas, not far from the Natchez, and sent word that he desired to

Battle Hollow, the Scene of Black Hawk's Defeat.

Photo. by E. J. Hall, Oak Park, Ill.

locate a mill or factory in the Natchez country. The chiefs of the latter tribe were suspicious but were finally persuaded to visit Bienville. The latter had sent boatmen past the Natchez capital, in the darkness of night, to post upon the trees *affiches* of warning to all Frenchmen descending the Mississippi. These untruthfully stated: "The Natchez have declared war against the French, and M. de Bienville is encamped at the Tunicas."

The Natchez chiefs arrived at Bienville's headquarters on May 8, 1716. When the calumet was offered to him, Bienville declined and demanded reparation for the murder of the Frenchmen. The chiefs were greatly surprised, supposing that the French Governor at New Orleans was uninformed of the tragedy. The envoys were put in chains. At nightfall, Bienville sent for the principal chief, "Great Sun" and his two brothers, "The Stung Serpent" and "Little Sun," and told them he would spare their lives on condition that the heads, not merely the scalps, of the murderers of the four Frenchmen were delivered to him. "Blood for blood!" he exclaimed. "I am known as 'The Arrow of Uprightness' and 'The Tomahawk of Justice.'" It was agreed that "Little Sun" should return to the Natchez and secure the heads of the murderers. He came back with three heads, but confessed that the principal culprit had fled into the forest; his head not being obtainable, that of his brother had been brought, instead. Bienville was not satisfied.

In the meantime, twenty-two Frenchmen and Canadians, descending the river, had seen Bienville's proclamations and had joined him. This brought his fighting strength to seventy-two men. The Tunicas gave information of an intended attack by the Natchez, to release their chiefs. The Tunicas offered forty braves; but Bienville, fearing treachery, declined their help. That attack was not made, probably owing to a threat by Bienville that he would cut the throat of each chief, big and little, the moment the Natchez made their appearance. The river began to overflow the island on which Bienville was encamped; he therefore executed a treaty by which the natives agreed to cut and deliver logs for a stockade at Natchez. Bienville released all his captives, except one, whom he connected with the murders. He, " Chief of the Beard," was shot, in the presence of the other captives. Bienville had conquered the Natchez by the trick of getting their chiefs into his clutches and keeping them until he secured terms that suited him.

The fort was built by the natives, in keeping with their promise, and was occupied on August 3, 1716. Thus did two distinct and antagonistic races sit down to watch each other.

Bienville left Aid-Major Pailloux in command at the fort and departed for Mobile, where he arrived on October 4th. He was rejoiced to find that Cadillac had been deposed, and Bienville received a letter from the Minister of Marine reappointing him Governor, to supplant De l'Epinay, Cadillac's successor.

Fully a century later, the scene shifts to the upper Mississippi. The French and the Chippewas between Lake Superior and the Wisconsin River had driven the Renards, or Fox Indians to the west bank of the great river, where they coalesced with another tribe of the Algonquin nation, the Sauks, or Sacs. After the Illinois country and the western bank of the Mississippi

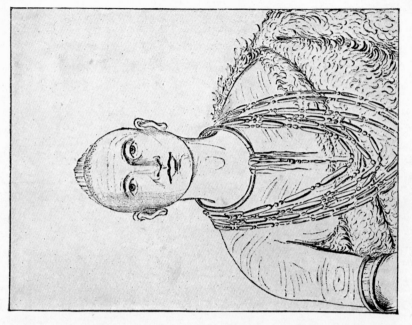

Muk-a-tah-mish-o-káh-kack.
(The Black Hawk.)
(From Catlin.)

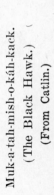

Náh-se-us-kuk.
(The Whirling Thunder.)
(From Catlin.)

came into the possession of the United States, the Sacs and Foxes maintained stubborn resistance to the advance of the white man culminating, in 1832, in what is known as the "Black Hawk War." Colonel Zachary Taylor took an active part in that campaign. The leader of the revolt against the Government was " Black Hawk," who had been chief of the Sacs for almost fifty years. Below Prairie du Chien is Bad Axe River; the last engagement of the Black Hawk War was fought five miles south of that point. The Sacs and Foxes were defeated by United States troops under General Atkinson, and " Black Hawk " was taken prisoner. Many battles of this campaign were outside what is strictly the Mississippi Valley, although the Sacs and Foxes belonged there.

A perpetual state of war continued between the Dakotas (Sioux) and the Ojibwas (Chippewas), for a hundred years. The conflict was waged without mercy! The year 1833 was particularly bloody. Almost every bend in the Mississippi above the entrance of Crow Wing River had its tragedy. A battle that lasted three days was fought at the last turn in the river before it takes the plunge at St. Anthony.

The Sioux outbreak in Minnesota in 1862 led by " Little Crow," was confined to the Minnesota River valley and hardly belongs in this volume; but it was probably the last open revolt of the natives that the citizens of that region will know, certain troubles with Chippewa Indian agents and lumbermen in 1898 being settled by arbitration. The Sioux knew that the Civil War was in progress and that the arms of the South were often triumphant over those of the North. In brief, the Indians realised that the white men were

16

fighting among themselves! It appeared to be an auspicious time in which to shake off a galling yoke and to destroy the intruders. The brutality with which the settlers at Redwood and that part of the valley were treated was typical of the worst period of aboriginal uprisings.

Fugitives fled down the Minnesota to St. Peters (now Mendota), Mankato, and St. Cloud. These towns were crowded. Forts Snelling and Ripley were places of refuge. Governor Ramsey asked Col. H. H. Sibley to take command of the militia and to hurry up the Minnesota Valley to the scene of disturbances. A detachment of troops and settlers sent from Fort Ridgeley, on the Minnesota, to quell disturbances and bury the dead at Birch Coolie, a trading post eighteen miles to the north-west, was surrounded at night by three hundred Sioux, and twelve soldiers and civilians killed. This was in the first week of September, 1862. Colonel Sibley attacked and captured the main band of Little Crow's army. The leaders and all participants in the outrages, some thirty odd, were hanged.[1]

II—BRITISH FINAL DEFEAT AT NEW ORLEANS

The splendid and decisive victory of the American troops on the Plain of Chalmette—known to history as the Battle of New Orleans, a conflict of several days' duration, culminating on January 8, 1815—was as essential to the future greatness of the American Republic as was any engagement of the Revolution. By Louis Jonté Meader, a Louisianian author, it has been very

[1] Heard's *History of the Sioux War*. New York, 1864.

prettily and accurately described as " our Thermopylæ."
Had that battle been lost, although fought after a treaty
of peace actually had been signed, and the city of New
Orleans occupied by British forces, England would have
attempted to hold what had been known as "The
Louisiana Province," despite the treaty, under the defensible claim that the Napoleonic sale of 1803, by which
the United States acquired the territory from France,
was void, because that nation did not possess a
valid title to the Province. The gravity of such a complication is tremendous, when we remember that another
war would have been necessary to acquire the vast
wedge of territory to-day comprising our Western
States. The Pacific coast might never have become a
part of this Republic!

The battle itself was a brilliant achievement,—one
that will always reflect honour upon the commander and
credit upon the brave frontiersmen who did such effective
execution upon the enemy. An invading army of fourteen thousand, including ten thousand seasoned veteran
British troops, was crushingly defeated by thirty-two
hundred raw Kentucky, and Tennessee militia and
Louisiana Creoles. The disparity of loss was as remarkable as the victory and was due to the fact that
the woodsmen used the musket of the period as an
arm of precision.

The abdication of Napoleon at Fontainebleau, April
11, 1814, and the temporary pacification of Europe
consequent on that event, decided the British Cabinet
to prosecute the war against the United States with
the utmost vigour. Veterans of the Peninsular Campaign were re-embarked at Plymouth in the fall, and
sailed under sealed orders. On their way across the

Atlantic, the ships touched at Madeira, October 8th, at Barbadoes and had rendezvous at Negro Bay, Jamaica. There, the British fleet was joined by four thousand troops under General Keane, a young Irish officer who had followed from Plymouth. The combined forces, in fifty vessels, reached the Louisiana coast on November 29th. Anchoring between Ship and Cat Islands, near the entrance to Lake Borgne, the commander of the expedition hoped to land before his presence on the coast was known and to take the Americans by surprise. Commander Daniel T. Patterson, in charge of the Naval Station at New Orleans, received word of the presence of the British and sent five gunboats, a tender, and a despatch boat to the passes of Mariana and Christian to watch the enemy. A preliminary fight occurred there. The American vessels, under Lieutenant Thomas Catesby-Jones were discovered by the British. His force consisted of only one hundred and eighty-two men and twenty-three guns. His flagship was a small sloop of eighty tons. The British attacked in sixty barges, under Captain Lockyer, and with such overwhelming numbers won a victory, giving to them control of Lake Borgne. Troops were landed between the 16th and 20th of December, under command of General Keane.

Jackson had reached Mobile on November 11, 1814, after the evacuation of Pensacola by the British and Spaniards. There he received despatches from New Orleans begging him to hurry to its defence. Several English vessels were already in the neighbourhood; their commander, Captain Lockyer, was in communication with British sympathisers ashore. In this connection, Lockyer committed a blunder that led to the disclosure of his plans by one Jean Lafitte to General Jackson.

Here occurs a highly romantic episode that must always be associated with the final grapple of American and Briton for the independence of the States. A community of smugglers had headquarters on a marshy island, Grande Terre, at the Gulf entrance to Barataria Bay, sixty miles south-west of New Orleans. This broad bit of bay afforded a sheltered harbour, in which the small craft of the Baratarians lay in shallow water beyond gun reach of ships of the line. Jean Lafitte, chief of these outlaws, is the American pet buccaneer. He is our " Pirate of the Gulf of Mexico," although he never was a corsair in the strict sense of the word, because never guilty of a crime against humanity but only a defier of revenue and neutrality laws. In this particular, he differed from Captain Kidd, who was an inhuman monster. Kidd was an Englishman. He once lived in Wall Street, New York. Curiously, the first " Trust " company was organised in his house, after he had been hanged in England. He proved his fidelity to his mother country by going home for trial and execution. Lafitte was born in Bordeaux, France, learned the blacksmith's trade there: he came to New Orleans, established a forge in St. Philip Street and was a law-abiding citizen for several years. But smuggling West Indian liquors and costly French merchandise into the populous city of New Orleans offered much greater prospects of wealth than shoeing horses. He assembled a band of associates and settled at Grande Terre. It became a smuggler's lair. Never outside the Spanish Main was a worse embodiment of dauntless courage and cunning than existed in Lafitte's followers. He had several hundred expert gunners and sharpshooters. In addition, the Baratarians, as they liked to be called, possessed a squadron of swift, well-armed vessels that would have been of inestimable service to the British commander. Knowing that the Government at Washington had proscribed Lafitte and that the brother of the Baratarian chief was already in prison at New Orleans, Captain Lockyer naturally expected to find Lafitte filled with hatred for the United States. He was in error. Lafitte had accumulated a fortune by unlawful depredations; he wanted to return to New Orleans to enjoy it and recognised an opportunity to make peace with the Americans. Self-interest, therefore, rather than patriotism, may have inspired him to send a letter he had received from Captain Lockyer to John Blanque, a member of the Louisiana Legislature. In an accompanying note, Lafitte said: "Though proscribed by my country, I never shall miss an occasion to serve her, or to prove that she never has ceased to be dear to me."

In his communication to Blanque, he also repeated details of interviews with two British officers, who had been sent ashore to confer with him and to deliver the letter from their commander. Plans of the intended British operations against New Orleans were also inclosed. To Governor William C. C. Claiborne, Governor of Louisiana, Lafitte addressed the following remarkable letter:

I offer to restore to this State several citizens who, perhaps, in your eyes, have lost the right to that sacred title. I offer them, nevertheless, and they are all you could wish to find them,—ready to exert their utmost efforts in defence of their country. All that I ask is that a stop be put to the proscription against me and my adherents by an act of oblivion for all that has been done in the past. I decline to say more on this subject until I have the honour of Your Excellency's answer; and should it not be favourable to my ardent desires, I declare to you that I shall at once leave the country, so that no imputation may be made connecting me with the contemplated invasion.

Governor Claiborne convened a council of leading citizens, before which he laid the letters of Lafitte; the decision was to reject the offer. An expeditionary force, under command of Colonel Ross of the United States Army and Commodore Patterson, was sent to Barataria, which attacked the smuggler's stronghold and captured his ships and took many prisoners. The latter were taken back to New Orleans and put in prison.

Governor Claiborne sent copies of the British documents and Lafitte's letters to General Jackson, who left Mobile for New Orleans on their receipt, arriving December 2, 1814. He established his headquarters on Royal Street.

The city was in an undefended condition, but, with his characteristic energy, Jackson organised the local military forces, obstructed the entrances to the large bayous, strengthened the fortifications,—especially improving Fort St. Philip, on the Mississippi below the city. He openly denounced Lafitte, and opposed " any alliance whatever with those infamous bandits," declaring, in the same breath, that his only hope was to get his hands upon them and to hang every one of them.

While seated at headquarters a few days after the affair of Barataria, General Jackson was surprised by a call from Jean Lafitte, who, taking his life in his hands, braved the sturdy soldier, face to face. Before

Jackson could order his arrest, the bandit chieftain renewed his patriotic offers. So well did he argue his case that his services were accepted and the two remarkable men shook hands. This conversion of Jackson proves the magnetic power of Lafitte, because " Old Hickory " was a man of usually inflexible will. All judicial proceedings against the Baratarians were suspended and their release from prison ordered. Jackson sent some of these erstwhile pirates to assist in the defence of the outlying forts, formed a corps of the remainder, which he placed under the command of two of their own officers, Dominique You and Bellouche. The importance of this acquisition to Jackson's forces cannot be overestimated. The Baratarians proved invaluable during the preparations for defence, and, when the death-grapple came, their bravery and heroism was dramatic in the extreme. Jackson never forgot their splendid conduct and made good his promise to secure from the President full pardons for every man of them. In his general orders of January 21st, after the battle, thanking his troops and particularly those from Louisiana, he mentioned most feelingly the signal bravery of Lafitte, Bellouche, You, and their men.

Meanwhile, Jackson put New Orleans under martial law and impressed all able-bodied men, except British, into military service. He summoned to his aid Generals Coffee, Carroll, and Thomas; and warned General Winchester, at Mobile, to be prepared for an attack at that point. The British occupied Fisherman's Village, at the head of the Bayou Bienvenu, twelve miles from New Orleans, seized the Villere plantation, and made it their headquarters. Carroll, Coffee, and other reinforcements had reached Jackson and the following stations

had been assigned to them: Carroll, at the upper branch
of the Bayou Bienvenu; Governor Claiborne, with his
Louisiana militia, farther up the Gentilly road; Coffee's
brigade, Planché's and Dankin's battalions, Hinds's
dragoons, and the New Orleans Rifles, under Captain
Beale, and a small band of Choctaws, under Captain
Jugeat, were ordered to assemble at Montreuil's plantation, thence to proceed to Canal Rodriguez, six miles
below the city, there to prepare for an assault upon
the British. Commander Patterson was ordered down
the Mississippi to the flank of the enemy at Villere's.

Jackson had run his lines across two plantations,
from the river to the edge of an almost impenetrable
swamp that ultimately became a part of Lake Pontchartrain. The land lying between the river and the marsh
was known as the Plain of Chalmette. There the
famous battle occurred.

At seven o'clock in the evening of December 23d, the
schooner *Carolina,* Captain Henry, anchored off Villere's and opened fire upon the British camp, throwing
the troops into confusion. Thornton, in command of
the British troops at that point, attacked Jackson and
was repulsed. Coffee, following the levee, flanked
Thornton and made his defeat decisive.

Lieutenant-General Pakenham, "the Hero of
Salamanca" and fresh from the Peninsular War,
landed on Christmas day to assume command of the
British forces, now eight thousand strong. He advanced his troops close to the American line of defence
and began the erection of earthworks near the river.
The men engaged in this fort-building were attacked
by Hinds; but the British destroyed the schooner *Carolina,* causing her crew to abandon her. Another en-

gagement occurred on the 28th, caused by an advance
of the British in two columns; Gibbs on the right, Keane
on the left, with Pakenham, in personal command, in
the centre. Keane was received with deadly fire and
forced to fall back. Gibbs, aided by the dauntless
Rennie who led an assault in person, made some progress but was ordered back by the commanding general. On the 31st, the British attacked again, threw up
redoubts, in which they mounted thirty guns, manned
with their best gunners. This battery next day shelled
Jackson's headquarters, at the château of M. Macarté,
a wealthy Creole, rendering it untenable. Jackson returned the fire on January 1st, with all artillery that
could be trained upon the redoubt. The British fled
and abandoned five guns.

On January 2d, both armies were strongly reinforced. Brigadier-General John Thomas came with
two thousand militia from Kentucky; Major-General
John Lambert, also arrived by sea with Pakenham's own
regiment, bringing British forces up to ten thousand
veteran soldiers. The British troops were then divided
into three brigades, under Keane, Gibbs, and Lambert.
The American forces were in only two divisions, the
right under General Ross and the left under Generals
Carroll and Coffee. Second and third lines of defence
were thrown up by Jackson. General Morgan was
posted on the opposite side of the city and divining that
he would be attacked by Thornton, Jackson sent five
hundred Kentuckians to Morgan's aid. Thornton as-
saulted Morgan, causing his men to spike their cannons
and retreat; Patterson, three hundred yards in Morgan's rear was next attacked and his troops took refuge
on board the *Louisiana*. Thornton, after this success-

ful foray, rejoined the main army confronting Jackson.

What is known as the real battle of New Orleans began on the following morning. The Americans fired the first gun. Lieutenant Spotts opened fire on the British; but General Gibbs advanced, under this fire, against the Tennesseeans and Kentuckians, who fought in a line four deep, protected by cotton bales. The accuracy of the woodland sharpshooters under General Carroll cut the advancing British line to pieces. Pakenham, in person, then led one of his veteran regiments to the support of Gibbs, and was mortally wounded. Keane also supported the assault with the famous Ninety-third Highlanders, who drove a wedge into the centre of Carroll's defence. Gibbs was fatally wounded. Soon after, Keane was wounded and the command devolved upon Major Wilkinson, who met the fate of his commander-in-chief. Of the nine hundred Highlanders, with twenty-nine officers, only two hundred and thirty-five men and nine officers were mustered at the close of this assault! All the attacking regiments on this part of the field suffered terrible losses.

The British right was more successful, where Colonel Rennie, with one thousand men, advanced in two columns, one by the road and the other along the levee at the river's bank, taking a redoubt at Jackson's extreme right but only holding it a short time, for although Rennie succeeded in scaling the parapet of the American redoubt, the New Orleans Rifles, under Beale, opened a terrific fire upon the heroic enemy, in which Rennie was killed. At this juncture, Lafitte, who had commanded a battery which was no longer serviceable at the close range, called to his lieutenants, Bellouche, You, and Sebastiano, to follow him. Seizing cutlasses, the pirate patriots swept upon the survivors of the assault like Arab fanatics, and although a few of the British sprang into the ditches, Lafitte's men followed them there and slew them mercilessly.

That night Patterson retook his line and at dawn opened fire from his former position. His were the last guns fired. The battle was over, and the British withdrew. Their losses were seven hundred killed, fourteen hundred wounded, and five hundred prisoners. The American casualties were eight killed and thirteen wounded. The British had to fight in the open, while the Americans were behind defences.

The British, under Lambert, wholly withdrew from the Mississippi banks on January 19th, and two days later reached their fleet. They were prevented from further attack upon other unprotected cities by receipt of the official despatches announcing the signing of the Treaty of Ghent, on December 24th.

III—THE CIVIL WAR

The western frontier of the British colonial possessions in North America, even at periods of most vain-glorious assumption, never had extended beyond the Mississippi. With a stubbornness and an activity that did not characterise the Spaniards in any other part of the world, the race of Narvaez, De Soto, Ponce de Leon, and Coronado claimed and held against French and English the vast, unmeasured wilderness beyond the mighty river that bisected the North American Continent. The same conditions existed when the thirteen States freed themselves from the British yoke and began to work out their own destiny. No man had arisen, who, like Rameses II. of Egypt, "fixed his frontiers where he pleased."

Thomas Jefferson, as we have seen, accomplished by one bold stroke the apparently impossible. The necessities of Napoleon, the promptitude of Jefferson to take advantage of opportunity, the acquisition of Florida, the bravery of the Texans, the results of the Mexican War, and the Gadsden Purchase extended the territory of the United States of America from the Atlantic to the Pacific and from the Forty-ninth parallel to the Rio Grande.

When the Civil War tore the Republic into two pieces, the prescience of learned tactitians was not necessary to comprehend that the rebellion ought to be confined to the region east of the national waterway. The problem of blockading the Atlantic and Gulf ports of the Confederacy is sufficient to excuse the Lincoln Administration for not taking prompt possession of the Mississippi from Saint Louis to the Gulf. The South was in a condition of preparedness; the North was in a state little better than panic. The slave States of Missouri, Arkansas, Texas, and three quarters of Louisiana lay west of the Mississippi. All of them were prompt to put troops into the field in behalf of the Confederacy. The importance of segregating them from the rest of their southern associates was too obvious to be discussed.

The troubles in Missouri delayed the seizure of important strategic points on the river below. A governor of that State declared for the Confederacy, organised rebellion to the national Government, and assembled hostile troops. Saint Louis was more turbulently rebellious than Baltimore. Months of valuable

time were lost in securing conditions of semi-peaceful-
ness within its borders.   Although the battles in Missouri distinctly belong to the reconquest of the
Mississippi, they need not be gone into.   The redemp-
tion of the Mississippi does not begin with the trifling
and inconsequential fight at Belmont, almost under the
guns of Columbus, then held by the Confederates, but
with the occupation of Cairo, at the mouth of the Ohio
River, by Ulysses Simpson Grant, then thirty-nine
years of age.   He possessed a West Point training and
had seen active service in the Mexican War,—at every
battle except Buena Vista.   Curiously, in that campaign he had attracted the attention of General Scott's
staff officer, Robert E. Lee, whom he was afterwards
to confront in Virginia and defeat in the final campaign
of the Civil War.

Had Polk seized Cairo, as he intended, and had
other Confederate generals fastened hold upon Paducah
and Louisville, the probabilities are that Kentucky and
Tennessee would have been dragged into the Confederacy, however unwillingly.   Grant's second act was
to occupy Paducah, at the mouth of the Tennessee
River.   The junction of the Cumberland with the Ohio
was less than ten miles distant.   This coup made possible the subsequent flotilla advance upon Forts Henry
and Donelson.   Grant's immediate objective point was
Columbus, situated a short distance below Cairo, on
the Kentucky side of the Mississippi, where General
Polk had a considerable Confederate force; but a descent of the great river would have been bad military
art, as long as formidable bodies of the enemy occupied
fortified points at Forts Henry and Donelson, on the
Tennessee and Cumberland rivers, at the Tennessee

State line.   The extreme right of the Confederate defence rested upon Bowling Green, Kentucky.

Forts Henry and Donelson

The movement upon the centre of the Confederate line was inaugurated on January 30, 1862.   Grant, with a force of seventeen thousand men on transports, escorted by four armoured and three unarmoured gunboats under Commodore Foote, began the ascent of the Tennessee River.   Here started a campaign that was to include the victories at Forts Henry and Donelson and the two days' battle at Shiloh, and to culminate in the siege and capture of Vicksburg.   It is doubtful if Grant expected this flank movement on the Mississippi's fortified places to develop into a year and a half of activity.   This land campaign, by which the Confederate positions at Columbus, Fort Pillow, and Memphis were turned is as much a part of the Mississippi's conquest as are the battles of New Madrid and Island No. 10.

Taking events in their chronological sequence, the fall of Fort Henry was inevitable, owing to the suddenness of the attack by Grant and Foote.   Its commandant, General Tighman, sent all of his thirty-four hundred men, except ninety-six, to Fort Donelson and maintained a show of fight until their retreat across the twelve-mile neck of land separating the two rivers and forts had been accomplished.   Then he surrendered.   The importance of the capture was that a new base for operating against Fort Donelson was created. A good and direct road connected the two places. Meanwhile, Foote's armed flotilla had to descend the

Tennessee to the Ohio and to ascend the Cumberland
to a position for using its guns upon Donelson. Fort
Henry was occupied on February 6th.

The advance of the troops upon Donelson began the
morning of the surrender of Henry. This fort occupied
a fine position upon a plateau, elevated a hundred feet
above the Cumberland, and consisted of " two water-
batteries on the hillside, protected by a bastioned earth-
work of irregular outline on the summit, enclosing one
hundred acres." [1] Along the western ridge of the
plateau was a line of fortifications for field artillery
and some rifle-pits. About the time Grant had deployed his troops, General Floyd, who had been
Buchanan's Secretary of War, superseded General
Pillow and took over the command of the eighteen
thousand Confederates.

The first assault was ordered by Grant on the 13th.
It was little more than a reconnaissance in force. The
fleet and transports arrived next day with five thousand
fresh troops. Seven mortar-boats rendered valuable
service. The Confederate water battery was shelled at
a nearness of six hundred yards, although the gunboats
finally were driven away. About daylight of the 15th,
Pillow, with eight thousand men, attempted a sortie
directed against McClernand who held the road to
Charlotte, and opened a way of escape. Had Floyd
acted promptly, he might have got away with his entire force. But, Pillow spent the precious hours in
another attack upon Lew Wallace until Grant had
time to reach the field and take personal command.
He saw that a fight to a finish then and there was
inevitable. He ordered a general charge upon all the

[1] *Rise and Fall of the Confederate Government*, pp. 11–28.

outlying earthworks, which resulted in carrying the
ridge and extending the Federal line completely around
the bastioned fortress. With the aid of the mortar-
boats, escape by land was completely cut off, and the
Confederates had lost in the fight about two thousand
men. During the darkness of that night, Floyd and
Pillow escaped up the Cumberland in a boat. The
" unconditional surrender " by Buckner of Fort Donelson occurred next morning (16th), and included fifteen
thousand prisoners, sixty-eight cannons, and seventeen
thousand muskets. This Federal victory was immediately followed by the evacuation of Columbus by
Polk, who burned his buildings and went by steamer
to New Madrid.

In the field, Corinth, Mississippi, became the natural
point for Confederate concentration. Grant sent his
transports to the Tennessee and began to move troops
and provisions up that river to the nearest location for
a base of attack upon that town. Thus was Pittsburg
Landing chosen; and Shiloh church, about two miles back
from the river, became the scene of a two day's battle that
has provoked more controversy than any other event
of the Civil War.

Meanwhile, Commodore Foote's squadron had been
ordered to dislodge the Confederates from Island No.
10, in the Mississippi, almost opposite New Madrid, to
which place General Polk had sent one hundred and
forty guns from Columbus and part of his force.

Brigadier-General W. T. Sherman occupied Columbus on March 4th. Brigadier-General John Pope was
on his way through Missouri and arrived before New
Madrid, on that shore of the Mississippi, March 3d. A
siege of a month followed. Foote was banging away

17

at the fortifications on Island No. 10, disabling gun after gun; and Pope was gradually tightening the lines about the town on the mainland. Polk surrendered to Pope on April 7th, about seven thousand men.

The intention of the Federals was to move down the Mississippi in transports, guarded by Foote's gunboats, to Fort Pillow, a defensive position created by the Confederates upon a high bluff on the Tennessee side. Plans were made for a combined attack from land and river on the 17th; but orders came from Halleck directing Pope to reinforce Grant at Pittsburg Landing for the attack on Corinth. Troops were hurried aboard the transports which steamed up-stream, en route for the Tennessee River. Fort Pillow was left to its own destruction. It was subsequently abandoned.

Shiloh

Albert Sidney Johnston was in command of the rapidly assembling Confederate forces at Corinth. That a great battle would be fought in that vicinity was obvious, even to General Halleck. Troops were hurried thither from many parts of the Gulf States. The flight of Floyd and Pillow had disgraced them in the eyes of the Confederate Government and they were removed from all command. Johnston's chief aid was Beauregard, who had ordered Fort Sumter fired upon, thus precipitating the war, and had covered himself with Southern laurels at Bull Run. Braxton Bragg was brought from Pensacola, with eleven thousand men.

The choice of Pittsburg Landing, as a base of Federal operations upon Corinth, was made by Gen. W. F. Smith. Endless discussion has arisen regarding the wisdom of selecting a site upon the west bank of the Tennessee, by that act, putting the river behind the Federal troops instead of in front of them. The Count de Paris did not settle the dispute when he declared in his *History of the Civil War in the United States* that " the position was extremely well chosen." It was a fighting man's selection, made for another fighting man! Smith and Grant were of the same metal. It is fair to state that Beauregard had seen the strategic importance of the bluff at Pittsburg Landing and had occupied it prior to the arrival of the gunboats; but these had shelled his small garrison and driven it away before Smith's arrival.

As long as the boats held the river, the position was a strong one,—a quadrilateral enclosed on three sides, by a river and two deep creeks, with an opening to the south-west toward Corinth. This latter feature was fully recognised as the weakness of the position, and the contention of critics always will be that a triple or quadruple line of Federal videttes should have been posted along the Corinth highway. From left to right, facing this obvious point of assault, if one were to be made, lay the commands of Stuart, Prentiss, Sherman, and McClernand. Inside this line were Hurlbut, and William Wallace, who had taken over W. F. Smith's command. Lew Wallace was on the Purdy road, near Crump's Landing, five miles to the northward. Buell's army was anxiously expected, because his advance guard under Nelson, had reached Savannah, a landing on the east side of the river eight miles from Pittsburg.

With an impetuosity that carried everything before it, Johnston attacked in great force at 5.30 on the raw Sunday morning of April 6th. The Confederate troops

had deployed during the night within less than half a
mile of the Federal lines. The blow brought consternation to the troops of Prentiss, upon whom it fell. If
it came not as a surprise, it was followed by a panic.
Many prisoners were taken in their beds. Grant had
his headquarters at Savannah and McClernand was the
only Major-General on the firing line, which did not
possess a single rifle-pit or other defence.

Johnston's attack was made in three parallel lines
of ten thousand men each, separated by half a mile.
Hardee led, followed by Bragg, and in the last line,
intended to cover and extend the flanks, were Polk with
ten thousand on the extreme left and Breckinridge with
six thousand on the right. In addition to the thirty-six
thousand infantry, some excellent Confederate cavalry,
that could have been used in the open, were valueless in
the underbrush of the forests. Of the forty thousand
Federal troops, Lew Wallace's seven thousand men did
not arrive in time to participate in the first day's fight.

Grant reached the battle-field at eight o'clock and
sent an order to Lew Wallace to advance at once.
Owing to a blunder in the transmission of the verbal
message or to ignorance of the roads, Wallace's command did not make those five sloughy miles until seven
o'clock at night, at which time the Federal line had
been driven back fully one mile, contesting every foot.
Prior to Sunday noon, great disorganisation reigned in
several parts of the Federal line. The loss of human
life was terrible. About 2.30 in the afternoon, General
Johnston sitting on his horse in the open was hit by a
rifle ball that severed an artery in his leg. It was not
a fatal wound, but Johnston paid no attention to his
injury until he suddenly collapsed and died from loss of

blood. President Davis asserted, years afterward, that " the southern cause perished then and there, on the field of Shiloh." General Beauregard succeeded to the command.

At six o'clock in the afternoon, twenty-two hundred of Prentiss's men were surrounded and captured by the Confederates, and William Wallace, who was commanding Smith's brigade, was mortally wounded. Before dark, the gunboats took part in the battle and probably checked the advance to Pittsburg Landing. Nelson was the Blücher of the day. He arrived in time to cross the river and to defend the landing of McCook and the rest of Buell's army.

The splendid bravery of the Confederates had not given to them decisive victory. Bragg advocated a final charge after nightfall, but Beauregard ordered a cessation of hostilities. " The battle is lost in that event! " exclaimed Bragg, protestant. Beauregard's defence of his action is to be found in *Battles and Leaders* (i., 590). He knew that fresh troops were crossing the river and believed a repulse of the charge suggested by Bragg to be inevitable.

In the Federal ranks, Prentiss was the chief hero of that terrible Sunday, because his command stood the brunt of the attack. About dark, Lew Wallace and Nelson each added seven thousand men to the Federal forces almost simultaneously. Crittenden arrived during the night.

Monday morning saw the Federal line, stretching from a bayou of the river (reading from left to right), held by Majors-General Nelson, Crittenden, McCook, McClernand, and Lew Wallace. Confronting them were the four divisions, right to left, of Hardee, Breckinridge, Polk, and Bragg. Grant assumed the aggressive at daylight. Nelson's fresh troops were thrown against Hardee's; Lew Wallace, anxious to retrieve the misfortunes of the previous day that had kept him out of the fight, made a savage attempt to get possession of the Corinth road in the rear of the Confederates. McCook did some brilliant work at the centre. Although Lew Wallace did not wholly succeed in his efforts, he compelled the beginning of a retreat by Beauregard that only ended when the defences of Corinth had been reached. During Monday afternoon, Generals Wood and Thomas, with twelve thousand fresh troops arrived, and Grant has been criticised because he did not follow and harass his retreating foe.

The battles of Iuka and Corinth were supplements of Shiloh. The Confederacy had shot its bolt in that battle, and, although the result was indecisive, the Southern arms had suffered losses that could not be repaired. Corinth fell by force of circumstances.

New Orleans

Upon the insistence of President Lincoln, as early as January of that year (1862), the assembling of a fleet of naval vessels and transports, for the capture of New Orleans and the opening of the lower part of the Mississippi River, had been actively begun. Wooden frigates and gunboats selected carried one hundred and fifty guns of various calibres. A lot of extemporised mortar-boats were added. The expedition was supplemented by a land force of about thirteen thousand troops, and Benjamin F. Butler was given command of them. The fleet commander was David Glasgow

Farragut, who, although a Tennesseean by birth, never had faltered in his fidelity to the Union.

There was not an armoured vessel in Farragut's fleet when it assembled in April off the mouth of the Mississippi. The debt of naval architecture to the designers of the *Merrimac* and the *Monitor* had already been recognised in the historic encounter at Hampton Roads, and the utter worthlessness of wooden ships against armoured ones was admitted. Farragut's flagship was the old *Hartford,* twenty-five guns; and with her were the *Brooklyn, Richmond,* and *Pensacola,* even inferior to her as fighting machines. Commander Porter, son of a famous United States naval officer, and who was afterwards to become an admiral of the Navy, commanded an auxiliary flotilla of nineteen mortar-boats, each having a thirteen-inch mortar for throwing spherical shells. Its work in the subsequent battles at New Orleans and Vicksburg proved to be of the highest importance.

The distance by the Mississippi from the Gulf to New Orleans is one hundred and twenty miles, and two antiquated forts, located at Plaquemine Bend, about ninety miles south of the city, had been strengthened to such a degree that the Confederates felt sanguine of their effectiveness. Fort St. Philip stood upon the right bank and twenty-four hundred feet farther downstream, upon the left bank, was Fort Jackson. The former was an open work and mounted fifty-three guns, but the latter was a casemated structure, with a ditch, and possessed seventy-five guns, some of heavy calibre. These strongholds had been well provisioned, were secure from land attack because of their positions upon the narrow strip of soil that served as a dyke to separate the river from the Gulf, and each was garrisoned by seven hundred men. A few water batteries had been begun between Plaquemine and New Orleans, but they had not been brought to any condition of armament, because the defence afforded by the two forts was considered ample. A line of schooners had been anchored across the river, held together by the heaviest anchor chains. Ten small armoured vessels were kept above Fort St. Philip; but the chief menace afloat—in the light of the devastation wrought by the *Merrimac* upon wooden ships in Hampton Roads prior to the arrival of the *Monitor*—was an iron-armoured ram, the *Manassas,* and the *Louisiana,* a small corvette, the bulwarks of which had been cut down and a sloping deck, similar in form to that of the *Merrimac,* added. This iron-covered superstructure and gun-deck carried sixteen cannons of large calibre for that period. The naval part of the Confederate equipment was under Commander John Mitchell; but several of the smaller vessels, furnished by the city authorities, had been given into the charge of a river captain, and conflict of authority was inevitable. General Duncan was in chief command of the Confederate land forces, with Lieutenant-Commander Higgins at Fort Jackson. In the city of New Orleans were as few as three thousand troops, all others having been drawn to support Johnston in his attack upon Pittsburg Landing.

Farragut was in readiness on April 16th, and began to get his ships across the bar. It was before the days of the Eads Jetties, and great trouble was experienced with shallow water at the mouth of the river. Porter's light-draft vessels were hurried up-stream and anchored close to Fort Jackson, behind the narrow neck of land

Point-a-la-Hache.

formed by a sharp bend in the river,—which in front of the forts flowed almost west. The mortar-boats were sheltered from view by a dense forest, but as an additional means of confusing the men on watch at Fort Jackson, the tops of the masts were trimmed with boughs from the adjacent trees. The appearance of the snug little flotilla recalled the advance of the woods of Dunsinane.

Porter began the bombardment of Fort Jackson on the 18th and during its continuance for five days and nights threw about seventeen thousand shells, exceeding one per minute. So accurate were the calculations of the gunners that Fort Jackson became a mass of ruins. Attempts to shell Fort St. Philip, half a mile farther up-stream, were not successful; but its guns were not so formidable as those at Fort Jackson had been.

At the end of five days, Farragut's patience was exhausted. Porter's argument was that it would be unwise to run past the forts, even if it could be successfully achieved, leaving formidable places of defence in the rear. In other words, he feared that the fleet might be " bottled up " at New Orleans. While the bombardment had been in progress, Lieutenant Caldwell had been directed to take the two little steamers *Pinola* and *Itasca*—how interesting that the name of the then accredited source of the Mississippi should have been thus attached to the battle at the mouth of the river!—and break through the line of chained vessels that blocked a passage-way up-stream. He successfully accomplished the hazardous undertaking on the night of April 20th. After failing to explode a mine under the central vessel of the row, he worked round an end of the line, in shallow water, ran up-stream a short distance, turned, and at full headway came down upon the chain, breaking it, causing the vessels to drag their anchors and to swing to right and to left, leaving the centre of the river open. It was glorious service that the little *Itasca* rendered that dark night.

Four nights later, at two o'clock, Farragut's squadron got under way. Every conceivable means had been adopted to protect the magazines and boilers and all light rigging had been taken down. The credit of leadership was given to Captain Bailey of the *Cayuga.* After him came the sloops *Pensacola* and *Mississippi,* the corvettes *Oneida* and *Varuna,* and the gunboats *Katahdin, Kineo,* and *Wissahickon.* What was left of the batteries in the two forts did everything possible to destroy the ships. At this point, the gunboats, five in number, closed in, going within two hundred yards of the shore, and threw sufficient grape and canister to drive the men from the guns of Fort Jackson. The armoured ram, *Manassas,* failing to injure the *Pensacola,* attacked the *Mississippi.* Owing to the attention given to the other ships, Bailey got the *Cayuga* past the forts without serious injury and became hotly engaged with the ships above. The *Varuna* set four of the enemy's ships afire, but in the contest was so seriously injured that she had to be run ashore to save the crew, which was rescued by the *Oneida.* The *Cayuga* destroyed three of the enemy's boats; but one got away to New Orleans.

About that time the *Hartford,* with Farragut aboard, and the *Brooklyn* had arrived opposite Fort St. Philip when the most serious complication of the night occurred. A fire-raft was observed coming downstream, pushed by a plucky tugboatman. The channel

The " Crescent " at New Orleans.
(Mississippi 100 Feet Deep.)
(Courtesy of M. B. Trezevant.)

was not broad at that point, and as the raft held to its centre, despite a storm of grape-shot poured into the tugboat behind it, the *Hartford* tried to avoid the blazing danger and went upon a bar. The raft was jammed against the side of the flag-ship and the flames leaped into the rigging. Farragut's supreme coolness at that time enabled the crew to extinguish the burning mass, after which the *Hartford* backed into the channel and, with thirty odd holes in her hull, proceeded. While this crisis was occurring, the *Brooklyn* was rammed by the *Manassas,* far under the water-line, but the hole was plugged and the dangerous ram driven off. Three of the Federal gunboats met with misfortune, among them the *Itasca,* that had so gloriously distinguished herself by breaking the line of obstructions on the night of the 20th. The *Manassas* followed the squadron almost to New Orleans, where, again attacked by the *Mississippi* that she had rammed early in the fight, she ran ashore, was set afire by shells from the attacking boat, and finally blew up.

The actual engagement with the two forts lasted less than one hour and a half.

A battery was encountered on the eastern shore, not far from the historic battle-field on the Plain of Chalmette, where " Old Hickory," with his Tennessee squirrel and Indian hunters had defeated the British veterans of the Napoleonic campaigns.

When the Federal squadron anchored off the Crescent City, the people of the town were not complaisant. The *Cayuga* went to a wharf-head and Captain Bailey, accompanied by Lieutenant Perkins, walking alone to the City Hall, demanded from the mayor the surrender of the city. The mayor temporised and, as the demand could not be enforced until General Butler arrived with troops, the Confederate flag continued to float over the municipal building. Of course, Farragut could have shelled the city, but he never contemplated such an act of barbarism. Porter, who had remained near the forts, compelled their surrender on April 27th. The ascent of the transports followed, but before Butler arrived on the 29th, a small body of marines had landed and replaced the Confederate flag over the City Hall with the Stars and Stripes. No sooner had the marines departed than a man named Mumford tore down the Federal flag, carried it to the street, where the populace trampled it in the mud and afterwards tore it into fragments. One of General Butler's first acts was to order the trial by court-martial of Mumford for "insult to the Federal flag." He was condemned to be hanged and was summarily executed. The Count de Paris did not think Mumford ought to have been hanged, but the people of New Orleans never shed a tear for him. He was a worthless fellow, like the chap, who, earlier in the war, had killed Ellsworth at Alexandria.

Several historians agree that the capture of New Orleans prevented a recognition of the Confederacy's independence by the Emperor of France, Napoleon III. That any negotiations were pending between foreign emissaries of the Confederate Government, looking to a surrender of a portion of Southern territory as a military base from which France could with greater assurance of success invade Mexico, is highly improbable. Much as Mr. Davis and his Cabinet would have welcomed Napoleon III.'s recognition of independence, any attempt to grant a foothold for French arms upon the Rio Grande would have met with stubborn opposi-

Ursuline Convent, below New Orleans.
(Showing High Wharf, outside Levee.)

tion from the most devoted adherents of " the sacred cause," and the Texans would have resented it to a man.

Vicksburg became the objective point.   It alone impeded the free passage of Federal traffic the entire length of the navigable river.

Vicksburg

The Vicksburg campaign naturally divided itself into two distinct enterprises, the first wholly military and the second naval-military.   An unsuccessful attempt by Grant and Sherman in 1862 to capture it becomes purely episodical considered in relation to the subsequent siege, which covers a period of twelve months.   Farragut was restrained from proceeding to Vicksburg by the Washington government.   At any time during that previous month of May, a few thousand men, accompanied by the gunboats of Farragut's squadron, could have seized Vicksburg and held it. The adjacent Federal army then could have been provisioned by river from North and South.

The Vicksburg problem, by the time it was put up to Grant, was one of grave seriousness and complexity. For this delay, which probably added half a year to the life of the rebellion, General Halleck always has been blamed.   It was a misfortune to South and North alike.   Farragut, with the same impetuosity he had shown at the forts, had attacked the batteries at Vicksburg on June 28, 1862, and passed them only to find the city impregnable to attack from the river.   He once more ran the batteries on July 15th, returning to New Orleans.

General Grant urgently suggested the investment

of Vicksburg and the destruction of the boats and traffic on the Yazoo River, but Halleck took no notice of the letter and Grant, after being kept idle at Corinth for months, of his own volition moved to Grand Junction and La Grange. The latter place is sixty miles east of Memphis, which had been occupied during the summer by Sherman, after the abandonment of Forts Pillow and Randolph. Grant then asked permission to move down the Mississippi Central Railroad to Holly Springs and Halleck consented.

About this time, Grant's troubles with McClernand, who had been his subordinate, began. The latter secured a leave of absence, went to Washington, and persuaded President Lincoln to organise an expedition to proceed against Vicksburg and to open the Mississippi to New Orleans. General Grant, on December 8th, sent Sherman to Memphis, with one division, where he was to mobilise all the troops he could gather; then proceed down the river and, assisted by Porter's gunboats, to reduce Vicksburg. Although McClernand had been directed to command such an expedition, a message wired to Sherman to that effect never reached him. Forrest had cut the telegraph lines. Sherman's expedition was then ready to start, and, in ignorance of McClernand's assignment, its commander was at Vicksburg before McClernand had crossed the Ohio River.

Sherman had asked the chief quartermaster at Saint Louis to furnish transports for thirty thousand men at Memphis at the earliest date. Sixty-seven steamboats arrived at Memphis December 19th, and embarkation began. Porter's gunboats were already at anchor off that city. Leaving Memphis on the 20th, a stop was made

at Helena next day to take aboard Steele's division, and
the boats ran their bows against the bank at Millikens
Bend, twenty miles up-stream from Vicksburg, before
dawn of the 25th. There, A. J. Smith's division was
landed to cut the railroad to Shreveport, which had
brought large quantities of supplies to the beleaguered
city. The three other divisions went to the mouth of
the Yazoo, and ascending that stream fourteen miles,
disembarked. Smith's division was reunited with the
main force next day, having destroyed the railroad to
the west. Sherman hoped to take Vicksburg with his
thirty thousand men, but, if that was impossible, he
intended to cut the railroad to Jackson and, with the
co-operation of Grant's army, to isolate the town.
The hope of a surprise failed utterly; raids by Forrest and Van Dorn destroyed the other part of the
plan.

General Forrest was raiding the region between
the Tennessee and Mississippi rivers and eluding
Grant's efforts to capture him. He fought about a
dozen skirmishes and battles but succeeded in returning east of the Tennessee, after he had broken up
Grant's railroad communication with Columbus, his
base of supplies. Meanwhile, Van Dorn, another Confederate cavalry general, successfully surprised Holly
Springs and took fifteen hundred prisoners. He
burned Grant's supplies at that place, valued at
$1,500,000. The efforts of these two raiders compelled
Grant to retire to Grand Junction, Corinth, and
Memphis.

The Confederates began to pour troops into Vicksburg. Pemberton went thither from the field. Sherman soon faced twelve thousand men, intrenched. The

bluff on which the city stands has a height of two hundred feet, which enabled the Confederates to maintain
close observation of every movement of Sherman's
troops in the Yazoo Valley. On December 29th,
Sherman made an assault upon an intrenched Confederate position at the top of a slope.   The attack
was unsuccessful.   The loss of life was severe, namely,
one hundred and ninety-one killed, ninety-eight
wounded, and seven hundred and fifty-six missing.
The Confederate losses were inconsiderable.   It
was a Federal defeat and resulted in orders from
Washington despatching Grant to the scene.   The
year 1862 closed dismally for the Federal campaign.

General Grant reached Memphis on January 10,
1863, and prepared to go to the aid of Sherman at
Vicksburg.   The project of a movement by river and
land was abandoned.   An opinion of General Francis
V. Greene, who has written a book on this subject, is
that the original plan for an advance upon Vicksburg,
down the Mississippi from Memphis is worthy of defence and discussion.   " The risks of such a movement
were far less than those of the final campaign from
Bruinsburg, through Jackson to Haines's Bluff," says
General Greene.   He also points out that " a direct
movement from Memphis against the rear of Vicksburg
was the one suggested by Grant in his letter to Halleck,
of October 26th."   There was not any co-operation from
New Orleans as had been expected.   General N. P.
Banks had reached that city to supersede Butler on
December 14th; and he sent a large force, without disembarking, to occupy Baton Rouge, which was done
without resistance.   An attack was not made on Port

Hudson until three months had passed. Its siege by Banks was dependent upon the success of General Grant at Vicksburg. On March 14, 1863, Farragut, (promoted to be rear-admiral on July 16, 1862), attempted to run the batteries at Port Hudson with a fleet of vessels but succeeded only in passing with his flag-ship, the *Hartford,* and a gunboat, which was lashed to her side.

When McClernand relieved Sherman, after the failure of the assault on Chickasaw Bluffs,—the supersedence having been decreed weeks before and not coming as a rebuke for defeat,—Sherman organised an expedition against Arkansas Post, up the Arkansas River. The engagement he fought there, on January 11th, was entirely successful. A Confederate fort that had interfered with traffic on that river was captured, several thousand prisoners taken, and sixty-six guns, and the place destroyed. It was a small affair, but Sherman was rehabilitated.

But the first movement against Vicksburg had been a disappointment and Grant began all over again.

After the harassing raids of Forrest and Van Dorn had been in part repaired, Grant began the investment of Vicksburg. Five distinct battles and continuous skirmishes occurred east of Vicksburg, all successful to the Federal cause. Porter ran the batteries on the night of April 16th, with the *Benton, Lafayette, Louisville, Mound City, Pittsburg,* and *Carondelet;* followed by three transports, convoyed by the gunboat, *Tuscumbia.* In the passage up-stream, these vessels were under fire for two hours but only one vessel was lost, the transport, *Henry Clay.* All the men aboard it were taken off by another steamer.

After preliminary fighting on the Big Black River on May 17, 1863, made memorable by Lawler's charge in his shirt-sleeves, Grant ordered an assault on Vicksburg on May 22d. It was unsuccessful. He then decided upon a siege.

The Mississippi was in Federal hands from Port Hudson to Vicksburg. This city was admirably defensible. Eight roads led into it from the East. The Confederate line was irregular, because it followed the crest of a ridge from the Yazoo River at the north, first eastward, then southward to the Jackson road (three miles behind the city), thence south-westerly to the Mississippi bank. Deep ravines lay in front. Grant's line of investment extended from Haines's Bluff (on the Yazoo) at the north, fifteen miles to Bruinsburg and thence to the Mississippi. Operating on lower ground, Grant's problem was more difficult than that of the Confederates. While intrenching, the efficiency of Grant's sharpshooters kept the engineers and workmen from serious interference. In few places were his lines of rifle-pits more than six hundred yards distant from the enemy. Many negroes, paid by the day, helped on the fortifications.

The first important engagement in the Civil War in which coloured troops took part was on the west side of the Mississippi, during this siege, at Millikens Bend, (June 7, 1863), where they showed excellent fighting qualities. An attack by the Confederates was repulsed.

Grant's forces at Vicksburg had been so strongly reinforced that on June 14th, he had seventy-one thousand men. He relieved McClernand of the command of the Thirteenth Army Corps on the 19th and sent

General Pemberton's Headquarters, Vicksburg.

him back to Illinois. The cause was a flamboyant order by McClernand, praising his own men to the prejudice of other troops.

Grant had two hundred and twenty guns mounted by June 30th, but the grave menace of Johnston's army in the rear still existed. Intercepted messages from the latter to Pemberton indicated that he was about to move westward to raise the siege of Vicksburg. This necessitated two lines for Grant,—an emergency for which he had carefully prepared,—one facing Johnston and the other confronting the beleaguered city. A mine had been exploded on June 25th, but the crater had not been sufficiently large to admit the entrance of the Federal column. In this situation, a general assault was determined upon by Grant. The date was fixed for the 6th; but at 10 A.M. on the 3d, white flags appeared over parts of the Confederate works. Pemberton sent a member of his staff with a letter to Grant. The Federal General would not entertain any terms but " unconditional surrender "; after personal interviews between the two commanders, however, and an all-night parley with his own general officers, some modifications were made by Grant. He agreed to parole the troops, to permit Confederate officers to wear their side arms, and to allow all staff officers one horse. On the night of July 3d, General Grant summoned all his division commanders, which, he says in his *Memoirs* was " the nearest approach to a ' council of war ' I ever held." The surrender occurred on July 4th, the day on which was completed the victory at Gettysburg. Grant says: " The fate of the Confederacy was sealed when Vicksburg fell. Much hard fighting was to be done afterward and many precious lives sacrificed; but the morale was with the supporters of the Union ever after."

Port Hudson surrendered to General Banks on July 9th.

Almost simultaneously with these two great Federal triumphs, the Confederate General Holmes attacked Prentiss at Helena, Arkansas, with eight thousand men and was defeated by a force hardly more than half as numerous. This was the final effort to relieve Vicksburg and was made too late to have been effective under any circumstances. There were thirty-one thousand six hundred prisoners surrendered at Vicksburg and six thousand at Port Hudson. When Grant entered the city, it was a community of cave-dwellers. Living quarters had been dug in the sides of the clay cliffs that afforded secure protection from shells that were constantly thrown into the town from Porter's boats upon the river. "The Father of Waters" was now in Federal hands from source to mouth. Fiercely as the conflict raged in the East, dwellers along the banks of the Mississippi knew only peace.

History's verdict will probably fix Grant's master stroke, as a military tactician, at Vicksburg rather than at Richmond or Appomattox. There is not a career in the annals of time exactly like his. A discredited tanner's clerk, who had set out in his fortieth year to fight such battles as the world never had known, ended by having command of half a million men and twice becoming President of the United States. It is more marvellous than the tale of Joan of Arc!

CHAPTER XVI

"The Mississippi Bubble"

THE only one to give the "Father of Waters" a bad name was a Scotchman named John Law. His schemes of "frenzied finance" had no more to do with the Mississippi than with the Ganges. The Province of Louisiana never profited to the value of a livre from all the notes issued in the name of "The Company of the Indies." Law's tremendous "gamble," is known in history as "The Mississippi Bubble," and, as such, it claims space in this volume.

It is the only Scotch twist ever given to the mighty river.

From the view-point of the bankers of to-day, John Law was misunderstood. In a broker's opinion, Law's partner in the "flotation," the Duc d'Orléans, "laid down on him" and caused the failure of an elaborate financial problem. Had Law lived in the twentieth century, his methods would have been described as superb finance. He was a promoter, and much is permitted to that branch of the profession in extracting money from the public. Modern "promoting" consists in unloading upon people who have money securities of real or apocryphal values. The problem is to sell certificates representing shares in "soulless" corporations and to get money for them. A writer in the *Bankers' Magazine* frankly says:

Like many reformers who succeed in unchaining pent-up social and financial forces, Law was unable to keep these forces under command, and for the chaos that resulted he is held responsible, although no one was more surprised than he that the spirit of peace and prosperity, which he summoned, changed so soon into a demon of discord and disaster.

There we have the American view-point, exactly as the failure of the attempt to pool the Great Northern and the Northern Pacific railroads under the title of "The Northern Securities Company," in May, 1901, would have been explained by the small group of New York bankers and promoters who attempted to carry the plan into effect. But the French of to-day, as of two hundred years ago, do not accept Law's ideas of finance. In less degree, history repeated itself in France when the Panama Canal "bubble" burst, at the close of the nineteenth century, and the good name of a more deserving man than John Law, the Count de Lesseps, was branded with similar disgrace. The historic imposition of the Assignats of 1789 had its counterpart in Civil War finance of the United States, in 1861–65.

John Law's preparation for a career that made him so conspicuous in the history of the eighteenth century was not that by which several of America's successful multi-millionaires equipped themselves for the acquirement and absorption of other people's money. He did not enter a broker's office and learn to hypothecate shares left with him as collateral, or to charge interest on loans that were not made, or to collect and retain interest upon stocks or bonds held as margins, and in that way eventually to become the heartless creature that the successful stock-broker must be. He did "get near" to banking methods in Amsterdam, later, as we shall see, but only after he had failed to carry out plans of his own.

The father of John Law was a wealthy Edinburgh goldsmith. At twenty, young John left home, saw Europe, and returned home an accomplished "specu-lator." In Law's time, there was not a stock exchange, and the only means of "speculation" was what is now indecorously described as "gambling," or "bucking the tiger." Otherwise, Law's morals were excellent. He went to Holland to study the financial methods of that wonderful people. The Dutch would "plunge" on anything from a tulip bulb to a new brand of schnapps. That rich, resolute Republic had inherited all the push of the Venetians, without their vices. Amsterdam was the commercial metropolis of Europe. Money could be had there for two or three per cent. Her celebrated and mysterious bank promised inexhaustible resources. Holland's financial system was an enigma. Law fathomed it before he was thirty years of age. He was a solver of riddles.

When Law returned to Scotland again and found that business was stagnant, he suggested a remedy. He ascribed the commercial lethargy to "a deficiency of capital." What Law had not learned was the difference between "capital" and "currency." He thought them the same. Law's utterances at the time are historic: "The proprietor needs money to clear up his land; the manufacturer must have it to multiply his looms; the merchant cries for it to extend his opera-tions." Law's meaning was that every business needs funds for first materials and manual labour. It was almost a gleam of our vaunted "protection," our Government and State land-grants to railroads.

When Law became convinced that the prosperity
of a country is gauged by the currency in circulation,
he lay awake of nights planning the creation of the
needed conditions. He offered the scheme to his own
country in 1700, but the canny Scots promptly
stamped it " Nae gude! " He exhausted all arguments
that the American " Greenbackers " employed at the
end of the nineteenth century. Then he crossed the
channel and was unsuccessful at Paris, although he had
the favour of the Duc d'Orléans. Thence, he went to
Italy. He was told at Turin to get out of the country
and he took the advice. Next, we hear of him in Germany; but no better success attended him. On the
green cloth, however, he won enormous sums. In
Germany, he gathered in fully two million livres. With
this capital, Law hurried to Paris,—much as a young
American takes his fortune, won in a wild-cat mine, to
New York, buys a seat on the Stock Exchange, and
plays broker and banker.

Louis XIV. had just died, after bankrupting the
treasury; but Law knew there were millions of livres
in the stockings, tea-caddies, and strong boxes of the
bourgeoisie throughout the beautiful land of France.
He saw an opportunity to try his experiment,—much
as Dr. Ox, when he reached the sleepy city of Quiquen-
done in the Low Countries,—and he sought his former
patron, the Duc d'Orléans, who had become regent.
The way for his historic enterprise was made easy.

The specie circulation in France at the beginning
of 1716 was supposed to be eight hundred million livres,
or,—quoting the French livre as of equal value to the
English shilling,—roughly, $200,000,000. This was
thought to be an intolerable burden, although it was

only one fifth that imposed upon the people of the United States by the Civil War. Previous fluctuations in weight of the livre were seized upon by Law to issue demand notes, payable in livres containing a specified quantity of "silver of established fineness." Just what was to be "established" was not stated. This act removed the stigma from the livre, when the coin was supplanted by Law's paper money. He contrived, by that means, to float fifty-nine million livres (say $15,000,000), of his paper! A mere bagatelle, as shown by the ease with which shares of the United Ship-building Company, having a capital of $100,000,-000, were put out in this country.

On January 1, 1719, the regent, in the name of France, took possession of Law's bank, due to some dispute over "graft" coming to him. His first act was to discredit Law by omitting from the faces of the notes the words, "of the same rate and fineness." The printing-presses then got busy and, in eleven months' time, issued ten hundred and ten million livres of paper money. Let us call this $252,000,000.

Here is where the name of the Mississippi becomes associated with Law. While the bank was in his hands, he and his partners had been granted the exclusive privilege of trading to the French possessions on the continent of America. This single fact has attached to Law's bold financiering in France the name of "The Mississippi Bubble." The charter also included the West Indies and " all countries to the east of the Cape of Good Hope." Law had incorporated under the title of "The Company of the Indies." This corporation soon absorbed remarkable powers. It "took over" the mint, to coin the livres any weight its directors chose; it engaged to lend to the Government sixteen hundred million livres ($400,000,000), at three per cent., and to do this the bank was restored to Law on February 22, 1720. Five days later, the infamous *arrêt* was issued which prohibited any corporation or individual from possessing *any* bullion, or more than five hundred livres in specie. The notes of the Company of the Indies were made the only legal tender. This compelled all hoarders of money to deposit it in the bank and to receive notes therefor. The value of a French mark of silver had been forty livres; but, on March 5th, an *arrêt* appeared fixing the value of the mark of silver at eighty livres. This was semi-repudiation; it enabled Law to settle at one half, *but that was not where the high finance came in.* It was a lure to draw into the company all the silver still outstanding. This is made clear by the next step. The announcement was issued that after April 1st, the value of the mark of silver would only be seventy livres and after May 1st, only sixty-five livres. That was a "hurry up" order of the rankest kind. The idea was worthy of Wall Street. Naturally, unthinking men desired to get as much paper for their coin as possible, and the rush to the bargain counter was unabated. In three weeks, in anticipation of the impending reduction in value of the mark, Law was given forty-four million livres of coin for his worthless paper. Thus, and through other channels, this frenzied financier issued, between March 1st and May 2d, notes equal to 1,626,672,910 livres. All told, notes were out for 2,235,085,590 livres, or double the average amount of money in France. This proves that people in other parts of Europe, looking for "good things," got "stung."

" In less than three weeks after the last issue of notes," says the unknown banker, writing in the *Bankers' Magazine,* "the bank was *murdered* by the Government: without that interference, the bank was due to have lived exactly three months longer." The misfortune that deprived Law of three additional months, in which to rob the people of Europe, appears to grieve the banker-author deeply. He had practically gathered in every livre of loose change in the kingdom; a fairly reasonable man would think the hour to stop had struck.

The collapse in value of the paper money was greater than that which came to the bills of the Southern Confederacy.

In the opinion of the editor of the *Bankers' Magazine,*[1]

The fatal errors of Law's " system " were: First, He held that paper money, if it rested upon any basis of solid wealth besides coin, was just as sound and as firmly established as if represented by specie in the vaults of the issuer. Second, He believed that an act of Government could give the potency and value of money to paper which had not that support of coin.

Similar theories have been argued in both Houses of the Congress of the United States during the last generation. Law's opportunity was offered by the revulsion of sentiment in France following the death of Louis XIV. During the King's life, he had been the object of popular adulation; but hardly was he laid in the grave before his statues were stoned and his name

[1] *Banker's Magazine,* 1874.

was execrated.[1] Law had his play, however. He made money " plenty."

[1] Charles Mackay's *History of the Mississippi Scheme* is worth reading; Emerson Hough's novel is highly entertaining.

St. Anthony Fall, 1910.

CHAPTER XVII

Great Cities of the Valley

FIVE great cities have developed along the Mississippi Valley. The one farthest north, Minneapolis, is at the head of navigation and within six hundred miles of the river's source. The one farthest south, New Orleans, is one hundred and twenty miles from the river's mouth. Community of interests makes of Saint Paul and Minneapolis one city. Saint Louis owes its location to the nearby outlet of the Missouri. Memphis occupies a point almost on an air line between the industrial and commercial centres of the North-east and the growing South-west.

Rivers are the foster-mothers of communities, small or large. In most cases, streams upon which large cities stand have been made to serve purposes of foreign or domestic commerce. When too shallow for ships that go down to the sea, they have been canalised and made to furnish internal transportation. Moscow and Madrid are two exceptional examples of cities independent of usable rivers. Madrid was built by Philip II. upon what he declared to be " an impossible site." It stands upon the top of a truncated cone, having a desert of sage-bush upon three quarters of its circumference. Cairo, " the City of Saladin," owes much to the wonderful river that has converted a long cañon, called the Nile Valley, and its own delta into the most fertile land upon this earth. Paris, as Violet le Duc demonstrates, never would have risen to greatness except for an island in the Seine that suggested a site for defence in a period when only the strongest and most wary survived. Chicago is upon the Great Lakes, having river outlet through the majestic St. Lawrence. St. Petersburg has the Neva, London the Thames, Vienna the Danube, and New York the Hudson and a salt water strait. Berlin, for example, could do without the Spree; but every city is made more self-reliant and prosperous by association with a river, although boats from across the seas may not come to its wharves.

The Mississippi is navigable for large freight-carrying steamboats from the Gulf of Mexico to Minneapolis, a distance of two thousand one hundred and seventy-nine miles. With the possible exception of Memphis, the cities and villages along its banks owe what they are to the river. Some communities that promised to achieve greatness have failed of their apparent destinies; but all are prosperous and their people are intelligent and happy.

SAINT PAUL–MINNEAPOLIS

The " Twin City " of Minnesota must one day become united in name and municipal government. The same fantastic, deterrent rivalry exists that deferred for fifty years a consolidation of Brooklyn and Manhattan, although the two cities were only separated by a narrow strait connecting Long Island Sound with New York Bay. The union of the two Minnesota cities would give to that State one community of half a million people.

Louis Hennepin probably was the first white man

City of Minneapolis, from the Eastern Bank.

to see the great fall in the Mississippi, which he named Anthony after his patron saint: therefore, he may be credited with discovery of the sites of Saint Paul and Minneapolis.   That was in 1680, sixty years after the Pilgrims had landed at Plymouth Rock.   For nearly a century, no record exists of any verification of Hennepin's statement.   Captain Jonathan Carver, of Connecticut, ascended the Mississippi, as far as the fall, in November, 1776.   The island now below the cascade was then upon its crest.   Lieutenant Pike, before setting out upon his historic journey up the river, held a council with the Indians above the fall.   Not long after (1819), Colonel Leavenworth, with ninety-eight soldiers, established a stockade upon the heights overlooking the junction of the Minnesota with the Mississippi, calling it Fort St. Anthony; but, in 1824, at General Winfield Scott's suggestion, the name was changed to Snelling, as a worthy tribute to the gallant commander of the post.   The first Mississippi steamboat, the *Virginia,* ascended to Fort Snelling on May 10, 1823.   Steamboat traffic to the head of navigation reached its highest point in 1857, when ninety-nine boats plied upon the Upper Mississippi, the annual number of their trips to Saint Paul exceeding nine hundred and fifty.

A town had grown at the east side of the fall, taking name therefrom.   On the admission of Minnesota as a State, and later, this town was a candidate for the capital site.   On the other side of the river a highly important incident occurred.   A Swiss watchmaker, named Perry, tried to establish a home upon the military reservation surrounding Fort Snelling. He was driven away and became the first actual settler

at the site of Saint Paul.   In 1841, Father Lucien
Galtier built a rude chapel of logs upon the river bluff,
near what was then the steamboat landing, and named
it " The Chapel of Saint Paul."   This humble church
gave name to the present capital of the State.   The
city's history really begins in 1849, in which year
Minnesota was organised as a territory and Alexander Ramsey was appointed its Governor.   Statehood
followed in 1858.

Meanwhile, another town had begun to form upon
the west bank, at the Fall of St. Anthony.   In 1849,
the War Department gave to one Robert Smith, a
member of the House of Representatives at Washington, a claim to one hundred and sixty acres of land
upon the west bank and guaranteed to him the right
to purchase the water-power upon that side of the river.
It was not the first example of special favours to Con-
gressmen, but memory thereof still lingers in Minnesota.
The new town was called Minneapolis, although legal
titles to land could not be had until 1855.   It was incorporated as a city in 1867.   The city of St. Anthony
was consolidated with Minneapolis in 1872, under the
name of the latter,—the two boroughs being distinguished as East and West.   The State University
was located in Minneapolis, East, bringing much pres-
tige to the combined city. (" Rah, rah, rah! Ski-U-mah
—hoorah! hoorah!   Varsity! Varsity! Minne-so-ta! ")
Minneapolis was by that time the manufacturing centre
of the young State.   The power of the fall at that point
was calculated at thirty thousand horses, and mammoth
saw and grist mills rapidly took form to utilise it.   The
splendid timber of the Upper Mississippi was " logged "
to Minneapolis, there to be converted into lumber.

Fort Snelling, 1908.

(Copyright, 1908, by T. W. Ingersoll.)

Grinding of flour grew to such mammoth proportions that the output of the Minneapolis mills at present is set down at eighty thousand barrels per day. The United States Government in recent years has done much to maintain the evenness of the water supply at St. Anthony. A system of reservoirs has been built for impounding the floods of the Upper Mississippi. These barrages constitute a unique feature of the economies of the stream. Like those on the Nile, their purpose is to secure a more even water volume, and they minimise the dangers of overflow by restraining the spring floods. A new dam at Grand Rapids is a small replica of that at Assuan, with its gates. In some instances, the value of the dams is yet to be demonstrated. They certainly have proved to be aids to navigation by small craft. Water storage occurs at the following points: The Winnebagoshish reservoir, with seventy-five square miles of surface; Leech Lake reservoir, one hundred and sixty-five square miles of surface; Pine River reservoir; Pokegama Lake reservoir, ten square miles, and Sandy Lake reservoir, area nine square miles.

Two features of special pride to the people of Minneapolis are Minnehaha Fall and Lake Minnetonka. The little stream that flows over the rocky ledge and creates the pretty waterfall often dries up in hot weather. In the words of Metellus Thomson, "It is like the Manzanares, at Madrid, it goes out of town in midsummer." The lake, however, is a charming and popular warm-weather retreat for the people of the Twin City.

Saint Paul always has been the capital of the Territory and State and is its political centre. It was incorporated as a city on March 4, 1854, a trifle more

19

than four years before Minnesota became a State of the Union. Saint Paul has become the railroad centre of the North-west. Seven different lines of rails connect it with Chicago. Two trunk lines to the Pacific coast start there. A magnificent State Capitol has recently been finished, at a cost of $5,000,000, and a Roman Catholic cathedral that will excel in beauty any religious structure west of St. Patrick's cathedral in New York. The Municipal Auditorium will seat ten thousand people. An island in the river has been converted into a public park and a comprehensive system of free public baths established.

SAINT LOUIS

The proud claim of the people of "The Mound City" is that Saint Louis "stands at the heart of the Continent." Its site is very near the centre of the Mississippi Valley, the basin of North America. It is about midway between Saint Paul and New Orleans; Pittsburg and Denver. Topographically, it covers a series of ridges between the Mississippi, the Missouri, and the Meramec. Its general altitude is about two hundred feet above the rivers, rising gradually to that height. It extends about twenty miles along the west bank of the Mississippi. It is one thousand three hundred and seventy miles from the Gulf of Mexico; one hundred river steamers are often seen at one time upon its levee.

Saint Louis dates from the arrival of Pierre Leclade Liguest, a New Orleans merchant who had obtained an exclusive concession to trade in furs on the upper Mississippi and Missouri rivers, and took up his

Saint Paul from Mississippi Bridge.
(Copyright, 1908, by T. W. Ingersoll.)

claim on February 15, 1764. Auguste Chouteau, a
companion, cleared the first ground and built the first
house. Liguest had left New Orleans, with a party
of French *voyageurs,* in August of 1763, for the avowed
purpose of founding a city on the Mississippi near the
mouth of the Missouri. Shortly after his arrival in
the north, the cession to Great Britain of the Illinois
country occurred and many French, who disliked the
British, moved to Liguest's settlement on the west bank
of the river, already named in honour of the patron
saint of the King of France. When the territory of
Louisiana was retroceded to Spain, the French Governor at Saint Louis died of a broken heart.

St. Ange de Bellerive became Governor-General in
1765. The first grants of land were made by Liguest,
—who often wrote his name Leclade in deeds,—to
Bellerive on August 11, 1766. The Spaniards never
exercised any control over the settlement; but, in 1767,
word was received that Spain intended to garrison the
site. This announcement created alarm and threats of
resistance. The fort was not built and the troops never
arrived. Bellerive was a warm friend of Pontiac, the
Ottawa chief, and after the Spaniards left, the famous
Indian visited him. At that time, with the single exception of Red Jacket, Pontiac was the greatest of all
living American Indians. His dream was to drive the
English into the Atlantic. To this day, French de-
scendants at Saint Louis believe that Pontiac was
poisoned by the British.

Don Alexander O'Reilly came from Spain to New
Orleans to assume command of the Louisiana territory.
He had three thousand troops and his reception by the
French population was very cold. He sent a deputy,

Piernas, to Saint Louis in 1770. This man was successful in ingratiating himself with the people. When an Osage chief announced the intention of killing Piernas, he was himself slain by a Shawnee. True to the mercurial French temperament, the Osage was buried with much honour upon the eminence that afterward was to give to Saint Louis the title of " The Mound City."

The Governor who succeeded Piernas was popular, but he was replaced by Don Fernando de Leyba in 1778. The American Revolution was then in progress. Both French and Spanish hated the English and sympathised with the Colonists. An intrenchment was thrown around the village; but, in 1780, a party of Canadian-Frenchmen, aided by one thousand up-river Indians, attacked the town, killed forty of its citizens, and took as many more prisoners. Francis Crozat, the next commander, so thoroughly fortified the place that it never again was attacked. The first recorded " June rise " of the Mississippi occurred in 1785 and threw the citizens of the town into consternation. Saint Louis was flooded to the present line of Main Street. The immediate effect of the overflow was to drive settlers from the lowlands to the city upon the hills; but, in 1790, it did not possess a post-office, ferry, or manufactory of any sort. The Saint Louis merchant of that time kept his stock in a chest holding a few tools, rifles, shot, powder, and red paint. A ferry was established in 1797, that is still in operation.

The history of Saint Louis really begins with the Louisiana Purchase (1803) that joined the destiny of that vast tract of territory with the United States. Lewis and Clark built their flat-boats and outfitted

The Minnesota State Capitol, Saint Paul.
(Copyright, 1909, by T. W. Ingersoll.)

their epoch-making expedition up the Missouri and down the Columbia River at this thriving village, then having a population of six thousand: but their report makes scant mention of the natural advantages of the site.   Lieutenant Pike began his memorable trip up the Mississippi from the budding city.   The first newspaper in the West, *The Republic,* was founded there in 1804.

Jean N. Nicollet, whose footsteps we have followed in the Itasca wilderness, was the first eulogist of Saint Louis.   " Future generations will inquire of us all that concerns the origin of this Queen City of the majestic Mississippi," he wrote in 1838.   " Saint Louis was born French," he said in 1842, " but her cradle was hung in the forest, her infancy stunted by unavoidable privations, and her early maturity retarded by the terror of the Indian cry.   Abandoned by her Castilian guardians, she was reclaimed by her first parent only to be once more repudiated."

The great Territory of Missouri was organised in 1813 and in the same year the first brick house was built in the young city, then boasting sixteen thousand people.   Saint Louis was so remote from the Atlantic seaboard that her citizens hardly knew of the second war with Great Britain.   The town had been incorporated in 1809 and a city charter was secured in 1822. General Lafayette was warmly welcomed in 1825. Cholera ravaged the city in 1849.   The first railroad was opened in 1851.   The Missouri Compromise gave a check to the city's growth; at the beginning of the Civil War, owing to the attitude of the Governor of Missouri, it became turbulent, like Baltimore, because many of its people believed Missouri to be in fact, as well as in name, a Southern State and obligated to secede from the Federal Union.

Saint Louis was swept by a tornado on May 27, 1896. The storm approached from the north-west, crossed the city from Tower Grove Park to East Saint Louis, on the Illinois bank of the Mississippi, destroying $15,000,000 worth of property.

The phenomenal growth of Saint Louis is indicated by an eight-fold increase in its assessed valuation in forty years. It occupies a unique position among all municipalities of the United States. It is a free city, absolutely independent of the county government. It has its own executive, judiciary, and legislature. In Tower Grove Park is a mulberry tree, reared from a slip brought from Shakespeare's grave at Stratford-on-Avon by the late Adelaide Neilson. Unlike New Orleans, the French characteristics of Saint Louis have almost disappeared, although the French language is spoken in many households. It is to-day the most German city in the American Republic, except Milwaukee.

MEMPHIS

Memphis occupies the only site on the Mississippi adapted for a town of large size between the mouth of the Ohio and Natchez. Prior to the treaty of Ildefonso, the Spaniards built a fort there; but the history of the city begins with a grant from the State of North Carolina to John Rice, by which, for ten pounds sterling per hundred acres, paid to the State, Rice acquired five thousand acres of land upon Chicasa Bluff. This elevated plateau had been the home of the

View of Saint Louis from the River, during the Visit of
President Taft.

(Copyright, 1909, by Verner White.)

Chicasa branch of the great Muskhogean tribe. The grant was recorded on June 24, 1784. The irregular tract began one mile below the mouth of Wolf River and extended north many miles: a description of the plot is very complex. Upon this five thousand acres, a large part of Memphis stands.

John Rice was owner of large tracts of land in middle and eastern Tennessee,—a very energetic man. He removed from North Carolina to Nashville soon after entry of these lands, and was killed by Indians in 1791.[1] Judge Overton, in 1794, bought for $500 from Elisha Rice, brother and an heir of the deceased owner, the Chicasa Bluff tract. The Judge was timid regarding the title to the land and insisted that Elisha Rice's three brothers join in the transfer. Next day after purchase, Overton conveyed an undivided half interest in the land to General Andrew Jackson. The two men were bosom friends, and the purchase was doubtless on joint account.

The North-west, except a settlement at Saint Louis, was unpeopled west of the Ohio. The Mississippi Valley was without population, except at Natchez and New Orleans. Jackson sold three quarters of his half interest, so that Chicasa Bluff was owned thus: Judge Overton, one half; Andrew Jackson, one eighth; William Winchester, one eighth; and James Winchester, one quarter. The property remained in these hands until President Madison's administration, when Isaac Selby and Andrew Jackson were appointed a commission to negotiate a treaty with the native tribes. By a covenant, signed October 19, 1818, the Chicagaws surrendered all claim to lands lying north of the

[1] Haywood's *History of Tennessee.*

Tennessee boundary. Memphis was plotted in the following year, while General Jackson was in Florida. Changes in the river front rendered a re-survey of the Rice tract difficult. Many years of litigation followed: but the Jackson treaty of 1818 extinguished all the Indian titles. There was a grant to one John Ramsey that conflicted, and although no consideration was mentioned, its genuineness never was questioned.

Memphis was named after the ancient city on the Nile, which stood twenty miles south of the present capital of Egypt, Cairo. The new Memphis was laid off to the cardinal points, parallel with the Mississippi, and upon the bluff, twenty-five to thirty feet above the highest flood. A cluster of islands in the river north of the city was known as " Paddy's Hen and Chickens "; three miles below is President's Island, containing several thousand acres of land, mostly fertile.[1] The first mayor of Memphis, M. B. Winchester, took office in March, 1827.

During the Civil War, Memphis became a point of strategic importance in General Grant's campaign which ended with the siege and capture of Vicksburg. Major-General Washburn put the city under martial law on July 2, 1864; but the rights of private property were fully respected and the order was revoked on July 2, 1865.

Among heroes of the city, Colonel David Crockett is the immortal figure. He crossed the Mississippi from Memphis for the last time on his way to Texas and to his glorious death at the Alamo, in San Antonio. He had spent considerable time in Memphis in 1823 and

[1] *History of Memphis*, by James D. Davis, p. 29.

The City of Memphis.

(From a Water-color Painting by T. F. Anderson.)

the local history literally teems with stories of Crockett.
Thomas H. Benton's name is also associated with the
early days of the city. An anecdote of Abraham Lincoln
is recorded by Davis: "In the summer of 1831, a steamboat bound up the river touched at Foy's Point, opposite
Memphis. A young man landed and asked one Wap-
panocha Furgason for work, saying he had been robbed
on the boat. He was put to chopping wood and worked
until he had earned money enough to proceed to his
home in Illinois."

The revival season of Lorenzo Dow, in 1826, is
mentioned in all histories of Memphis. The parson is
described by the historian thus: "He was below me-
dium height, awkward, with swaggering walk and
gesture; but he possessed much natural drollery
by which he could rouse his hearers from tears to
laughter."

The recent growth of Memphis has been phenomenal.

NEW ORLEANS

After Quebec and Mont-Real, New Orleans became
the "dream town" of France in the New World. It rose
upon the wreck of John Law's preposterous Mississippi
scheme which almost bankrupted the people of France
but served to draw universal attention to the Province
of Louisiana, that up to that time had received little
popular thought. The first act of Bienville's second
administration as Governor of Louisiana was to select
a site for the capital of the colony. He chose the spot
where now stands the City of New Orleans. There he
erected a stockade. Bienville not only showed his

sagacity but his courage, because he dared to ignore
the preferences of the home government for Manchac,
where communication was open with the Gulf through
the Bayou Manchac and the Amite River. The land
now occupied by the "Crescent City" was marshy and
covered with a scrubby growth of semi-tropical verdure.
Bienville foresaw that ships of deeper draught than
those then in use would be built and that the river
must be the city's outlet to the sea. Remember his Canadian birth and his close acquaintance with the gigantic
St. Lawrence,—the one river of this continent great
from beginning to end.

Then followed the capture of Pensacola, its re-
capture by the Spanish, through bad faith of the Spanish commander at Havana, to which port the two French
corvettes carried their prisoners only to be seized, loaded
with Spanish troops, and sent back for the reversal of
a short-lived victory. But, additional aid coming to
Bienville at Mobile, whither he had gone, he returned
to Pensacola and turned defeat into complete victory.
Deserters from the French to the Spanish were summarily punished with death. Bienville began to encounter renewed opposition to the transfer of the seat
of government to the site of the capital of his choice.
An unexampled overflow of the Mississippi that year
(1719) was urged, with much force, against the location. Hubert, a special messenger from the King
of France, insisted upon Natchez; but his pleas were
inspired by self-interest, because he was a large land-
owner there. Bienville promptly exposed this propen-
sity to "graft" and stood firmly by his choice. Three
agents of the Company of the Indies appear to have
had more power than Bienville or the royal commis-

L'Union Française, New Orleans.

Moss-covered Oak, Audubon Park, New Orleans.

sioner, for they fixed the capital at New Biloxi, on the bay of that name. Extortionate taxation was then imposed upon the colonists of Louisiana by the company's agents. Not until 1722 was the site chosen by Jean Baptiste Lemoyne de Bienville officially proclaimed as the capital of the vast province. The exiles from Acadia settled there in 1765. The people of the town rose to arms in 1768, against the cession of Louisiana to Spain, but were compelled to submit under the menace of a large Spanish force in 1769. Two fires devastated the city, the first in 1788 and the second in 1894. The destiny of New Orleans followed that of the Louisiana Province, which was returned by Spain to France in 1800 and by France ceded to the United States. Aaron Burr's conspiracy was defeated in 1807 and the battle of New Orleans occurred in 1815.

An interesting incident in early colonial days was the arrival of "the Casket Girls," in the spring of 1728. Unlike predecessors, they had not been taken from correctional institutions but were daughters of respectable, although poor, bourgeoise parents. When they sailed from France, the India Company gave to each girl a casket containing some useful articles of dress, and this fact gave to them the designation of "*les filles à la cassette*." The Ursuline Sisters cared for them until they were married: owing to their good character, it subsequently became a matter of distinction to claim descent from "the Casket Girls," rather than from the earlier arrivals.

To this day, the nomenclature of the streets tells the story of French and Spanish domination. Names chosen by Le Blond de la Tour, when he plotted the city, remain, especially such evidences of French-Creole gallantry as the pretty feminine names of Suzette, Angelie, Annette, and Celeste. Several hundred saints thus honoured proves the religious character of the early citizens. Although the Creoles were overawed by the Spaniards, during the French Revolution they imitated the classic tendencies of their "dear Paris," and named many streets in honour of Greek and Roman heroes or statesmen. The three graces, twelve gods *persona grata* on Olympus, and the nine muses were thus honoured. The water-works had place in the streets of the Naiades and Dryades.

The Creoles regard the language they speak as "a beautiful French." They are so much a part of New Orleans that even their caressing, delicious dialect is worth journeying thither to hear. One can begin at 253 Rue Royale, in "a region of architectural decrepitude,"—where is the snug cottage of "Madame Delphine," with its bristling, sierra-like ridgepole of tiles, —and, by the route of the French market, travel through the dreamland of the Creole quarter, finding wonderment everywhere. A typical corner exists at Toulouse Street. A few steps' divergence along that quiet lane is the French Opera and under its shadow is the rendezvous of artists, "Au Point d'Orgue," where painters have congregated for more than a hundred years to take cognac and absinthe. Once in a generation, a new door is hung, but nobody remembers when a key was turned in a lock. It is the abode of yesterday and to-morrow. Its shabbiness endears it to Bohemia,—and all the French quarter, like the *Quartier Latin* of Paris, is Bohemian. At St. Anne and Royale is the "Café des Exiles," where every chord of a happy-

A Typical Corner.

Café des Artists.

hearted life finds its responsive note. The Creole girl is always attractive, rarely beautiful, and, as a matron, she grows old with the same gracefulness that marks every step in her life. Mr. Cable is the troubadour of the Creole; one may not intrude upon a field so pre-empted.[1]

There is a street play and pageant in New Orleans every February. " Mardi Gras " is conducted by carnival secret societies. It is a French importation, brought over during the reign of Louis Philippe. Long preparation and lavish expenditure of money characterise these parades and the ball that closes the festivities.

Voudouism is still practised among the negroes dwelling upon the shores of Lake Pontchartrain. The annual service of worship of the Evil One occurs on St. John's eve.

The Cathedral of St. Louis, on Chartres Street, the fourth church upon the site, embodies the history of Catholicism in Louisiana. The Capuchins originally gained control of the religious element in the province; but in 1721, Father Charlevoix, a Jesuit missionary, came from Canada, by the familiar Illinois and Mississippi rivers route. He found the Capuchins so thoroughly intrenched that he threw mud at their service. Some of his reports sent back to France contain venemous attacks upon the morality of the Capuchin priesthood. Similar bitterness between various

[1] The writer of this volume is under obligations to Professor Armour Caldwell for original photographs of the French quarter of New Orleans. Mr. Louis Jonté Meader, formerly of New Orleans, kindly placed his library at the writer's disposal. If one wants to understand the New Orleans of the eighteenth century he must study Mr. Cable.

branches of the Christian faith is seen in Jerusalem to-day. Religiously, the Louisiana territory was ultimately divided into three districts. The Capuchins retained jurisdiction from the mouth of the Mississippi to that of the Illinois. The barefoot Carmelites were given stewardship over Mobile, Biloxi, and Alebamos. The Jesuits had the country watered by the Illionis and Wabash, practically what is to-day Indiana and Illinois. Governor Bienville was very intolerant; no religion except that of the Roman Church was permitted. All Jews were expelled. The arrival of the Ursuline nuns in 1727 is an important episode in the history of the city. They occupied a convent on Condé (now Chartres) Street from 1730 until 1824, when they removed to spacious quarters on the river's bank, south of the city. During the intervening century, they toiled namelessly and without earthly reward in the hospitals and among the poor. War between the Capuchins and Jesuits was most violent in 1755; but the former won and the latter were expelled. All Jesuit property was seized and sold at auction for $180,000, an enormous sum in those times.

When Spain resumed authority over the province, six Capuchin friars arrived from Spain in 1789, chief of whom was Father Sedella, remembered best as "Father Antoine." He was fifty years curate; but the actual founder of the cathedral appeared in the person of Andreas Almonaster-y-Roxas, who, in 1792, undertook to build a superb edifice in place of one destroyed by fire. At the time the United States took control of Louisiana (1803), there was not in the entire colony a single Protestant church or Jewish synagogue. The religious heroes of New Orleans are Father Dagobert,

The Monk's Court. (Cathedral on the Right.)

The Cathedral of Saint Louis.

Superior of the Capuchins in Louisiana, a typical Amador of Turpenay, and Padre Antonio, mentioned above under his French name. The latter came from Madrid as Commissioner of the Holy Inquisition; but the then Governor of Louisiana, Don Eslevan Miro, promptly told the monk that heretics were not to be arrested, tried, or burned while he held the post. The zealous priest was forcibly shipped to Cadiz; but he returned as a humble servant of the Faith to become universally beloved.

Jean Lafitte, smuggler, pirate, and hero, the antithesis of all that was good or noble, belongs to any sketch of New Orleans, however brief. He has been mentioned in our account of the final grapple with Great Britain upon the Plain of Chalmette. His loyalty preceding that important event, at a time when such fidelity was ungratefully received, and the splendid heroism of Lafitte and his Baratarians in that decisive battle go far to atone for his lawless acts.

In taking farewell of the grand river at New Orleans, one comprehends for the first time the enormous assemblage of forces concentrated in its majestic movement toward the Gulf. It has received its last affluent. The Mississippi, as we see it, is the product of the drainage of one third of the territory of the United States (exclusive of Alaska and the colonies), divided into the following basins, with their respective areas in square miles: The Missouri River, 518,000; the Upper Mississippi, 169,000; the Ohio, 214,000; the Arkansas and White, 189,000; the St. Francis, 10,500; the Red, 97,000; the Yazoo, 13,850; and thirty small tributaries, 28,688. This aggregates a drainage area of 1,240,038 square miles.

TO THE RIVER

" Chucagua " and " Mechesepe "—these are names for Mississippi.

   .   .   .   .

Dead are now the scalping warriors! But the music of the
    river,
And the sweet, syllabic rhythm of its name, shall live for
    ever.

           M. V. MOORE, *Harper's Magazine*, 1883.

Men may come and men may go,
But I go on for ever.
           TENNYSON, *The Brook*.

The Tomb of Dominique You, the Pirate Hero of Chalmette.

South Pass, Rear Range Lighthouse.

INDEX

A

Admiral's Map, the, 3–5, 63

Alexander VI., Pope, and his Bull of 1493, 17

Allen, Lieut., U. S. A., his bitterness toward Beltrami, 117

Allouez, Father, brings back a name for the great river, 43

A-ze-wa-wa-say-ta-gen portage between Red River of the North and Mississippi, 142, 155

B

Beaulieu, Henry, famous guide and woodsman, 133, 143

Beltrami, Giacomo C., his trip down Turtle River to Cass Lake and thence to Saint Louis, 102–105

—— Injustice done to, 116

Boutwell, Rev. W. T., guest of Schoolcraft, at Itasca, 106

—— states purpose of expedition of 1832, 107

—— suggests " ver-i-tas ca-put," 111

Brower, J. V., estimate of Nicollet, 126

—— estimate of Pike, 100

—— explorations and surveys, 110, 127, 202–207

C

Capuchins, troubles between Jesuits and, in New Orleans, 302

Cartier, Jacques, voyage of, 18–20

Carver, Jonathan, at the Mississippi, 81, 287

" Casket Girls," the, of Louisiana, 299

Cass, General Lewis, trip to upper Mississippi, 99–102

Cass Lake, description of, 161

Chambers Creek, described by H. Clarke, C.E., 152

Chicago Drainage Canal, 224

Chouteau, Auguste, builder of first house in Saint Louis, 291

Clarke, Hopewell, C.E., estimate of Nicollet, (note) 127; 128–130

—— his survey of Itasca region, 128–130, 152

Columbus, Christopher, 3, 4, 5, 6

Crockett, Colonel David, a hero of Memphis, 296

D

Delta of the Mississippi River, 208

E

Eagle's Nest Savannah, description of, 164

Eastman, Mary H., her fanciful account of " Itasca," 117

Elk Lake, beyond Itasca, 148

—— how named, (note) 150

F

Fort Snelling, as it is to-day, 175

305